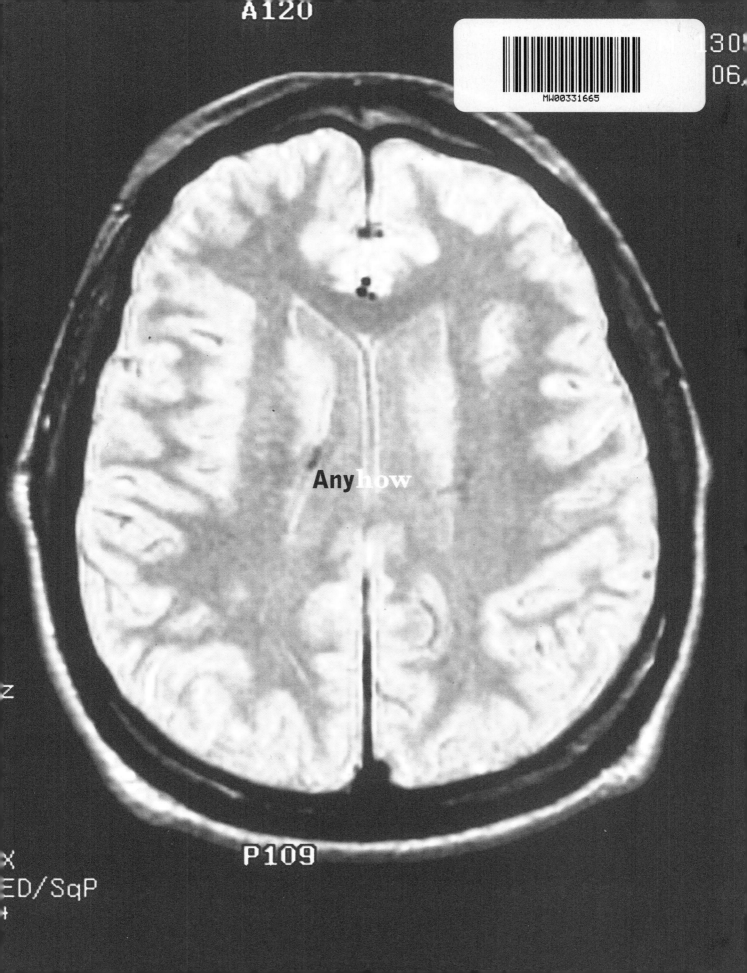

Anyhow

Edited by Cynthia C. Davidson

Anyone Corporation
New York, New York

The MIT Press
Cambridge, Massachusetts
London, England

Editor
Cynthia C. Davidson

Associate Editors
Matthew Berman
Paul Henninger

Copy Editor
Lois Nesbitt

Design
2x4

Anyhow is the seventh in a series of 11 planned volumes documenting the annual international, cross-disciplinary conferences being sponsored by the Anyone Corporation to investigate the condition of architecture at the end of the millennium.

Printed and bound in the United States of America.

Library of Congress Catalog Card Number: 98-66485

ISBN 0-262-54095-9

Anyone Corporation is a not-for-profit corporation in the State of New York with editorial and business offices at 41 West 25th Street, 11th floor, New York, New York 10010.

Photo Credits
Images of Rotterdam: Panorama taken from Het Witte Huis, Rotterdam, 1947. Photo: © Steef Zoetmulder/Netherlands Photo Archives (pages 2–3, top)

Same panorama taken from Het Witte Huis, Rotterdam, 1962. Photo: © Steef Zoetmulder/Netherlands Photo Archives (pages 2–3, bottom)

Again, same panorama taken from Het Witte Huis, Rotterdam, 1997. Photo: © Hans Bol/Netherlands Photo Archives (page 6)

Portraits: All photos © Bert Nienhuis except Arata Isozaki, © Museo Nacional de Bellas Artes, Buenos Aires, and Kristin Feireiss, © Tom Croes Fotografie

Section breaks: © Dawn Barrett

Group photo: © Bert Nienhuis (pages 262–63)

Translations
Matthew Berman (Spanish/English): Letter from Ignasi de Solà-Morales

Sabu Kohso (Japanese/English): "From Molar Metabolism to Molecular Metabolism," "Architecture's Impurity," Letter from Kojin Karatani

Graham Thompson (Spanish/English): "Liquid Architecture"

Gila Walker (French/English): "Tunneling"

TABLE OF CONTENTS

Acknowledgments

How things happen — how ideas are generated and disseminated, how money is used, how people collaborate — was not only the subject of the Anyhow conference in Rotterdam in June 1997 but also what made the conference and now this book possible. The idea began with Ole Bouman and Hans van Dijk, who, after the 1994 Anyplace conference in Montreal, first proposed to host an Any conference in Holland. Through their initiative and the added input of Anyone board members John Rajchman and Rem Koolhaas a concept for Anyhow was conceived. Implementation was made possible first by the generosity of Kristin Feireiss, director of the Netherlands Architecture Institute, who agreed to host the event, and then by NAI staff Caatje Peeters, Billy Nolan, and Gabri van Sluis, led by the indefatigable Ton Idsinga, whose steady helmsmanship led Anyhow safely into port. In addition to the NAI, financial support was provided by the City of Rotterdam, the Dutch Foundation for Architecture, and the Bilderberg Parkhotel in Rotterdam. This book documenting the event required another dedicated team and additional sources of funding. Edwin Gunn transcribed audio tapes; Matthew Berman, Paul Henninger, and Lois Nesbitt carefully edited and reedited; photographer Bert Nienhuis shot the excellent portraits; and Michael Rock and Katie Andresen of 2x4 designed the final product. Two generous grants made publication of **Anyhow** possible: from the Consulate General of The Netherlands, New York office, and the Graham Foundation for Advanced Studies in the Fine Arts in Chicago. How this international endeavor is made at all possible is through Mr. Harusuke Imamura, president of the Shimizu Corporation in Tokyo. Not only his investment but also his faith in the 11-year Anyone series of conferences and books is unparalleled in architecture today. **Anyhow** is the seventh volume. — C.D.

Title page: (top) Panorama taken from Het Witte Huis, Rotterdam, 1947; (bottom) Same panorama, 1962. Left: Again, same panorama, 1997.

A book with the word **how** in its title might rightly be thought to be an instruction manual, a "how-to" for something. The word **anyhow**, however, and this annual, **Anyhow**, refer to and represent something else altogether. How, according to Webster's English language dictionary, means "in what manner or way; for what reason; with what meaning; to what effect"; the word anyhow, "in any manner whatever; in a haphazard manner; at any rate." The difference between these terms, between "in what manner," which suggests a directed course of action, and "in a haphazard manner," which implies an undecided randomness, is perhaps subtle, since both define a manner of operating, of some kind of practice. Nevertheless, with respect to architecture, this subtlety became the focus of a heated debate, not only while planning the Anyhow conference but also at the conference itself, which this book documents.

It has been the difficulty of each Any conference – from Anyone to Anybody, from Los Angeles to Buenos Aires and all of the conference sites in between – to focus on the often fuzzy concept of undecidability, to open up something such as architecture, which has flourished in its precise and definite terminology, to indeterminacy. In planning for Anyhow there was an obvious, growing anxiety about the idea of undecidability that has been the basis of Any and a growing desire to see Any begin to deal with the global infrastructure of the 21st century. How should the term **how**, which deals with practice, deal with the theoretical Any? Anyhow committee members in Rotterdam, notably Ole Bouman and Hans van Dijk, seized on the pragmatic aspect of "how," disregarding the "haphazard" any, as the moment to argue for a new Any agenda, a productive Any that sets examples of, even writes prescriptions for, how architecture and urbanism can be done. Not surprisingly, this position strongly mirrors the pragmatism and social responsibility that seem to be standard policy in Northern Europe. For some, the responsibility to produce an outcome weighed heavily in Rotterdam, for even after the conference Bouman wrote, "If [Any] is a project for a new architecture, my question is, did Anyhow in Rotterdam contribute to that project?" (page 262).

Indeed, if Any is perceived as a project for a new architecture, then the absence of a plan for operation and result, perhaps especially when attached to the idea of how, may be unsettling. Any's **only** project is simply to open a free space for a multidisciplinary, multicultural dialogue that finds a home, even if temporarily, in architecture. At each conference Any introduces a theoretical possibility, in the case of how, the introduction of undecidability into practice. This theoretical possibility proposes to transcend the limits or thought-to-be boundaries of practice to open a free, boundless space in which previously and narrowly defined architectural practices, such as the use of the diagram or the trope, can float into and through each other; where an exploration of the digital and digital space can be conflated with a discussion of flows without any pressure to produce a result or a form, without any demand to adopt a particular method of operation or to subscribe to a particular ideology.

The pressure now exerted on Any to produce something real, to direct a new movement in architecture, seems to originate in the struggle to move theory out of architecture. Richard Rorty, in his new book **Achieving Our Country: Leftist Thought in Twentieth-Century America**, blames the post-Vietnam "New Left" for retreating from pragmatism into theory, which, he argues, has led the left "to give cultural politics preference over real politics" and because of its disenchantment with democratic institutions that have failed to serve social justice, has led them "to prefer knowledge to hope."

In a chapter titled "The Cultural Left," a group with which some Any participants might identify, the pragmatist Rorty writes:

> The difference between this residual Left and the academic Left is the difference between the people who read books like Thomas Geoghegan's **Which Side Are You On?** – a brilliant explanation of how unions get busted – and people who read Fredric Jameson's **Postmodernism, or The Cultural Logic of Late Capitalism**. The latter is an equally brilliant book, but it operates on a level of abstraction too high to encourage any particular political initiative. After reading Geoghegan, you have views on some of the things which need to be done. After reading Jameson, you have views on practically everything except what needs to be done.[1]

Jameson, who has become a mainstay of Any conferences since participating in the first event, Anyone, in 1991, is anything but "the academic Left" in the context of many Any participants. Yet Rorty's cursory summation of Jameson would apply to Bouman's and others' idea of undecidability: that undecidability allows for views on practically everything except what they – and "they" is the critical factor – believe needs to be accomplished. With slight adaptations, Rorty's views could easily be Bouman's argument: to use knowledge to meet hopes; to engage the institution of architecture in order to "transcend" (Bouman's word) and change how that very institution is thought and operates (page 145).

The operative terms for Anyhow – tools, money, policy, etc. – originate in the so-called realm of the pragmatic, reflecting the real-life conditions that bear on the making of architecture but that seen through the lens of undecidability are freed of their customary definitions and ideological associations. It is in this free space of Anyhow, in fact, that

1 Richard Rorty, *Achieving Our Country: Leftist Thought in Twentieth-Century America* (Cambridge, Mass., Harvard University Press, 1998), 78.

John Rajchman proposes a "new pragmatism" (page 212), one that he calls "a pragmatism of diagram and diagnosis" and defines as being "about forces that we can't predict, with which we can only experiment – about what William James once called 'things in the making.'" This new pragmatism, he writes, "is concerned in the present with those multiple unknown futures of which we have no image just because we are in the process of becoming or inventing them." This new pragmatism of diagram and diagnosis comes out of the Foucauldian idea of the diagram and the belief that theory is a form of practice. Rajchman now proposes that the "diagrammatic 'mobilizes and connects' us in other, indirect ways that work more through linkages . . . that grow up around new questions or in response to new conditions. . . ."

This new pragmatism might seem to apply to Rem Koolhaas's research in China's Pearl River Delta. Working with students, his Harvard Project on the City compiles cultural, social, and economic data and then represents it as sheer information in the form of bar graphs and charts that allow him to question the validity of current form-producing practice, if not the entire question of form production. (How an architectural practice as opposed to a purely theoretical practice can be non-form producing is a question that Koolhaas often avoids.) Copyrighting familiar terms such as **tabula rasa** and **infrastructure**, Koolhaas acknowledges and names conditions in the Pearl River Delta, but takes no action on that condition other than to bring it to light. This research-based text then becomes both a diagnosis of and a critical attitude about architecture and urbanism. At first glance this seems to be similar to the critical distance proposed by indeterminacy. In any case, this is not the pragmatic solution to making architecture and cities that Bouman sought for Anyhow. Rather, Koolhaas could be said to be operating a Deleuzian "abstract machine" that is neither physical, corporeal, or semiotic but is "**diagrammatic** (it knows nothing of the distinction between the artificial and the natural either) . . . operates by **matter**, not by substance; by **function**, not by form."[2] Again, this could be seen as an example of the new pragmatism that Rajchman proposes.

However, the situation is more complex than it might at first seem, for Koolhaas's work may not be indeterminate simply because it proposes no formal resolution. In this sense, Sanford Kwinter's attempt to present a manifesto, what he called an "aborted manifesto," on behalf of another way to think of architecture, might be more useful: "Architecture is no longer the familiar cult of objects. It is becoming an organon, that is, a system of investigation, invention, and technique," Kwinter said. "[A]rchitecture has begun to vanish as a discipline, and some of us are not mourning . . . we like to think of

2 Gilles Deleuze and Félix Guattari, "587 B.C.–A.D. 70: On Several Regimes of Sign" in *A Thousand Plateaus*, trans. Brian Massumi (Minneapolis: University of Minnesota Press, 1987), 141.

practice in more generic and elastic terms: we think of what we do as **design**" (page 22). Among his group Kwinter counted Greg Lynn, Alejandro Zaera-Polo, and Ben van Berkel. Each attempted to lay out a kind of architectural practice that in various ways deals with a shift from analysis to design research, with matter and technique, and, most especially, with motion, what Lynn called "motion techniques [to] be added to the architects' toolbox" (page 164).

If architecture is thought to be a waning discipline, whether because of its loss of power as an image or sign, because of such practical issues as the expanding role of engineering, or even the rampant uncontrolled building that Koolhaas studied, then rethinking architecture as a design practice and rethinking the tools of architectural design keeps it alive, even if the product of that practice may change. This is already evident in the form expressions derived from Lynn's motion techniques, work such as his H2 House for Schwechat, Austria, the shape of which is inflected by the movement of passing traffic and the movement of the sun, expressed and imaged through the use of animation software. For all the variation in technique, however, Lynn's final product resists gravity, provides shelter, and accommodates program, the old pragmatics of architecture. Are these pragmatics that architecture can escape?

Under the old idea of pragmatism, architecture is the pragmatic art: it must resist gravity, it must provide shelter, it must accommodate a social function. Architecture is also never truly free of ideological or political associations, whether those associations are symbolized or accommodated. Undecidability, on the other hand, is neither form nor function, neither theory nor practice, neither ideological nor political. Undecidability is a free space; and in that free space such things as a new pragmatism can emerge; such things as Koolhaas's research and Kwinter's manifesto, which come down on two different sides of design, can be explored.

3 Rorty, *Achieving Our Country*, 91.

When Rorty speaks of pragmatism he speaks of an ideological belief that the function of thought is to guide action. He suggests, in fact, that "the Left should put a moratorium on theory . . . should kick its philosophy habit"[3] in order to implement real and needed social change. Today we are more and more in the mood to "get going," to keep up with the relentless production that has come to characterize our age. Architecture, however, so bounded by pragmatism, cannot effect change either within its own discipline or in society at large without theory, without the time for contemplation. In the planned 11 years of Any conferences leading up to the next millennium, the undecidability of Any provides the opportunity to explore theory's contribution to architecture. Perhaps that is the instructional message, the pragmatic message, of **Anyhow**.

HUBERT DAMISCH

CHRIS DERCON

KOJIN KARATANI

ARATA ISOZAKI

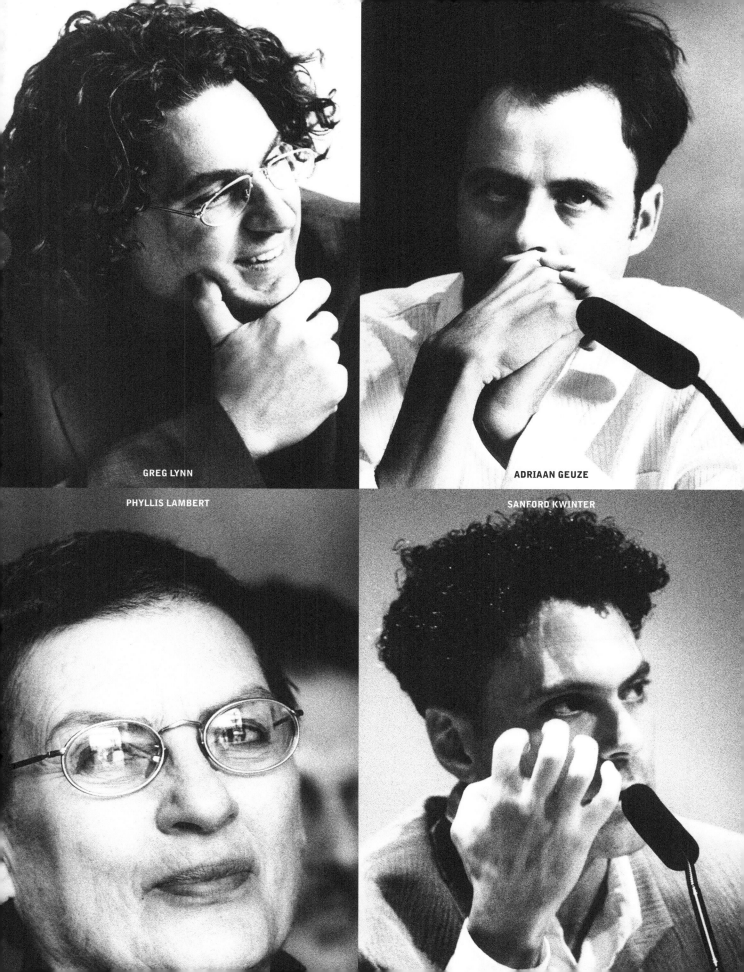

GREG LYNN

ADRIAAN GEUZE

PHYLLIS LAMBERT

SANFORD KWINTER

CHARLES JENCKS

ROSI BRAIDOTTI

FRANCESCA HUGHES

BERNARD TSCHUMI

ALEJANDRO ZAERA-POLO

PAUL ANDREU

CYNTHIA DAVIDSON

FREDRIC JAMESON

HANS VAN DIJK

SASKIA SASSEN

BEATRIZ COLOMINA

PETER EISENMAN

KRISTIN FEIREISS

AKIRA ASADA

NASRINE SERAJI

IGNASI DE SOLÀ-MORALES

JOHN RAJCHMAN

BEN VAN BERKEL

ED TAVERNE

OLE BOUMAN

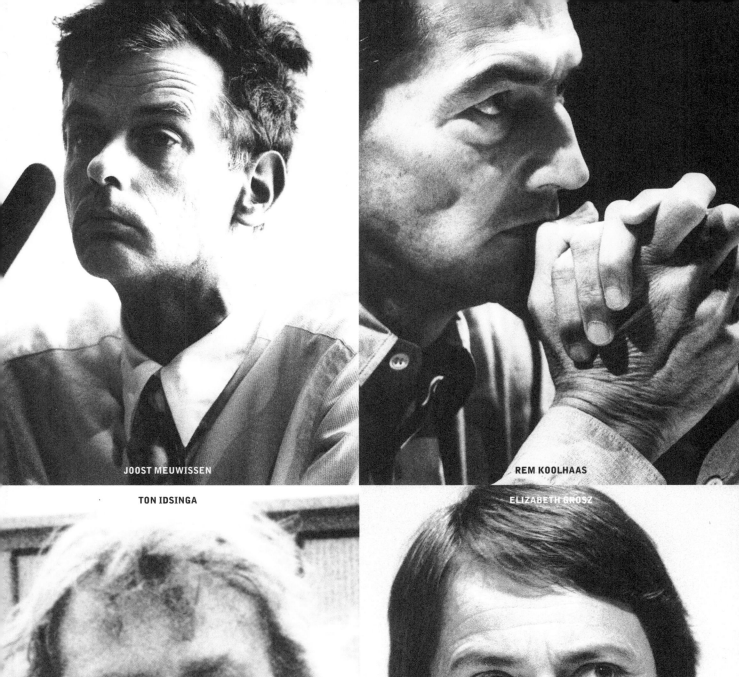
JOOST MEUWISSEN

REM KOOLHAAS

TON IDSINGA

ELIZABETH GROSZ

Tools, Organization, Process

Sanford Kwinter

Leap in the Void: A New Organon?

For this year's meeting, some of us wished to try an experiment – to arrive en masse or en bloc, to manifest, in the old way, as a collective and a front with pack loyalty, shared concerns, a willingness to appear faintly ridiculous and to defend one another in the act, to display some courage by declaring to one another publicly things that we have not yet had the opportunity to work out or to test even privately.

Jeffrey Kipnis and I had wished to present together as theorist-critics and sometime historians wearying quickly of that role and to make that weariness into a point of departure, a place for change, and a challenge to the activities that practitioners have for too long, and in too complacent and circumscribed a way, called "practice." His absence here means that it will be my honor and duty to risk ridiculousness by myself.

It is very hard to work as a group – but it is very important, and even if for certain historical reasons it is arguably no longer so important, it is worth doing for at least two other reasons: first, because it could be great fun, and second but most important, because it goes so against the grain of our times. We ourselves have been pretty much a failure up to this point: travel schedules, time zones, egotism, laziness, grotesque career and business pressures, remoteness, etc., have all prevented us from coordinating our efforts and thoughts in the natural and customary ways. It unfortunately goes without saying that these comments (and those that follow) have not yet been shared with the others. But it is them whom I should like to address

today – and "them" includes "anyone" who should feel him- or herself interpellated (to use that hideous old word), especially all of our known and as-yet-unknown Dutch friends in the audience, who, like us, are looking for and just now beginning to find something different.

It is absolutely not a club that we are trying to form but rather a "front," a line of resistance, a point of catastrophe. A group needs many relays, diversity and dissent, and rich and responsive feedback mechanisms in order to become robust, flexible, intelligent, and alive. To those who came here with the explicit anticipation that this conference would be a deliberate, collaborative meeting, let Anyhow serve as our "host" in the biological sense of the term; let us have a working session, let us publicly acknowledge our commonality, whether real or only willed (and all the more open for that).

The comments I will make today are but little sparks, provocations meant to start fires in the most- or best-kindled camps. They are brief. If what follows is a text, it is incomplete, an aborted manifesto. When I began writing yesterday, I called it "A New Organon" (after Aristotle, Bacon, and Brecht). Manifestos, after all, even aborted ones, need to be about a "new" something.

Any conference themes have never suffered from excessive focus or explicit relevance to problems in contemporary culture. This year's Anyhow, I believe, may be an interesting exception. That is because it no longer matters what one does – the genius of the market will

Previous page:
Michael Whelan,
Leap of Faith, 1997.

cut a convincing swathe for anything, however hollow. What does matter, more than ever, is *how* one does it.

This is where a subtle "coup" is today taking place in architecture. The practitioners whom I might cite as examples – and more than a half dozen are by no coincidence here today – would not themselves immediately recognize their practices in the following descriptions. Yet once they have done so, they will realize that they have already abandoned architecture in the traditional sense and, once so emancipated, they will not willingly be going back. Architecture is no longer the familiar cult of objects. It is becoming an organon, that is, a system of investigation, invention, and technique.

We – whoever we turn out to be – are no longer interested in what the last two decades of pedagogy and advanced practice have referred to as "process." Process, in this tradition, has become little more than a poor man's Game of Life, a board game for those short on intuition, a ruse with which to cloak the deep fear of matter that has characterized architectural enterprise since its mathematization and routinization by medieval template stonecutting and renascence perspectivalism. The ideology of process – often a desultory fishing expedition for a formal *parti* based in unrelated, more rigorously organized forms of knowledge – is a postmodern crypto-transcendentalism that does little more than impose arbitrary routines onto the logic of formation. For a period of time design process ideology, in schools and in so-called advanced

offices, permitted a necessary opening of architectural practice away from the parochialisms of styles and manners. It permitted, during the postwar pseudo-avant-garde era, a brute engagement of architectural discipline by the most sophisticated concerns of cultural and intellectual practice. But this engagement was at best clumsy, graftlike, adversarial, at once forced and ponderous. Process almost always meant "automatic process," for it was naively believed that removing the human substrate from the design loop would free the resultant work from regressive forms of subjectivity while preserving the potential and rich endowment of the mind and of pure thought. This was wrong on both counts. The ensuing stylistic cults of complication did little to hide from the historical record the fact that this was just a new logico-mechanical reductionism. The new poverty was mistaken for antihumanism. In America, its remnants can be found everywhere and no less amid our own ranks.

Today, from a particular perspective, architecture has begun to vanish as a discipline, and some of us are not mourning. More and more, we like to think of practice in more generic and elastic terms: we think of what we do as *design*, and we too, like the generations before us, feel the need for an escape velocity that might carry us beyond the sclerosis of inherited boundaries. For us the new design envelope is an organon-in-the-making; it is comprised of a will to technique and an ethos of research in real domains.

What are technique and research in real domains, and how are they being used to achieve an escape velocity sufficient to free us of the gravitational field of "mere," or reductionist, architecture? Technique, as we understand it, is quite simply the authentic and *immanent* version of what process ideology of the 1980s and 1990s could only seek crudely to simulate. Technique is the engagement of real logics present in the human or nonhuman environment and their conversion into potential, specifically, into apprehensible *formative* potential. Technique is design from within.

Real research represents a more classical formulation: investigation is not simply a *part of*, a preparation or inducement for, design practice; rather design practice is fully coextensive with investigation and the production of knowledge and correlative design culture. In the case of technique, the logics are there as a kind of immanence or *pregnance* in matter, and they are followed in matter because the world is matter and its products and nothing besides. For this reason we have referred and will continue to refer to ourselves as materialists. Real research adds a dimension of ecumenism: it claims that the entire material world is the product of shaping logics and that these are in turn the proper subject and domain of design research. To follow the grain of the world and to see in this infinite twisting dance the expression of multiple, converging formal and diagrammatic logics is both the a priori and the mandate of design research. As materialists, we do not approach linguistics or economics to extract a method or to pillage their banks of metaphors; we see them as material expressions of exogenous (external) and endogenous (internal) shaping forces.

We do not believe in models, and we do not seek to "apply" anything external to architectural or design practice. Rather, we extend the domain of design possibility by following research to its inevitable, yet unforeseeable conclusion. We produce works of incredible ugliness, novelty, elegance, and naivete. Yet such adjectives apply only provisionally, for these are not works of architecture *but experiments in design logic, research, and potential*. Some of us are engaged in what might be called teratological practices, others in extreme hybridization and cosmopolitanization. Either way, we all seem to specialize in what might be understood as monstrous evolutionary deviations from common or standard types. The crux here may be found in the word *evolutionary*; it claims that the logic of development forms the substrate of design action and intervention, not arbitrary production ex nihilo. The immanentist credo holds fast: design accelerates, channels, or modulates flow, and it does so as an embrace, as a flow itself.

The ultrahybridity, the teratological, in relation to a norm, is commonly said to present a *pathological* phenomenon. Yet as the great neurologist Kurt Goldstein once argued, there is substantially "greater revelation" of a living logic in pathological rather than in "normal" phenomena. He stated that it is a mistake in both method and understanding to see in the altered or impaired organism a merely reduced state; rather, we must see in the whole constellation of disease's bizarre behaviors and morphologies acute and creative expressions of a robust will to actualization that actually *builds* innovative behavioral pathways around the damaged parts.

Herein lies the key to a successful escape velocity: let research follow the real, let it be encumbered by no moral and aesthetic preconceptions, and design will follow as an integrated process.

The late 20th century may one day be known as the dawn of the age of the algorithm. If so, we wish to be the first to embrace the new rationality that sees space and matter as indistinguishable, as active mediums shaped by both embedded and remote events and the patterns they form. Ours is a transactional world – in nature as well as in society and economy – not a deterministic one, though we do not deny the efficacy, the economy, and the beauty of the mechanistic and ultimately classical methods that have brought us to where we are. Yet architecture is among the few arts that have not undergone anticlassical revolutions in this century. After all, even late-modern fragmentationist ontologies were deterministic. Now, however, seemingly indifferent to the pressures of the fin de siècle, that revolution is taking place in spite of itself, silently and ineluctably. Henri Bergson referred to reality as an "intensive manifold," a matrix of interpenetrations whose fundamental characteristics are tension and necessity. As the first philosopher of evolution, he had to explain how matter came to be fraught with necessity, how indetermination came to inhabit the actual compounds that make up our world. We too believe in this necessity of matter, its impatience to become. At root it may even be construed as a political concept: evolution is nothing other than the gradual insertion of more and more freedom into matter. In that sense we humans, custodians of the most advanced form of Mind,

are simply the most free material entities in the universe. But the universe itself is not all that far behind; it too pullulates with openness and indeterminacy, different from us, though perhaps only in degree.

The computational paradigm that is overtaking us – and this paradigm has nothing whatever to do with computers! – has extended our concept of materialism to regions of reality – that is, of society and economy as well as of nature – that, paradoxically, are often fully incorporeal, though no less replete with agency, with tension and viscosity, with necessity to organize, to change, and to move. The shapes of our world, those which determine our being, are today more than ever invisible, embedded – they are the shapes of time.

Matter has always given special importance to transitions, to thresholds and discontinuities, to *pregnances* and to differences (to the ΔT, or changes over time) because this is where "potential" to change or to become is lodged.

By bringing the seed of "form" and "design" to these wet sites of spontaneously unfolding potential we believe it is possible to offer shapes and diagrams to the intuition that go beyond the three-dimensionality of the mechanistic worldview, indeed that allow a more or less faithful "reading out" of the "intensive manifold," of the increasingly obscured dynamo of interpenetrating forces that drives our social, economic, technological, and natural worlds today.

If such a program were somehow to be construed as merely a new form of mimesis and we as "expressionists," then I, for one, am happy to be one.

SANFORD KWINTER
TEACHES AT RICE UNIVERSITY AND IS A NEW YORK-BASED WRITER. HE IS COFOUNDER AND EDITOR OF THE JOURNAL ZONE.

Peter Eisenman

Zones of Undecidability:
The Processes of the Interstitial

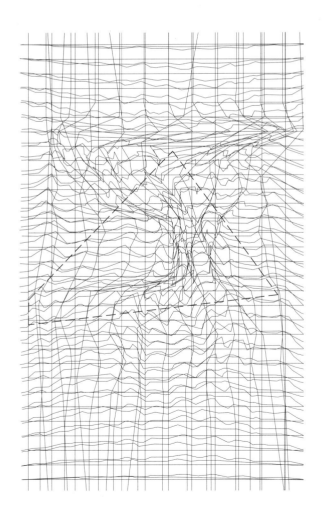
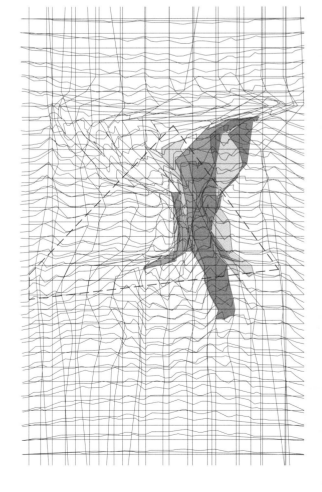

The architect Harry Cobb has said, "There is a difference between design and architecture. Design is about giving satisfaction and architecture is about subversion." That statement is made all the more interesting by the fact that Cobb is a partner in one of the most prestigious corporate architectural firms in the world, Pei Cobb Freed & Partners, a practice one would generally associate with satisfaction rather than subversion. However, the difference between the two may not be as great as it initially seems, for subversion is often a form of satisfaction.

One idea of subversion in an architectural context exists in a purely theoretical and perhaps political sense. A second idea, and more relevant to this discussion, is the possible subversion of our preconceived notions of what constitutes real space and time in architecture and suggests that other processes are present but suppressed by what is considered the normal. Since architecture's structure cannot be subverted – that is, architecture must always stand up – subversion must deal with some other aspect of architecture. It can be argued that those other aspects lie fundamentally in architecture's rhetoric. This condition of rhetoric is ultimately different from the idea of literary rhetoric. This is particularly true when it comes to the issue of the architectural trope. Jacques Derrida would argue that spatial or architectural metaphors cannot be found in what he calls "literary ideality." In architecture, unlike literature, the trope is a condition of excess and not of structure. When most people think of rhetoric in architecture they think of visual metaphors, such as "a house looks like a ship at sea" or "a classical facade looks like a bastion of democracy." Even Le Corbusier's famous dictum, "A house is a machine for living," has more to do with a visual image than it does with processes. This is because it is thought that tropes attach themselves to stable conditions which are necessary for any static image. However, rhetoric may produce what can be called affective conditions of space that relate the subject to the object by means other than visual recognition. For example, when it comes to the physical conditions of solid and void, metaphors are active in a different way. Metaphors such as "carving away solid" are just that, metaphors. Architecture is never actually carved away, but because of certain solid/void relationships, it appears that it has been. This appearance of carving away is not in itself destabilizing. Rather, when such a metaphoric carving away produces a condition that can no longer be read simply as carving away, the reading becomes blurred or multiple, critical of any one stable reading; the metaphor itself is destabilized by its own processes. Thus it is not the fact of architecture that is subverted but rather only its rhetoric.

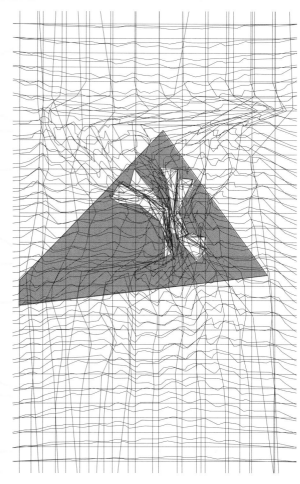

Eisenman Architects, Bibliothèque de L'Institut Universitaire de Hautes Études Internationales, Geneva, competition entry, 1996.

Two-dimensional representation of memory consolidation: (left to right) Incorporation of the site; Solid/void overlap; Building form.

In this sense it can be argued that the trope is the most active process of subversion in architecture. Tropes are conditions of architecture that have existed since the time of the Renaissance, that is, from the time when architecture became representational, began to be seen as something more than structure and use. While clearly any form of representation makes use of some form of metaphor, not all of these metaphors are in any way subverting. Early Christian, Romanesque, and Gothic architectures were metaphoric, yet the intention of these metaphors was hardly subversive. It was perhaps only in the Renaissance that tropes became subverting, when architecture first attempted to overcome the present (i.e., the Gothic) with a conscious use of the past as a form of representation. The trope in architecture is commonly used to distinguish the discourse of one architect from another. The way a facade is developed or a plan is organized can define differences in what is traditionally referred to as the style or "signature" of an architect. Equally, tropes also define how architecture is commonly perceived and experienced. For example, space is usually deployed and understood through a narrative continuity or sequence, usually about an axis of circulation. Such organizations have become almost natural tropes and have rarely been challenged. But in fact, the possible transgression and subversion of these tropes not only defines differences from one architect to the next but also provides for the possibility of change in the discourse of architecture itself.

In order to understand how architectural tropes work to destabilize, it is possible to look specifically at the relationship of solid to void, of structure to space, to illustrate the operation of a trope as subversive of the normative, binary condition of container and

Building sections.

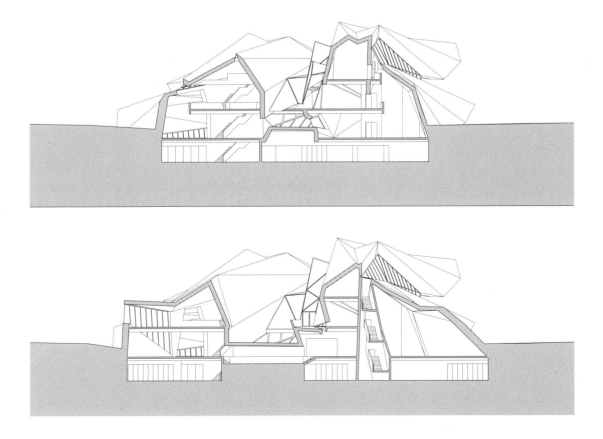

contained. The relationship of solid and void is by itself not a trope. It becomes tropic as the fact of that relationship is rhetorically both presented and represented ina building.

For example, it can be argued that Alberti's interpretation of the Vitruvian *firmitas* had nothing to do with the firmness or stability of structure, but rather was a suggestion that what was in fact stable in architecture should look like it is stable, that is, it rhetorically had to represent stability. Thus from Alberti's idea of *storia*, architecture became representational in a way that it previously had not been. And as these representations were made manifest, they often became destabilizing tropes of architecture. This can be seen in the development of the relationship of solid and void from Brunelleschi's San Lorenzo to his church of Santo Spirito, and then from Bramante's Pavia cathedral and St. Peter's projects. The work of the trope, in particular as related to the development of what is now called *poché*, becomes active.

In Brunelleschi's San Lorenzo, structure is articulated as a basic grid not very different from the structure of Gothic cathedrals. The difference, however, is important in that the solid material of the structure is organized to clearly define a perspectival depth down the side aisles and the main nave. The change in the solid material at Santo Spirito does not reflect a structural change so much as it does a rhetorical one. Here the solid material is organized to create a layering across the aisles, establishing a continuous series of frontal or picture planes as one proceeds from the front of the church toward the transept crossing. In both churches the presence of new solid material acts rhetorically to subvert both the clarity of structure and the narrative conditions of space present in Late Gothic structures. It is not so much that the structures themselves are different from Gothic structures, rather it is their rhetorical deployment as manifest in an excess of solid material that has changed.

This is also true of Bramante's cathedral project for Pavia, which must be seen as a transitional work in this context. Here the solid of the piers has less to do with the perspectival subject in space and begins to articulate an autonomous relationship between the solid and its effect on space. The autonomous character of this relationship becomes more apparent in the first project for St. Peter's, in which an entirely new relationship between solid and void is proposed. No longer are the solids seen as *poché*, as structure, or as enclosing. Rather, the solids now appear as a molten mass imbricated with the space in such a way that the outline of the space has lost its definition. The relationship between solid and void has lost much of its iconic content as either symbolic or structural form. While the issue of a figure/ground dialectic between solid and void has yet to become a conceptual issue (it will arise with Serlio and others), there is something else at work: first, there is the movement in Bramante's organization of space and structure from the mechanism of structure to the organism of successive scales of solid and void nested within one another; second, the iconic qualities of circle and square have been reduced and subverted by these new quasi-amorphous relationships of solid to void. For the first time a rhetorical form has been turned into pure material through a subversion of what is normally indicated by the structure or the container. In this context, normal vision has been subverted in order to conceptualize architecture differently. This transformation of what could be called *poché* from an inert mass between forms, or as something from which void is cut, to something highly mobile and volatile can be seen as a subversion of the form of both traditional solids and their traditional organizations in space. This modification of the material condition can be given a new name – the interstitial. The interstitial, it can be argued, is achieved through a rhetorical trope rather than through the modification of a structural organization. While rhetoric is active in the definition of any artistic act, it does not always act transgressively or else there would be no continuity in any discourse. However, when tropes act to displace continuity, they can open a discourse to new conditions of being. Bramante articulated something that had never been conceptualized as the interstitial. As a tropic process of displacement, the interstitial is still being used today. This trope denies the stability of the image and produces change in it throughout different periods of time. It is possible to suggest that the transformation or deformation brought about by the processes directly related to the trope of the interstitial might provide us with a way to look at architecture again. Not to abandon architecture as others have suggested, but in fact to look at what has been previously repressed in its received history.

This leads to the idea of zones of undecidability, or the processes of the interstitial. This idea of the interstitial is different from and at the same time subverts Bramante's interstitial. It is a condition between form and space, between figure and ground, between an affective and a conceptual experience of space. The processes of the interstitial do not begin from either a container or a contained, even though all architecture is in some way traditionally legitimated by its function as container. This is not to say that there is no container or contained, only that these terms are no longer used to legitimate the work. Instead, it is possible to think of a container that is more amorphous and mutable, like a series of balloons filled with sand that conceptually can both push into space and be pushed into. These zones of alternation or pulsation produce an interstitial condition that is neither all solid nor all void but rather something that contains both. This condition, while ultimately stable in real space, produces a disjunction in rhetorical or narrative time. This alternation of void and solid is no longer experienced in a linear sequence; it is understood as a nonvisual sensation that also requires the experience of the subject in space. This affective experience begins to question the hegemony of visual representation in architecture.

Our project for the United Nations in Geneva is one in a series of projects that explore different conditions of the interstitial and how they can be used tropically to destabilize the traditional spatial organization of any program. The process initially begins with an attempt to destabilize the idea that buildings are containers of meaning, structure, and functions, dependent on their visual recognition as such. While these conditions will always in some way exist, they are not necessarily the only legitimating conditions for architecture.

The process began from a diagram of functions outside of architecture, chosen because it would not produce in architectural space and time a recognizable image or figure. This diagram must contain a series of stages of transformation of the original condition so as to blur the connection between a recognizable image of the original and its function. In this case the diagram, which depicted a moment of neurological activity illustrating a combination of individual synaptic movements separated from each other in space, had no immanent relationship to the program of a library. A membrane that recorded the deformations of this diagram through its various stages also recorded each individual synaptic stage as a difference in height. This diagram was separated into two frequencies that recorded the traces of their individual activity. Thus as the neurons pushed past their thresholds, the membrane recorded these as height differentials which would eventually become the three-dimensional aspects of the initial diagram to be

Sections of
computer model.

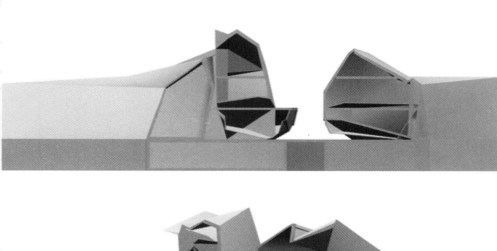

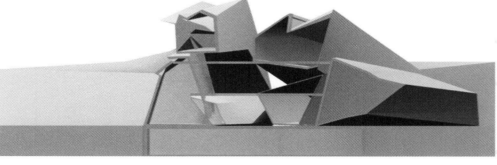

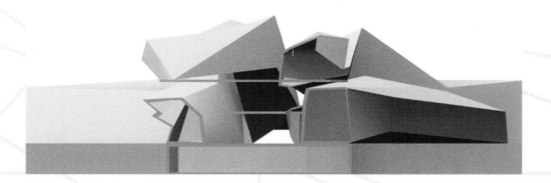

incorporated into the project. The relationship between trace and frequency is interpreted as part of the three-dimensional solid/void relationship. In this case, these relationships produced a series of overlaps that twist through the initial matrix of the spatial diagram, producing, at an arbitrary moment in the time of this activity, a series of blurred and thus potentially interstitial conditions which could then be assigned library functions. The result is neither programmatically based nor an object of personal expression, but rather produces in its processes a series of formal structures that have the potential to constitute a condition of the interstitial. These potentials can be seen as different from previous incarnations of the interstitial in that they do not rely on the visual dialectic of figure and ground.

The resulting three-dimensional matrix is composed of four linear elements which are the material that acts in a similar fashion to the previously mentioned balloons filled with sand. The voids between these elements then participate in an evolutionary process that leads to a complexity in which they are no longer either solid or void. Lateral sections of these voids can be compared to some normative condition of solid and void sectioning in order to understand their affective difference from such norms. These sections between the voids and the normative conditions can be seen as different stages in the development of an interstitial condition containing a fluid relationship between solids and voids, their figural qualities containing little resemblance to any known figuration. At any moment in the process, the voids could be frozen in space and time, thus engaging the form of the original solid components. Each of these frozen stages is superposed on each other to produce the resultant interstitial condition as an overlay of both solids and voids.

Thus from seemingly value free or arbitrary origins, a series of interstitial conditions were produced that contain both a memory trace of their processes as well as an object, the final form of which could not have been predicted from the beginning. Here the ground no longer frames the object but becomes part of the object itself, thus transgressing both the conditions of container and contained and the figure/ground dialectic. The result is not so much a recognizable "building" as it is a potential matrix for a series of affective experiences in space and time. This matrix is the result of a process that produces a figural condition of figure/figure through the transformation and recording of vectors, of energy flows that have a mass and a density. This energy produces not just a container and contained but a series of interstitial layers from the periphery to the interior. These reveal, in the internal structuring of a building, alternative spatial possibilities.

Site model.

PETER EISENMAN IS AN ARCHITECT AND THE IRWIN S. CHANIN PROFESSOR OF ARCHITECTURE AT THE COOPER UNION IN NEW YORK. HE ALSO TEACHES AT PRINCETON UNIVERSITY AND THE UNIVERSITY OF ARKANSAS.

Ignasi de Solà-Morales

The classical definition of architecture is based on the triad of Vitruvian concepts *utilitas*, *firmitas*, *venustas*, which can be literally translated as function, structure, and beauty.[1] Of these three concepts, *firmitas* most clearly determines architecture's material characteristics. *Firmitas* expresses the physical consistency, the capacity of stability and permanence to stand against the passage of time. Of course the physical consistency of architecture also relates to the formal solutions that allow it to respond to the laws of gravity and the actions of external agents. A firm, stable architecture is also a solid architecture whose dimensional and formal characteristics do not change in spite of changes in temperature, humidity, wind, and so on. If we cross this notion with those derived from the myth of the primitive hut, also recounted by Vitruvius, it becomes apparent that the individual who abandons a nomadic existence to settle in one place constructs (with branches, stones, and mud) a closed, roofed precinct the primordial objective of which is to enclose, to delimit a space in which the fire and the word can have their domain.[2] Western culture has maintained this principle of stability, permanence, and spatiality as one of three defining features of architecture; only at its margins has it been possible to conceive of other structuring activities.

1 Vitruvius, *De Architectura* (Perugia: Volumnia, 1985), book 1, chap. 6, 7.

2 Vitruvius, *De Architectura*, book 1, chap. 11, 5–32.

If Vitruvian *firmitas*, or consistency, relates to architecture's delimitation of space, its will to permanence and stability relates to the solidity of its material form. The general rule in architecture is that determination is effected by means of solid materials. Here again, if we refer back to that strange, ambiguous yet decisive text by Vitruvius, the anthropological and aesthetic definition put forward in his last two books is immediately developed in the materials that ensure the consistency of architecture and in the construction techniques that guarantee its solidity.

It is neither through caprice nor pragmatism that Western treatises on architecture focus from the start on materials and construction. Indeed, the material condition – physical consistency, solid construction, delimitation of space – has for more than 25 centuries linked the knowledge and technique of architecture to permanence.

What happens if we try to think from the other side of these traditional concepts? Is there an architecture that is materially *liquid*, that configures and is attentive not to stability but to change and is thus at one with the fluid and shifting nature of all reality? Is it possible to think an architecture that is more of time than of space? An architecture whose objective would be not the ordering of dimensional extension but movement and duration?

Liquid

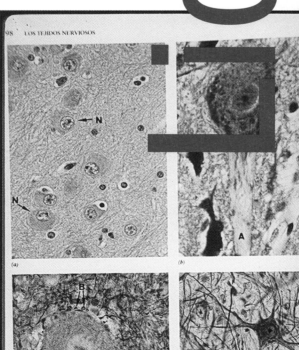

98 LOS TEJIDOS NERVIOSOS

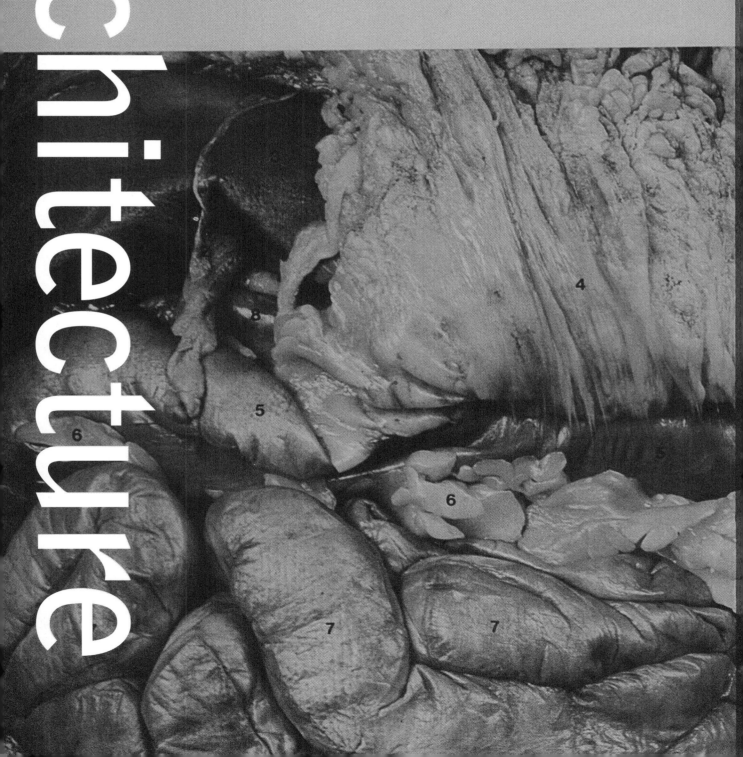

ceras abdominales superiores,
el epiplón mayor levantado
a arriba
bulo derecho del hígado
igamento falciforme
óbulo izquierdo del hígado
uperficie posterior del epiplón mayor
olon transverso
péndices epiploicos
ntestino delgado
orción superior (primera) del duodeno
Para más detalles del peritoneo y el epiplón mayor
ujetos ... vea las páginas
- 218.

● Los apéndices epiploicos son bolsillas peritoneales de grasa en los varios segmentos del colon (ascendente, transverso, descendente, y sigmoideo). No están presentes en el intestino delgado o el recto, y pueden ser rudimentarios en el ciego y el apéndice vermicular. En las intervenciones quirúrgicas abdominales, los apéndices epiploicos ayudan a distinguir el colon de otras partes del intestino.

● En la nomenclatura estrictamente anatómica, el termino intestino delgado incluye el duodeno, el yeyuno, y el íleon, pero clinicamente este término con frecuencia incluye el yeyuno y el íleon, haciéndose referencia al duodeno por su nombre específico.

● Las partes del duodeno se denominan

correctamente la porción
descendente, la horizontal
son más comúnmente lla
segunda, la tercera, y la
respectivamente.

It now seems more apparent than ever that Western civilization has abandoned the stability of the past in order to embrace the dynamism of the energies that shape our surroundings. In contemporary culture our first concern is with change, with transformation, and with the processes set in play by time, modifying through time the being of things. We can no longer think only in terms of solid, steady precincts established by lasting materials but must consider fluid, changing forms capable of incorporating; make physical substance not with the stable but with the changing; not search for a fixed and permanent definition of space but give physical form to time; experience a durability in change completely different from the defiance of time that characterized the classical method.

A *liquid architecture* will replace firmness with fluidity and the primacy of space with the primacy of time. This displacement of the Vitruvian paradigms is not effected so very simply; it calls for a *process* to establish all of the intermediary stages.

Today more than ever we are interested in architectures that are half way between space and time, existing in the tension of opposing priorities. Any architecture that takes up this process as that which is most essential will situate itself within the late-modernist values explored by current architecture.

The table below identifies the three states of architecture (solid, viscous, and liquid) in a sequence that moves from the traditional to a new structural mode that bears little relation to classical Western architecture. These states are based on three distinct material conditions: firmness, ductility, fluidity. Three different modes of the materiality intrinsic to architecture in turn produce three distinct dominant categories: space, process, and time.

Previous page: Photographic images of a real body; (left) Human nervous system; (right) Human abdominal cavity.

Above: Marc Boyle, Thermophotograph of a crosswalk, 1971. Below: Constant, New Babylon,1969, 122 x 133cm, collage.

States	Material Conditions	Categories
Solid	Firmness	Space
Viscous	Ductility	Process
Liquid	Fluidity	Time

BERGSONISM

Gilles Deleuze from his first writings points to the importance of French thinker Henri Bergson, who enjoyed great prestige and popularity in the first decades of the 20th century but was subsequently superseded by phenomenological and structuralist currents.[3]

What Deleuze finds of interest in Bergson's legacy is his reflection on the concept of space-time as put forward by modern physics and the way in which these are proposed

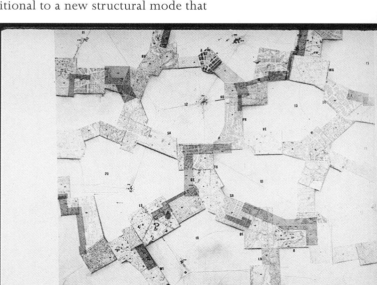

3 Gilles Deleuze, *Bergsonism*, trans. Hugh Tomlinson and Barbara Habberjam (New York: Zone Books, 1988).

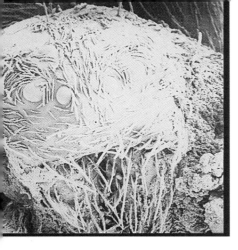

as two poles, at once opposed and totally related to one another. From the viewpoint of modern science the reality of space and the reality of time are two sides of the same coin, the inseparable relationship of the two fundamental Kantian categories that Einstein's relativistic physics and Riemann's mathematics were to bind together indissolubly.

In the 20th century, the notion of space-time has become the most decisive theoretical support for the task of formulating a theory of modern architecture. From Alois Riegl to Sigfried Giedion, the elaboration of the aesthetic notion of space unfolds as indissoluble from temporal experience in such a way that, as postulated by relativistic physics, space and time are reversible in art and architecture. They are both forms of Cartesian extension postulated on one another in order to address the need for a total description of experience.

The so-called fourth dimension is, with all of its sophisticated support in quantum physics, a mechanistic category, an inflexible rule extended to every kind of phenomenon. Space is perceived in time, and time is the form of spatial experience. The inflexible rigidity of this pair of concepts relates to the rigidity of gestalt perception and the mechanistic description of constructed space.

Top to bottom: Marc Boyle, Microphotograph of an insect's body, Cerdeña 1966; Marc Boyle, Thermophotograph of a playing field, 1970; Constant, New Babylon, partial section, 1969.

From the outset Bergson called into question this mechanical polarity of space-time. For Bergson, the experience of duration (la durée) is an intuition that reveals the continuity of the multiple. The theory of relativity resolved the spatial in the temporal and vice versa. The experience of becoming, of la durée, introduces plasticity into spatial and temporal experience. Dilation, expansion, strength are data at once external and internal to our experience of the multiple. The multiple has an internal continuity that makes the experience of duration an absolute diversity. Notions such as disturbance, modification, and flow are not thinkable in the schematism of the space-time of modern physics but rather are thinkable in internal experience, in the consciousness of duration.

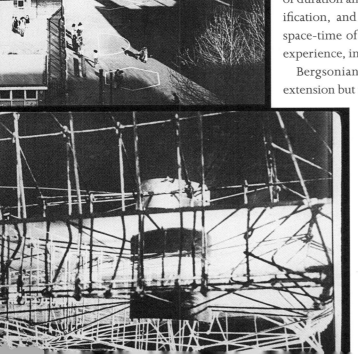

Bergsonian space contracts or dilates not through external extension but through the multiplicity that our internal intuition, real and physical but of consciousness, is capable of experiencing. The time perceived by consciousness is a succession, a fusion, a qualitative discrimination, a virtual and continuous multiplicity that is only experienced through consciousness and never reducible to an actual and discontinuous multiplicity determined by number. Bergson for Deleuze divines in modernity the plurality of durations. Reality appears as constructed by events recorded by our consciousness, opening the experience of space and of time to multiplicity.

An architecture based on the intuition of becoming as *durée*, as a multiplicity of the experience of spaces and times, must be founded on this principle of multiple continuity in which events neither fix objects, delimit spaces, nor detain times. The modern experience of space-time in consciousness reveals continuity and multiplicity; thus fixed spaces become permanent dilations in the same way that measurable times become flows, experiences of the durable.

This upholding of intuition and multiplicity means that today we can think of architecture in terms of categories that are not fixed but changing and multiple, capable of bringing together on the same plane diverse experiences that are in no sense either exclusive or hierarchical.

A *liquid architecture* signifies, first and foremost, a system of events in which space and time are simultaneously present as open, multiple, nonreductive categories and as organizers of this opening and multiplicity, not driven by a desire to impose a hierarchy and an order but by a composition of creative forces.[4]

4 Gilles Deleuze and Félix Guattari, *A Thousand Plateaus*, trans. Brian Massumi (Minneapolis: University of Minnesota Press, 1987).

LIQUID ART

The artistic experience of the Fluxus group reveals a series of recurring referents. Perhaps the most important of these is music, not only in terms of the central role occupied by the contributions of Nam June Paik and John Cage but in the whole musical environment in which the movement originated. Both the character of George Maciunas, the principal instigator of debate from the movement's founding in 1961, and the activities of the whole group, whether at the Wiesbaden music festival (1962) or in the role repeatedly accorded to music in its artistic actions, from performances to installations,[5] demonstrate that music assumed a fundamental and leading role. The very use of the word *performance* derives, in large part, from that musical context. The Fluxus artists adopted the form of musical performance as the paradigm for all artistic activity.

5 Michael Nyman, *Experimental Music: Cage and Beyond* (New York: Schirmer Books, 1974); Alan Kaprow, *Assemblage, Environments and Happenings* (New York: Harry N. Abrams, 1966); Jacques Attali, *Noise: The Political Economy of Music* (Minneapolis: University of Minnesota Press, 1985).

Extending the active idea of Fluxus performance, time becomes the most evident material support, so that the actions, the concerts, the installations set out to explore not only new possibilities for the production of sound and silence but also the musical sense of every other type of action, understood precisely in its limited, instantaneous, conditional temporal value. When Emmet Williams performed his *Continuing Song for La Monte Young* at the Fluxurum Festival in Düsseldorf (1963), the movements of the actors —

Top to bottom: Wolf Wostell, Cathedral of Colonia, 1967; Alan Kaprow, **Yard**, 1961; Yves Klein, Anthropometries, 1960; Louis Kahn, Plan for the Center of Philadelphia, 1956–62.

climbing up a ladder, tearing up papers, painting their faces, and pouring water down from the top of the ladder – expanded the musical form of the performance with events that were not only musical but physical, corporeal, visual.[6]

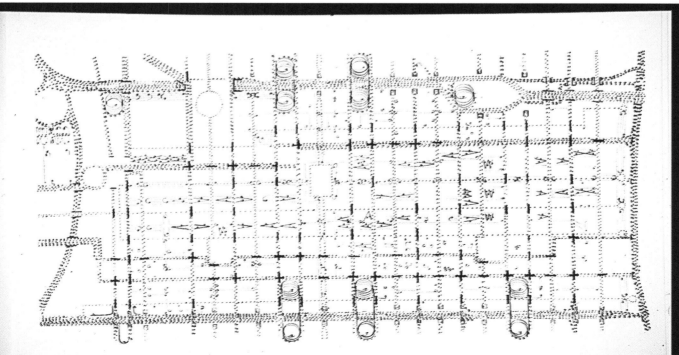

6 Elizabeth Armstrong and Joan Rothfuss, eds., *In the Spirit of Fluxus* (Minneapolis: Walker Art Center, 1993).

It has been said repeatedly that Maciunas – who studied architecture at The Cooper Union in New York – took the inspiration for the name Fluxus from the pre-Socratic philosopher Heraclitus, for whom all reality formed by the four elements – air, water, earth, and fire – was a permanent flowing. The summoning up of these four changing and fluid elements was part of the iconography frequently featured in Fluxus actions.

I want to note in particular the reference to water and, more generally, to the liquid state as a recurrent feature of Fluxus presentations. On many occasions the source of music in their concerts was liquid. Also liquid or viscous, certainly fluid, were the dyes and color daubed directly onto bodies and then transferred to floors, walls, and canvases. Liquid water fell on and unified the materials in many actions. Blood, urine, vaginal secretions, and gastric juices were evoked in many performances. Kristine Stiles, in a highly intelligent essay on the Fluxus performances, suggests that they created a space "between water and stone," using an expression borrowed from the anthropologist Bengt af Klintberg.[7]

7 Kristine Stiles, "Between Water and Stone: Fluxus Performance: A Metaphysics of Acts," in Armstrong and Rothfuss, eds., *In the Spirit of Fluxus*, 62 ff.

Fluxus developed a radical critique of everything in art that was conventional, classifiable and divorced from life, yet it also showed a particular sensitivity to the contemporary environment of mediatic, metropolitan, postconsumer, agnostic space. The primacy of the event, the occurrence, implies a fundamental shift away from a concern with perma-

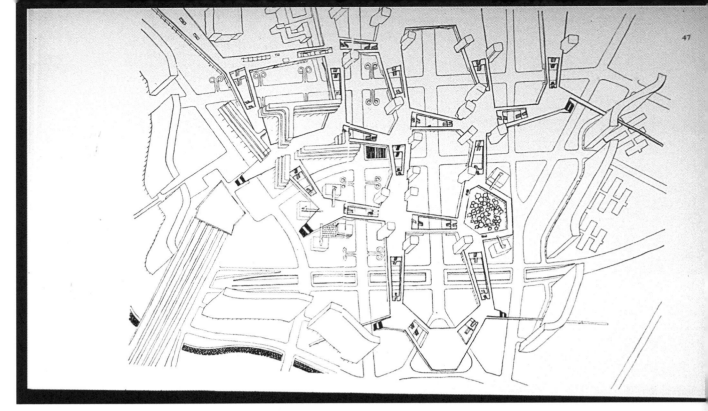

nence and durability and toward the instantaneous, occasional, unpredictable, and fleeting. This shift was not effected on the basis of some theoretical premise but by embracing the multiple condition that enfolds every event. It is important to note the differences which existed, historically, in the 1960s and 1970s between minimalism — always more abstract, essentialist, and reductive — and the more specific interests of Fluxus. The protagonists of the latter current show no signs of the presence of Zen and the pursuit of the liberating void derived from Buddhism that we find, for example, in Cage, Cunningham, and those minimalist artists who at one time or another were associated in some way with the Fluxus movement (Robert Morris, Sol Le Witt, Walter de Maria, etc.). On the contrary, it is not the search for essential unity but accumulation, succession, repetition, and chance that define the specific sensibility of Fluxus; real time as this is intuited and experienced is the fundamental thread of continuity, with no need for abstractions or schemas.

Top to bottom: Alison
and Peter Smithson,
Plan for Berlin; Rino Tami,
Porta di San Gotardo,
1980; Rino Tami, Highway
to Baschia, 1975.

As Andreas Huyssen has observed, we are dealing with a time of distribution — in other words, a time that springs from the real universe of the everyday and the production and consumption of merchandise of all kinds. A time that does not stop and cannot be invested with individual positions.[8] A collective, anonymous, enveloping time in which art is sublimated into pure inclusive becoming and in which space is constantly produced by the instant and devoured by the action.

8 Andreas Huyssen, "Back to the Future. Fluxus in Context," in Armstrong and Rothfuss, eds., *In the Spirit of Fluxus*, 140 ff.

LIQUID ARCHITECTURE

The Fluxus experience puts before us a completely *diverse* notion of architecture.

In 1953 Louis Kahn proposed a strategy for the center of Philadelphia based on a representation of motion: the conventional plan was rendered completely dynamic by thousands of signs indicating the movement of urban flows.[9] The city could not be

9 Louis I. Kahn, "Toward a Plan for Midtown Philadelphia," *Perspecta* 2 (1953): 10 ff.

understood as a system of spaces generated by the mass of the buildings or the gaps between them. Rather, buildings were merely the edges around which flowed cars, public transportation, and pedestrian traffic. The structure of urban space was seen as the result of systems of frictions of varying degrees of viscosity, producing turbulences at the points of contact and different densities within the flows themselves. The possibility of representing these phenomena proved itself to be seriously limited. Kahn's beautiful drawings are in effect a kind of palimpsest of a form that could only be measured and shaped from

the inside. The metaphor of the liquid form may prove deceptive if we think about its representation, that is, about the classical form of aquatic architecture such as the plays of water, the fountains, and cascades of the gardens at Tivoli or Versailles.

A liquid, fluid architecture is not oriented toward representation or spectacle but is the result of a fold, a folding in on itself, like a Möbius strip from which it is impossible to escape the form created by its own permanent fluctuation. An architecture that engages human flows in traffic interchanges, airports, ferry terminals, and railway stations cannot be concerned with appearance or external image. Becoming flow means manipulating the contingency of events, establishing strategies for the distribution of individuals, goods, or information. An architecture that continues to regard these places of flow as spectacle will fall into the same contradiction that Marcel Duchamp sought to cancel out when he abandoned retinal painting (based solely on the gaze) and ventured into an art of the event.

We lack, to a great degree, the instruments to control this space/time/event that is the place of flow, of liquid architecture. Conventional representation, perspective, continues to be entirely wrong, even when it makes use of sophisticated computer design programs. It is no use continuing to present *visions*, even if they are animated, in motion, virtual, etc. The experience of the place of flow is synaesthetic, *distracted*, as Walter Benjamin would have said, on the basis of his far-reaching intuition that the attentive, visualist gaze pertained to the experience of a disappearing culture.[10]

10 Walter Benjamin, "The Work of Art in the Age of Mechanical Reproduction," in *Reflections*, trans. Edmund Jephcott (New York: Harcourt Brace Jovanovich, 1978).

To produce forms of the experience of the fluid and to make these available for analysis, experimentation, and project design is today still more a desire than an attainable reality. To give form to the synaesthetic experience of flow in the movement of the metropolis, of the *dérive* or drift that distances itself from purely visual programmatic planning and pre-established regulation in order to experience other happenings, other performances, is one of the fundamental challenges for an architecture that looks to the future.

IGNASI DE SOLÀ-MORALES IS AN ARCHITECT, CRITIC, AND PROFESSOR AT THE ESCOLA TÉCNICA SUPERIOR D'ARQUITECTURA IN BARCELONA. HIS ESSAYS ON ARCHITECTURE ARE COLLECTED IN **DIFFERENCES: TOPOGRAPHIES OF CONTEMPORARY ARCHITECTURE**, PUBLISHED IN ANYONE CORPORATION'S WRITING ARCHITECTURE SERIES WITH MIT PRESS (1996).

Nasrine Seraji

Tools
Organization
Process

To get attention in the global marketplace,
you need the proper tools . . .

– Newsweek, June 9, 1997

Organization: Nexus–Atelier The studio as a nexus of fabrication (of thoughts, of things, of architecture) is a fixed place where manpower, machines, techniques, and references are confronted and put into conflict, creating a process of constant fluidity. This nexus is flexible and porous in nature; it is small, yet has the potential to become a large and complex structure. It brings various minds together: architects, philosophers, artists, art critics, engineers, and students. This combination allows for a variety of projects, resulting in the visibility of numerous architectural issues; this visibility results in a variety of forms. Buildings, theoretical projects, books, exhibitions, critical debates . . . The buildings finance the unpaid projects, the unpaid books, and the unpaid exhibitions. The latter activities have one aim – to introduce and expose us to criticism. This exposure allows us to negotiate a constant critical position.

Our Tools Juxtaposition, deformation, displacement, justification, legitimization, delirium, surprise, punctuated past, temporality, instability, superimposition, war, grounds, peeling, insertion, embedding, autonomy, and the magic wand found in the tool bar of Photoshop. The tools unravel the process of making. . . . The right tool is that which can announce, be seen and heard everywhere . . .

Our Processes Repetition, resistance, fluidity, derogation, competition, elasticity, concentration, colonization, reconfiguration, redefinition. . . . Significance needs amplification . . .

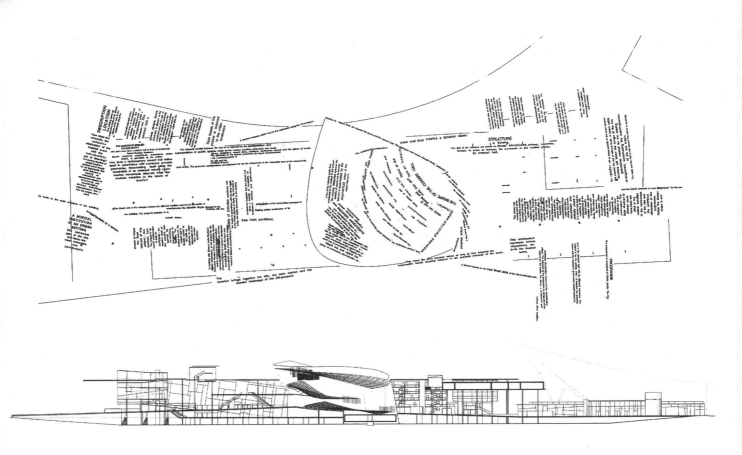

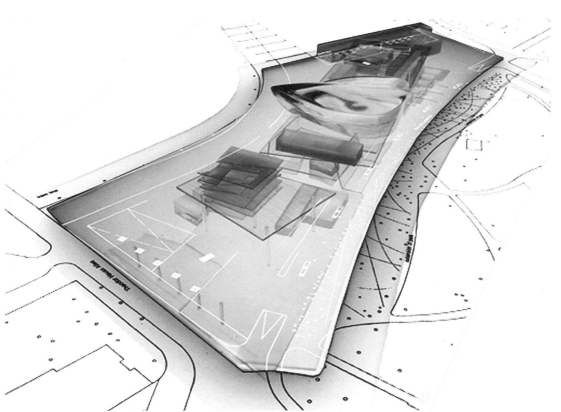

Atelier Seraji, Musicon Bremen, Bremen, Germany, competition entry, 1995, 2nd prize.

Architects: Nasrine Seraji, Andrés Atela, Micha Manz, Gian-Luigi Cito; CAD: Alice Y. Hwang; Consultants: Jean Attali (philosophy), Danièle Cohen-Levinas (philosophy/music); Jacques Sautereau (architecture); Engineers: Terrel Rock Associates.

NASRINE SERAJI IS A PARIS-BASED ARCHITECT. SHE IS A VISITING PROFESSOR AT PRINCETON UNIVERSITY, A UNIT MASTER AT THE ARCHITECTURAL ASSOCIATION, AND A PROGRAM DIRECTOR AT THE AKADEMIE DER BILDENDEN KÜNSTE IN VIENNA.

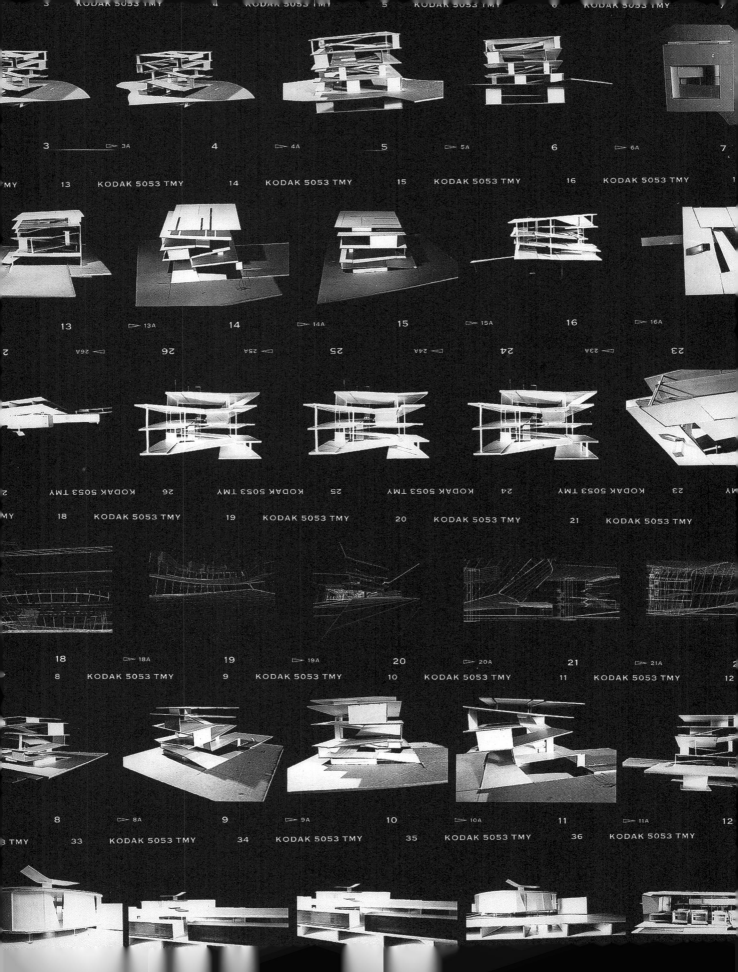

Discussion 1

Phyllis Lambert Before opening a general discussion, I want to give Sanford Kwinter an opportunity for rebuttal.

Sanford Kwinter I want to make a little point. Peter Eisenman is not exactly right when he says that the kind of flow he's interested in wouldn't be of interest to us. Peter is primarily interested in the flow of rhetoric through a person's mouth. Our position is to reject rhetoric itself as a basis of analysis and knowledge in architecture.

Peter Eisenman In favor of what?

Kwinter I said my piece; I thought it was clear.

Ignasi de Solà-Morales Sanford, you used a very precise word. While Peter was presenting, I was thinking about two different words from Aristotle that form the very basic philosophy of our Western culture: **poetics** and **rhetorics**. We know that the theory of tropes is central to the organization of rhetorics. The theory of tropes suggests that there is a language and that this language must be used. Peter, you emphasize your special interest in Palladio, who is a mannerist, an architect who understands the well-established classical language yet tries to go into the zones of instability. But you don't explain what Bramante means, that is, what poetics means. Poetics is the moment in which language is established, produced, invented. These two different moments are present at the same time. We can talk about architecture from within, meaning that architecture is a language that is the extension of but also the limits within which we can operate. For me, the objective of the Any meetings is to have people from outside architecture fertilize and stimulate zones outside the established architectural language, in other words, to produce a new poetic act, which is the moment of invention. Peter presents his building in Geneva as a play between the zones of instability of an established system of forms, but he seems not to pay attention to the fact that he's either playing with existing works or with a very orthodox avant-gardist idea that art is supposed to go into these joints of the established language. He doesn't pay attention to the strong poetic aspect of his architecture, as Bellini did in painting and Bramante in architecture. In other words, several architects —

and I consider Peter as one of these — are capable not just of playing with an established language — using the rhetorical possibilities of a language — but of showing new situations that are beyond architecture, that are part of our perception of the world. But this poetic side, which is a production of a language fully pregnant with other intuitions, other perceptions of the reality beyond architecture, is part of the fundamental nature of these Any meetings. We try to address the city and architectural progress today not just to analyze other possibilities inside an established system but to study the new aspects of our contemporary experience.

Eisenman In a conference like this, I've always found it difficult, Ignasi, to teach poetics. I think you can teach rhetoric, but I think it's very difficult to teach poetics.

Solà-Morales But we are not in a classroom.

Eisenman But I am a teacher and my work deals with the kinds of things that I teach and what develops out of that. The architect is the last person to ask about poetics. In our office we deal with these tropic conditions as rhetorical devices. Some projects are better than others; some succeed and others don't. I don't disavow that there is a poetic aspect to the work, but to present that poetic aspect is problematic. Thomas Pynchon's **Mason & Dixon** is basically a rhetorical, not a poetic exercise. At the same time it doesn't deny it's poetic.

Solà-Morales I understand that it might be embarrassing for you to talk about your poetic condition, so let's talk about architecture and cities today. Our situation today is not that of the Five Architects from New York who worked in a game that was basically rhetorical vis-à-vis the modern tradition; they used a more or less established language as something that could be changed, transgressed, deformed, etc. The discussion today could be the same, but it could also be another discussion, and Any is a good forum for this other discussion. We don't just play inside the discipline — the word **discipline** is always something of a security net — but rather find ways to go into the problems that architecture faces outside itself.

Eisenman Most of us in Any are accused of not sticking to our discipline but rather of taking from other disciplines and bringing them into architecture. This is the first time I have given a talk at Any in which I didn't refer to a philosopher or any other superannuated figure. I did refer to Thomas Pynchon — sorry about that. But my discussion was purposely pointed at the younger generation of architects, to Nasrine Seraji and Sanford's **novum organum**, in the sense that I believe that there's a big difference between the illustration of architecture as l'**espace indicible**, that perhaps deals with a sort of ephemeral poetics, and the discourse of tropes. Most of these younger architects have no discourse of the trope. They will argue that such a discourse is not necessary today, and I would argue that the trope defines the discipline and defines the difference between illustration, painting, literature, and architecture.

Nasrine Seraji I don't know if I should answer on your terms or go back to l'**espace indicible.** I want to bring attention to an organization upon which we base our research and the way that we work with projects. I talk about spatiality both in terms of our architecture and in terms of the organization of a group of people who allow for that architecture to happen. When you introduce the idea of the trope, I am not quite sure what you want to get at in terms of the younger generation.

Jesse Reiser I want to address Peter's discomfort about the discussion of poetics in relation to work. The trope in today's usage is seen as an aftereffect of a work rather than something on which one would want to base a work. There would naturally be a semiotic condition to any project, but it wouldn't be a generative condition of a project.

Eisenman Jesse, I can't read **Mason & Dixon** any other way. Pynchon's plan was precisely to transgress the tropic structure of the 18th-century novel. In **Gravity's Rainbow** he transgressed the tropic structure of the then contemporary novel. Having done that, he can't do it again, so he goes back to an 18th-century novel on which to base a contemporary critical project. That's what's so interesting about his project.

Kwinter Peter, I didn't mean to be aggressive. I meant exactly what Ignasi more explicitly pointed out, that your use of the concept of trope, somewhat predictably, is a model from rhetoric, yet it is also potentially a model from the materialist point of view. Trope comes from the Greek word **tropos**, which means a turning. It is precisely this turning that we find in the materialist Democritean tradition, a tradition that can be traced through Lucretius right up to thinkers like Marx, Bergson, and others. It seems to me that if Pynchon, in his greater work **Gravity's Rainbow**, did anything for the history of these rhetorical features, it was to have changed the literary centrality of troping to a problem of **en**troping. The entropy model, as it emerged full-force in that book, was a thoroughly materialist hypothesis about history and knowledge in the 20th century, almost to the point of declaring that this transformation is precisely what the 20th century had become. It had become a materialism of information science, essentially a comprehensive military campaign, by war as well as by other means, a systematic engineering of techniques as well as of the forms of knowledge and death that subtend them.

Eisenman Aren't entropy and the tropic enfolded, as it were, within one another? Don't they exist together?

Kwinter A work can be read from a structuralist and a rhetoricist point of view, and I agree entirely with Jesse that as a rule the same objects interest us. What is different is the fundamentally different approach to facture, to generation – not with respect to age but with respect to production or genesis. What are the genetic bases of understanding with respect to where forms and other manifestations of matter come from? I would be surprised if the revolutionary depth of what Pynchon achieved in **Gravity's Rainbow** would even begin to show a glimmer of itself in **Mason & Dixon**. I found your comments on the latter work extremely interesting yet entirely at odds with the rest of your presentation.

Hubert Damisch As an art historian, I am very uncomfortable with your distinction between artists who create a new language and artists who use a well-established language in their own way. As a mannerist Palladio simply used a well-established language in his own way. It seems to me totally outdated. As a philosopher, I'm totally uneasy with your distinction between language and rhetorics. I am reminded of a discussion between Lev Kuleshov and Sergei Eisenstein in the 1920s. Eisenstein was right when he said that film is not a matter of rhetorics but a matter of trope, which is totally different. Similarly, in the 1950s Emile Benveniste persuaded Jacques Lacan that the unconscious does not have to do with language but with the use of tropes. And you have to understand that, there is no language without tropes. There is no state of language in which words are used in their proper sense. Words are metaphors. You cannot oppose moments in language in which you use words in their proper sense and words in their metaphoric sense. Even the word **flow** is a metaphor because it has no proper sense. There are flows of cars, flows of people, all of which are metaphorical.

Eisenman Hubert, I really wanted to use Bramante and Palladio because I think that Palladio was not a mannerist deviating from a known language, but he took material that had already been. The language had been taken out of it by Bramante; it was there to be deformed into some other discourse. I never refer to Palladio as a mannerist. I would argue that he is the first modernist. I was suggesting there are moments in time where there is material on the table. Le Corbusier took an idea and worked it into material. I'm suggesting that perhaps we're at that moment when material is again on the table. We cannot move it back toward language without the notion of the trope.

Rem Koolhaas Sanford, you made a very bold suggestion at the beginning as if you were announcing a new manifesto. I sensed an undercurrent of generational conflict, and a desire to claim the mantle as part of the spectacle of Any and as part of a changing of the guard. At the end of the presentation, however, it was very unclear what the manifesto was, who the group was, and whether the abortion was caused by you or by some kind of extraneous force. I would find it very interesting if you simply had the courage of your initial apparent conviction. Is there in the house already, are we among, a new generation? If so, who are they and where are they and what do they do?

Kwinter The McCarthy Hearings will be held at . . .

Eisenman Booooooo!

Kwinter The aborted manifesto was explicitly a challenge to some friends — you among them. Some people who "belong" don't necessarily know that they do; many don't even want to. You are one of the former. My aborted manifesto was purposely left incomplete because I wanted others to complete it if they felt that they had a part to play in completing it.

Koolhaas Actually, it was a twisted intention to make a new kind of beginning in this very tired condition of Any.

Kwinter It's going to be a long two and a half days. I know many people who were addressed have been truffled very systematically throughout the rest of the conference.

Eisenman Will you tell us at the end?

Kwinter Peter, it's very clear that I meant to provoke you as much as possible. I had no idea you were even going to be on my panel, and I was absolutely crestfallen to find out that you were. I wouldn't insist on a generational thing. The assertions have primarily to do with how one works today, with the type of data that one gathers and organizes (the stuff I will simply call material for now), that one takes as one's intellectual and visceral point of departure. You've already announced yourself very clearly on the side of what I call the sort of brute, crypto-transcendentalists, the process ideologists. There is today a move beyond and below the apparent liquidity that Ignasi is talking about, one which has to do with — which embraces — certain liquid and superliquid states of contemporary economy, culture, society, etc. I have written about Peter's work, using the exact opposite argument to the one he's arguing for today. I always come up on his interstitial as the very thing in the work that is rigid yet absolutely worth investigating. I have argued that Peter's work kept the particular materiality of the so-called "in-between" alive for an otherwise mechanistic quasi-avant-garde in the 1960s and 1970s. Today this arena is being picked up by a lot of designers in a way not hampered by the anxiety about absolute states characteristic of the earlier generation. For us, in-between-ness is not a transgressive concept, it is **substance** itself.

Ole Bouman Sanford stated at the end of his lecture that evolution is nothing more than more freedom in matter. As a summary of his so-called manifesto, this presupposes a positive value to freedom. Do you believe that freedom has a positive value, and why do you give a positive value to the notion of evolution's next steps?

Kwinter I have a very old-fashioned idea of freedom. The sense in which I am using the word **freedom** comes out of an organicist or vitalist philosophy that argues against the idea of a universe fixed once and for all and merely rearranged in its parts for time immemorial. From a purely physics and philosophical point of view, one may ask: Is the universe deterministic, determined in advance, or is there a possibility for things to happen and for us to participate in what happens? The foundations of such a worldview cannot be simply political; they have to be material and philosophical as well. When one looks at evolution in a certain way one is forced to notice how inert matter gave way to life, how life gave way to botanical forms that had slightly greater torpor than the more autonomous animalian forms. Freedom in such a continuum becomes the possibility of possibility itself. Thinking, when we do this formally, with discipline and precision, helps free us from mechanistic habits of thought, habits that foster the complacency such that a common-sense outcome for a set of data or a set of givens is understood to be the logical and inevitable outcome — which of course it isn't. We think precisely because we need to produce alternative possibilities, and this is only possible if one can lay down a transcendental foundation (conditions of possibility) for what I've called freedom and generalize it to the material universe.

Renato Rizzi Sanford, you ended your talk using a very interesting and important term, mimesis. If you put the terms **trope** and **mimesis** in opposition, one suggests the notion of freedom and the other, the notion of law. Mimesis is not simply the replication or duplication of something, rather it is the active production of the correspondence between law and freedom; but today neither law nor freedom exist, only arbitrariness.

Kwinter That is an extremely beautiful formulation. Where did you get it?

Rizzi Massimo Cacciari, who spoke about mimesis by investigating the work of Mies van der Rohe. He said that Mies was the real classic architect because he denied the notion of arbitrariness; his work was exactly balanced between law and freedom because law is the way to maintain freedom and freedom is the way to produce law.

Kwinter If that is how the word **mimesis** is to be construed, then I would be happy to face accusation, but I also used the term **mere mimesis** because there is a tendency to see mimesis as merely copying something. For example, the relationship of what is to what might be was the subject of much discussion a few weeks ago in New York at a conference on complexity. The problem was broken down into different categories and ontologies, yet most of what was discussed was couched in the same Bergsonian ontology that has come up today in Ignasi's paper. We are interested today in the Bergsonian ontology as an absolute, as a necessity, a dynamic system and phenomenon. This so-called virtual/actual model of coming-to-be contains a radical and continuous turning and troping from what already exists, a ceaseless development of latent, potential, and virtual data. This model espouses so much more of the minutiae of reality and of materiality as it expresses itself in the process of coming-to-be.

Akira Asada As a rejoinder I have a very simple question for Sanford: on the one hand I understand your criticism of linguistic and rhetoristic imperialism, even though I don't necessarily agree with you. On the other hand, I cannot yet see the difference between your position and a certain intuitionism that pretends to grasp directly a prelinguistic, prerhetorical process of becoming from within. It would be wonderful to intuit and follow the line of becoming – a sort of Bergsonian elán vital – but I don't know how you can justify your choice in the social situation.

Kwinter It is, in fact, an intuitionism. It tries to embrace the philosophers who have been interested in such an intuitionism, including of course Deleuze and Guattari. But let's not forget what Deleuze took such pains to point out to us, the postwar generation: that in Bergson's philosophy intuition was meant to be nothing less than a science. There are, for example, structures distributed at such long periodic waves throughout time that their forms simply cannot be made directly available to intuition due to the constraints or limitations of the human nervous system. Yet once modeled within an environment such as a computer, these structures can take on an apprehensible plastic and temporal quality that can enter into intuition. One aspect of the "scientific intuitionism" that some are embracing today is the attempt to follow a movement that is happening in epistemology and mathematics. Quite simply this involves a shift toward the understanding of **qualitative** structures and away from the purely **quantitative** ones with which architecture – often unbeknownst to itself – has been traditionally obsessed.

Hilde Heynen Kristin Feireiss said that this would be a conference about the condition of globalization and how architecture is reacting to that condition. This panel was supposed to be about tools, organization, and process, thus I was expecting a questioning of the role of architecture vis-à-vis globalization. I am surprised to find myself in a highly interesting discussion about tropes and the language of architecture, but not about this globalizing condition, not about how architecture relates to building processes. There seems to be a narrowing of focus here.

Kwinter Given the question of globalization, I did my dutiful best to set up discussions that I anticipate from a variety of respondents — from Saskia Sassen, Rem Koolhaas, and others — about the corollary phenomena associated with globalization. Among the significant problems one faces today is exponential ultrarapid growth and development — possibly a new **type** of phenomenon. These processes must be engaged by design propositions, but forcing design to engage a problem like **growth** is very different from attacking a problem as simple, as inert, and as normative as **space**. It is important to have a worldview that accompanies the emergence of a whole new lexicon, a whole new "plasticity."

Saskia Sassen The category of globalization is enormously ambiguous and complicated; it needs to destroyed, to be exploded. Second, from where I sit and the way I work, this is the "how" of globalization. It is very important to identify the strategic sites, the planetary, the universal, to move away from the notion of the world, and to isolate what are the strategic in-betweens that allow you to elaborate a discourse. I am not an architect, a philosopher, a linguist, or any of the other professions presented at this table, but I could resonate with quite a few of the statements that were made. This question of globalization needs to be embedded in a whole series of specific meta-realities and strategic dynamics, and it also needs to be hijacked out of this very global category that is globalization, but for shorthand we need to use it because it does signal a whole number of discourses, events.

Greg Lynn I want to resuscitate a couple of the initial discussions about technique. Damisch made an incorrect argument for an architecture conference when he said that there's no language that doesn't already reference something. In fact, there is: it's called geometry. It's what architects deal with all the time. It's interesting to take some of Sanford's comments and rather than looking at the linguistic look at techniques to discover what kinds of metaphors and rhetoric they might generate. Looking at technique precedes a linguistic model, and that's really the cause of the tension on this panel. How do you start a discussion of technique? When Sanford says he's going to be ridiculous, it's because techniques now make someone seem very adolescent. Most design culture seems very adolescent right now because it's dealing with new techniques without any idea of the rhetoric that goes with them. Sanford's point that some people at the conference might risk being adolescent at the cost of talking about technique has nothing to do with age. The debate is simply between a mature architectural position and an adolescent position on architectural techniques.

Solà-Morales One of the interesting ideas that Sanford proposed is that technique is one of the most evident ways in which architecture is asked to move out of itself. The discourse of rhetorics is basically an internal, solipsistic process of self-analyzing and in some cases looks for an internal lack of order or instability. One of the strangest aspects of contemporary architecture, especially in schools, is that it has nothing to do with real weight, dimension, and resistance in physical terms. It's necessary to establish a certain movement from inside to outside. Changes in architecture have occurred because technical aspects have changed. In other words, instead of privileging the internal game of architectural language, now the technical problematic, the technical innovation, and technical possibilities are ways to move outward, to establish an alternative that holds possibilities of growing and producing new messages.

Reiser I am interested in the primacy of geometry and how one could instrumentalize geometry in relation to architecture. One thing that has preoccupied me is the question of how, if we are interested in dynamic systems and in flux and change entering into the instrumentality of architecture, that precisely enters into the work? I see it even in Peter's presentation, although he doesn't talk about it, because the diagrams are there. One should not look to a rhetorical or tropic base for this material but to how a real geometry might be carried from some other realm from within architecture itself, rather than reducing it to a representation of the place it came from. To speak as an adolescent, it would be in terms of actually working out a project, in a propriety sense of the diagram. How would it actually work within a particular context and how would it respond to, or be able to be changed within, a context, rather than seeing it as somehow a mere representation from some other realm?

Seraji Given the question of geometry and the question of tropes, I want to suggest that the structure of architecture can be made apparent through a colony of people working toward an object and not through the object itself. In this case representation becomes more social and political as opposed to the idea of representation as being a formal object. For me, representation exists already in political and social structures.

Infrastructure, Distribution

Paul Andreu

Tunneling

Paul Andreu with Anne Brison (ADP), The Sheraton Hotel, Charles de Gaulle Airport, Roissy.

What I am about to say is more of a "statement" than a speech, which gives me a good deal of freedom in expressing myself, but maybe also makes things a bit too easy. We have been speaking of flow, process, and interaction. I will talk about these without theoretical pretensions, simply by bringing up a few ideas and leaving it up to you to decide whether to provide them with a coherent order or give them no further thought. They are not ideas that I will try to prove. Indeed, for once I feel as if I were playing the part of an agitator. If I run the risk of rambling a bit, of sounding hesitant, somewhat vague, or repetitive, that's part and parcel of an agitator's role, and I must admit that in certain respects this can be quite convenient.

Let's take a step back and start by straying from the subject and considering the place of paths and roads in the landscape. I was thinking about this not so long ago while driving along the serpentine roads in the center of France and reflecting on a recent book by Michel Serres. These roads hug the landscape; like the fields and the stone walls, they marry the topography of the land. As I followed the road, winding my way around each bend, enjoying the smooth, flowing movements of the steering wheel, I felt as if I were coasting over the surface, exploring and discovering it. The journey was in a time linked to space, in a harmonious,

coherent whole. This is what happens when the path is an integral part of the trip, when the process of getting there is virtually as important as the goal.

But with the increasing importance of the desire to reach the goal, roads have been stretched tight, straightened and set apart from the land, remote from it. The outcome is a different view of the landscape, with the eye skimming over it in a more general, synthetic, and rapid way. Because nothing matters but reaching the goal quickly and travel time is seen as a negative factor of excessive duration, our relationship to the landscape has been destroyed. We need security barriers to protect us from our own speed, sound-reduction walls to shield us from the excessive noise, and bridges and tunnels to yield the straightest, quickest course. Ever quicker and straighter, the road requires our undivided attention. Ultimately, the epitome of the efficient road is a tunnel.

We are all aware that space and time are linked — no need to call on Einstein to explain that. It's an everyday experience. When one loses its value, so does the other. They only exist together. The greater our desire to be there already, the less our pleasure in being here and now.

In physics, the passage or instantaneous transition from one state to another of minute particles through seemingly impassable force barriers is

called tunneling. In our search for maximum speed, roads have been turned into tunnels. But this "tunneling effect" is not only confined to roads: present in all modes of transportation today, tunneling isolates us from reality and cuts us off from the intelligible world. This is the case with trains and even with airplanes. What are planes, with their portholes closed and the movie screens on, if not traveling segments of a tunnel? You were there, now you are here — nothing has changed. All you have to do is reset your watch.

Isn't this the ideal of transportation? In a way, it is. But what price has been paid? And can we continue pursuing this path? At the risk of seeming ungrateful when it comes to modern technology and progress, I cannot help wondering how far we can stretch this frantic race to reach the goal with ever increasing speed. There is something desperate about this negation of time. It ends up making time even more boring and stressful. Is it really progress to accept not living in reality so often? Is time really diminishing, and, in any case, can we accept wasting it?

I spoke of country roads — no doubt for the sheer beauty of a Rousseauean image — but nothing is really different in cities. Nothing but the fact that the difficulties that need to be overcome, the fatigue, the deterioration of the cityscape, and the "tunneling effect" are more extreme there than elsewhere. The very prototype of efficient urban transportation (which is, to be sure, the goal of all major cities) is the subway and its tunnels. Once again, I do not mean to be casual or irresponsible, nor to express ingratitude. Obviously, such tunnels and the parenthetical time spent in them is better than being stuck for hours in traffic jams. No doubt about it: just call to mind Cairo as it was 10 years ago, or take a trip to Bangkok today. But that does not mean that this development is good in and of itself. It is merely the lesser of two evils.

I tend to get on the nerves of many contractors – who have their drills ready and waiting at the snap of a finger to bore a hole here and there and in all directions – when I tell them that people should not be buried underground before they die. I also tend to get on the nerves of politicians when I tell them that after neglecting the comfort of residents and local voters for the sake of transportation as a matter of general interest, they are now with equally blind efficiency neglecting the people who travel daily across their district but do not vote there. I might be mistaken, but too bad! You cannot be an agitator and arouse public opinion without displeasing and without sometimes making mistakes.

At any rate, I challenge the blindness that regards a lesser evil as a good. Progress cannot amount to drilling further and better and increasingly shutting ourselves up in a negation of time and space. The lesser evil quickly becomes an evil, period.

Do I have a solution? Unfortunately, I do not. But I have dreams, and that is significant. I have a dream of paths running through the country and the city that would no longer be incisions or entrenchments. I have a dream of above-ground transit, with elevated transportation in cities made possible by significant progress in the field of noise reduction. I do not think that my dreams are all that remote. Witness the talk these days about a tramway in Strasbourg. Why should we give up so easily? Why shouldn't we maintain our high standards and be demanding? Why don't we do an about-face, make a kick-turn like skiers do, and look at things from a different perspective?

As we stretch our roads, tracks, and paths tighter and tighter to the point of isolating them from nature, we stretch our own frayed nerves to the breaking point, and this tension is present throughout society. How many of us resort to the use of tranquilizers? Here I am not merely playing the role of an agitator. I myself am truly disturbed. I am worried as a responsible architect. I do not want to lose hope and end up producing lesser evils. I want to work on what makes me dream and turn these dreams into practical and economic realities.

If we are to make that kick-turn, to shift our standpoint, we will have to do so as much in our relationship with time as with space. Not so long ago, not knowing how to accomplish this and having no solution, I would have kept silent on the matter. After all, haven't we had enough of all the absurd theories and utopias leading nowhere? Perhaps now it is time to resume the "project" of facing up to the difficulty, squarely and resolutely. What destroys space, destroys time. The tunneling effect destroys spatial continuity, breaking it up into small islands that cannot be connected mentally. This discontinuity – living in one place, working in another, and shopping in a third – resembles zapping, the instantaneous transition from one screen to another, be it on a television or a computer screen. It has become an isomorphic mental structure, a world in bits and pieces, incomprehensible yet beautiful and exciting in certain respects. But for whom? For what lot of disoriented, hedonistic "nomads?"

I have said enough about the shape of roads. Running straight from one point to another, they form networks and connect places and "non-

Charles de Gaulle
Airport, Roissy.

places." Places of passage — exceptional for some, commonplace for others — are always singular, ambivalent sites associated with pleasure and sadness, danger and security, and a sense of transformation. Ports, entrances to bridges, intersections, caravansaries, train stations, and airport terminals at all scales are important places. They are sites of transformation and gathering, sites that engender economic activity and trade. Nothing new in this today. Markets are set up at crossroads; Japanese stations occupy the ground floor or basement level of huge shopping centers. The only novel thing, at least in terms of scope, is the variety of activities involved and the extent of the interconnection between networks. This is true of all modes of transit and at all scales. Interchange sites have become more and more important when it comes to meeting new standards of comfort. Users hate the ruptures in conveyance associated with such sites, be it a matter of changing from one bus to another or from a train to a plane. How to enhance the value of such ruptures opens a huge field of reflection. With cities coming undone and losing their coherence, such points of interchange constitute lively sites full of energy and new possibilities. Projects abound in the field, whether

they involve train stations, subways, bus or airport terminals, or any combinations thereof. For cities such interchange points provide an occasion for reflecting upon and modifying themselves, for devising new models of organization and new spaces. It is a field full of hope and enthusiasm because everything seems to coalesce here, from the simple concern for the difficulties that some people have in getting around to increasing service and leisure facilities. Meeting and interchange are empowering in and of themselves, in the social field as in the sciences and the arts.

Having given thought to some of these points in my work at Charles de Gaulle Airport, at La Défense, and on the left bank of the Seine, I believe that the greatest difficulty resides in creating an organic space, by which I mean a space whose boundaries and visible circuits have a sense other than the mechanical addition of one functional space to another. Many problems arise in getting different authorities — each with its own status, mode of financing, and company identity — to work together to create an interchange center unmarred by overt signs of separation that are utterly meaningless to users. Current organizational modes and the growing importance given to economic and individualistic values do

not make matters any easier. Who will sustain and coordinate a common project? What solutions can be found for combining the technical requirements (which are important but can always be circumvented) and the economic, social, and political requirements? Few fields of research and experimentation are as important these days. For society it is an opportunity to organize itself and crystallize its nature.

I hold that we must invest enough in such places to make them not only convenient and practical but also beautiful. I also hold that we must not, for commercial or aesthetic reasons, artificially exaggerate the state of excitement in these places. Excitement thrives naturally, as it should, in places of passage and movement. It is not good to provoke or manufacture it. Just offer people a calm, generous, simple space and let them live.

The comparison may seem shocking, but to my mind the need to create artificial excitement resembles the need for drugs. Public places should allow all individuals freely to develop their own feelings and states of mind. They should be places where people can grow. Finally, they should be beautiful because beauty is good and necessary for all.

Of course, the question of what defines a beautiful space is another vast issue.

Charles de Gaulle Airport, Roissy.

PAUL ANDREU HAS DIRECTED ARCHITECTURAL DESIGN AT CHARLES DE GAULLE AIRPORT IN PARIS SINCE 1970. AMONG HIS WORKS ARE AIRPORTS IN ABU DHABI, JAKARTA, CAIRO, DAR ES SALAAM, SANTIAGO, AND HAINAN, AND THE FRENCH TERMINAL FOR THE CHANNEL TUNNEL. CURRENT WORK INCLUDES AIR TERMINALS IN MANILA, HARARE, LARNACA, PAPHOS, AND SHANGHAI. HE IS A MEMBER OF THE ACADÉMIE DES BEAUX ARTS AT THE FRENCH INSTITUTE, AND IN 1995 HE RECEIVED THE AGA KHAN AWARD FOR ARCHITECTURE.

Akira Asada and Arata Isozaki

From Molar Metabolism to Molecular Metabolism

A-1

Our plan is to approach two problematics of "how" simultaneously: "how to plan" and "how planning is surpassed by reality." To open such a discussion, we will take up the metabolism movement in a broad sense, including both the metabolists of the 1960s – which we call "molar" – and the new metabolism – the "molecular."

Let's begin with the earlier one. On the occasion of the World Design Conference held in Tokyo in 1960, a group of young 30-something Japanese architects – Kiyonori Kikutake (1928–), Kisho Kurokawa (1934–), Fumihiko Maki (1928–), and Masato Otani (1923–) – proposed "metabolism" as a new ism for architecture and urban planning. Their idea was quite simple: architecture and the city should constitute an open, living organism that grows through metabolism, instead of an enclosed, static machine. In certain ways, this is an extension of functionalism. Given a certain function, an architecture can be designed as a solid machine that fulfills that function. But what if the function fluctuates as time goes by? Architecture then should also fluctuate metabolically. In this manner the metabolists began to conceptualize architecture and the city, and metabolism in this sense was expected to generate a "becoming" of a complex structure, more open and dynamic than functionalism.

A vision common to metabolism also appears in the work of Kenzo Tange (1913–), a leading modernist under whose influence the metabolists came of age. "Tokyo Plan: 1960" by the Tange Studio is one example: in this city on the sea there is a stem, called an "urban axis," that encases the infrastructure; branches and leaves are grafted freely onto the stem. The whole structure can expand indefinitely over the ocean – if and only if an unlimited budget is available and one ignores environmental problems.

At this stage we can already observe two basic issues of the metabolists. First, while metabolism intended to radicalize functionalism, its structural model was the organic whole, based on a hierarchy – stem (or spinal cord), branch, leaf, organ, cell. No matter how complex metabolist projects seem, this hierarchical schema of the organic whole can be easily detected behind that complexity. Because this 1960s metabolism was strongly influenced by a holistic and organicist macroscopic view of life, we call it "molar metabolism." Second, metabolism took for granted the possibility of infinite growth based upon linear time. For this reason, it was extremely fashionable in the 1960s, during the Japanese economy's tremendous growth; the flip side is that it ended up functioning as an ideological expression of the movement of capital, a cycle of unending building and demolition, massive production and massive waste – the opposite of what it originally intended. The end result – the landscape of "delirious Tokyo" or "delirious Japan" – was a metabolist's worst nightmare. This same process is now accelerating even more deliriously in the cities of Southeast Asia.

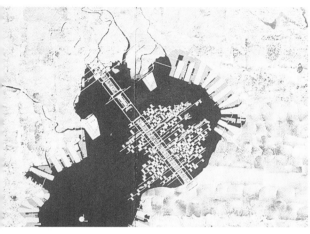

Kenzo Tange, Tokyo Plan: 1960, model.

Christopher Alexander fundamentally criticized this first aspect in the context of modernism in general, rather than of metabolism per se. In his classic article "A City is Not a Tree" (1965), he lucidly explains that while artificially planned cities – by the metabolists or whoever – consistently assume a tree structure, the naturally generated city has a much more complex structure that he identifies as a "semi-lattice." The tree structure – no matter how much potential it seems to contain for free development – is essentially homogeneous, implicitly determined by a single designer. It cannot accommodate the formidable complexity engendered by social reciprocity. (Ironically, Alexander's own projects are not free from this critique.) In *Rhizome*

Kenzo Tange, Tokyo Plan: 1960, detail.

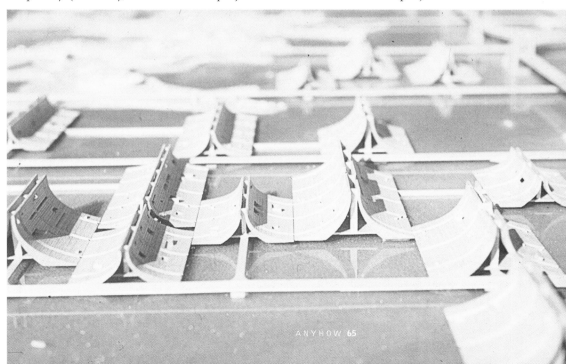

(1976), Gilles Deleuze and Félix Guattari counterpose the *rhizome* as a dynamic vision of the semi-lattice versus the tree structure. The problematic here is also to criticize the unified hierarchy of the spinal-cord-organ-cell and to unleash the multiple body they call the "body without organs." Although the metabolists were aware of Alexander's critique, they were unable to respond to it.

Here I would like to introduce an architect who might be called a postmetabolist: Arata Isozaki. Isozaki's early project "City in the Air" (1961–62), has a strong tinge of metabolism. It literally assumes a tree structure: offices and residences plug into a vertical column called the "joint core" that encases the infrastructure. But what he really intended to construct was not a tree structure but a forest, with the expectation that in the end the mingling of the branches in the air would become as complex as a labyrinth. It appeared to Isozaki that, no matter how he tried to design the city to be anarchic, inasmuch as he had designed the city by himself any result would be too consistent and transparent. On the occasion of a 1962 exhibition of metabolism, "Future City and Life," Isozaki presented a radical experiment: "Incubation Process." Instead of designing a project by himself, he installed a large table covered with an aerial photograph of a part of Tokyo, along with a hammer, nails, and colored wire for the audience to use. Hammering in a nail would produce a joint core; the wire that connects the two joint cores would represent offices and residences. Leaving the installation by itself, the architect disappeared. The result was astounding. By the end of the exhibition, a three-dimensional labyrinth as chaotic as a spider's nest of wire stretched not only all across the table but also to the walls and ceiling, all over the exhibition space. Perhaps it is this becoming that became Isozaki's metaphor for the city. Fascinated as he had been by the image of the city as ruins, Isozaki buried the model by dripping enormous quantities of plaster over it. For Isozaki this was symbolic of the end of metabolism. Thirty-five years later he presented the same exhibition at Art Tower Mito and developed

methods of interactive design using the Internet in the Haishi Exhibition at the InterCommunication Center in Tokyo.

Before leaping across this time span, however, I would like to point out that Isozaki was from the outset critical of the second aspect of metabolism – faith in the infinite possibility of growth based on linear time; this was expressed in his ritual of burial by dripping. "City in the Air" began as a "plan to develop the remains of the Yodobashi filtration plant in Shinjuku." As if "Incubation Process" were the negative of "City in the Air," in the drawing for "Incubation Process," he superimposed "City in the Air" onto an image of ruins. The accom-

Photo: Osamu Murai

Photo: Yoshio Takase

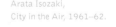

Arata Isozaki,
City in the Air, 1961–62.

Arata Isozaki,
City in the Air, 1961–62.

panying text read: "The ruin is the future of our city; the future city is the ruin itself." Obsessed with nonlinear time in which future and past are overlaid – that is, time in the last instance, the time of the eternal return of ruins – Isozaki always questioned metabolism's naive progressivist belief in infinite growth based in linear time.

The 1960s critiques implicitly or explicitly posed against modernism in general and metabolism in particular eschewed organic holism and teleological time. The true complexity that architecture and urbanism must deal with can be accessed only when they are released from organic holism. We have to go beyond the biological model – or the biological model must become molecular rather than molar in the sense of Deleuze and Guattari. Either way, we must reject the sovereignty of individual architects and accept the intervention of others in the process of social reciprocity. At the same time, complexity can be realized only if it is released from linear teleological time. Under the domination of teleological time, everything is programmed by the one and only telos of growth, leaving no space for heterogeneous emergence and dissipation. To resist this domination we have to pay attention to layered, multiple temporality. We have to listen to ghosts from both the past and the future. This lesson may sound mundane. In fact, the same problematic has persisted for 30 years. But at the present moment, when the dreams of the 1960s seem to be reappearing in various guises, we need to remind ourselves of metabolism's failure.

I-1

Unfortunately, I could not attend the conference, so I entrusted Asada with slides of my two projects, "Incubation Process" (1962) and "Haishi" (1997). Though 35 years apart, both assume a critical approach toward metabolism: the former is postmetabolist and the latter, molecular metabolist. As the designer, I will offer an ex post facto interpretation.

The metabolist group was established for the occasion of the World Design Conference in 1960. At this conference, most of the main members of Team X, which began a sectarian movement within CIAM (Congrès Internationaux d'Architecture Moderne), apparently participated, with an eye on the prize of being recognized as the Tokyo faction of CIAM. Following the conventions of architectural avant-garde movements, the metabolists (Team X) appeared with a manifesto. Then, seeking to undermine CIAM from within, Team X attempted to express the theme of "growth and change" in an existential and brutal architectural style. Only the metabolist group posed a biological model in place of the mechanistic model upon which architectural modernism had relied. It was already the tendency of CIAM to liken the gestalt of the city to the anthropomorphic structure of the human body: brain, heart, circulatory system, and spinal cord were used as models to arrange functionally central business districts, plazas, circulation, housing, offices, and green zones. In contrast, for the metabolists, the metabolic mechanism on the molecular level commanded special attention as a technical solution to the general thematic of "growth and change." This resulted in an application of combinative capsules – based on biomorphic metaphors such as stem and leaf, spinal cord and organ – that could replace the megastructure. This became the model for architectural design throughout the 1960s and corresponded to the economic development spurred by Japan's industrial production. Then came EXPO '70, the occasion for metabolism's grand display.

Evident in the theme "progress and harmony," EXPO '70 exhibited the image of modern society progressing along linear time. It goes without saying that progress (following the metabolist's linear axis) and harmony (an orderly replacing of the old with the new) were totally congruent with the objectives of the festival. At the margins of the metabolists in the early 1960s, I was critical of their methodology, for I believed that the contemporary city is characterized by discontinuity and contingency; it does not progress according to a predetermined harmony, and we had to reconstruct our methodology by confronting the repetitive cycle of becoming and destruction. I call my way "process planning," which I made into a project on the level of urban planning in "Incubation Process" and on an architectural level in the Oita Prefectural Library (1962–66). In these projects the problematics of uncertainty and undecidability came to the surface.

As Asada mentioned, "Incubation Process" was the performance of a model in progress that concretized the contingent urban becoming by organizing the interventions of a multitude of others; finally the flow of time was severed, and the whole was buried under dripped plaster. The end result is on view at a gallery called Oita Art Plaza, which is the transmigration of the Oita Prefectural Library.

The architecture of the library/gallery has been explained as an application of the theory of "process planning." This was concretized when the design had to be presented before the scale, budget, and program had been determined. First, functional concerns were categorized into several bundles of emerging conditions; each category was kept flexible so that it could expand or contract. At this point, the whole of the imaginary architecture could expand and contract in total fluctuation like an organism – a state of undecidability.

To transpose this into actual construction drawings, however, the fluctuation had to be frozen at a certain moment. The imaginary expansion and contraction – becoming – would be fixed: the moment of death. I called the decision "severance." When flow is severed, an open wound is exposed through which we see an image of ruin. Architecture that has been enjoying its becoming in undecidability is suddenly deprived of its continuous time by a violent intervention of the design subject. At this moment it is given life

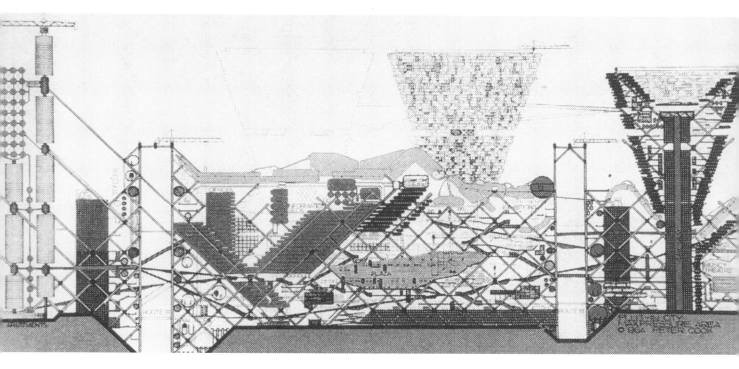

for the first time; simultaneously, linear time is put to death. It is the point at which another time begins.

These two projects have the following common inclinations: (1) making the future open-ended, without imposing any telos, (2) paying attention only to the process of becoming, (3) an incessant occurrence of uncertain elements – "process planning" – that organizes an unconditional intervention of others (an audience) and a coexistence of elements with different emergents, (4) a violent intervention of the design subject at a certain point – the ritual of burial by dripping and the determination of design by severance, and (5) one time dies and another begins – irreversible time (an image of ruin) and nonlinear time (the articulation by termination or freezing).

Manifest here is a radicalism that, by returning to *arché*, delivers a shock to the conventional avant-garde claim to produce a new idea in order to change the status quo and lead toward a target fixed in the future. In 1968 this radicalism was a death sentence for the old avant-garde, and it finally self-destructed. For this reason, in the 1960s there were many projects that aimed at not being built. The problematics of uncertainty and undecidability that had emerged during this time carried over to the 1990s, the age of post-polar-opposites. While the methodological tools of design have shifted from hard to soft technology, from actual to virtual, the climate of framing institutions has shifted from nation-state to regional blocs. Consistent, however, is the methodology of taking the thinking model as a clue.

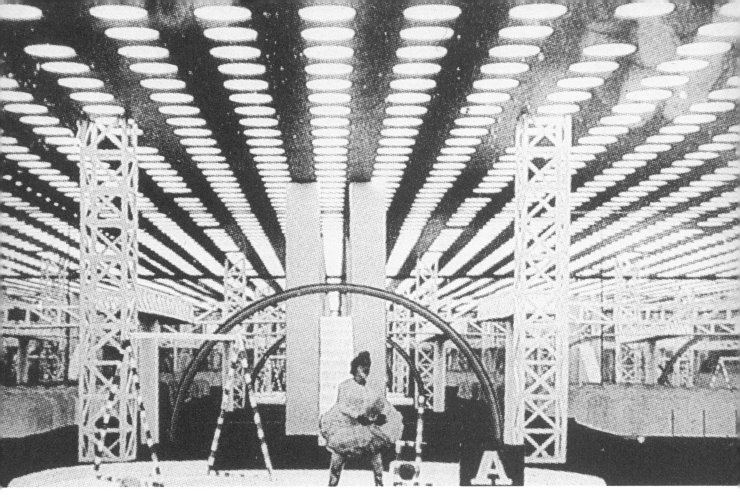

A-2

Metabolism conceptualized a paradigm shift from a physical to a biological model, from architecture as a solid machine to architecture as a metabolic organism. Beginning in the mid-1960s, however, parallel to the development of information technology, another paradigm shift – from the biological to the information model – occurred. This was evident not only in Isozaki's work but in that of his contemporaries, whom he introduced in his book *Demolition of the Canon of Architecture* (1975) – Archigram, Archizoom/Superstudio. They had arrived at the concept of "invisible architecture," that is, architecture as a cybernetic environment. On the one hand, they proposed a megastructure of ungraspable boundaries because of its enormity of scale (prescient of Rem Koolhaas's "bigness") and, on the other, they focused on events – information exchange rather than material production – occurring within the indefinite interior space of the megastructure (a precursor of Bernard Tschumi's "event city").

In the case of Archigram, for instance, Peter Cook's "Plug-in City" (1964) had many similarities to metabolism, but Ron Herron's "Walking City" (1964) was designed as a constantly moving city; Cook's "Instant City" (1968–69) reduced the city to a stage for happenings. In Archizoom's "No-stop City" (1971) the whole of urban space became an unlimited interior space, presenting various activities within it in close-up view.

Within this context Isozaki designed "Festival Square" for EXPO '70 in Osaka. It was intended to be "invisible architecture" – "faceless architecture" as a cybernetic environment for information exchange. The concept, though only partially realized, was quite vanguard for the time. Unfortunately, however, the state's requirement to have a visible

Archizoom, No-stop City, 1969–72.

face symbolizing the national event persuaded them to build an anthropomorphic tower with two faces – "The Tower of the Sun" by Taro Okamoto – in the center of the square. Isozaki's defeat was evident. He was hospitalized for overwork. Afterward, withdrawing from the experiment of large-scale urban planning, he turned toward the rhetorical manipulation of architectural language, that is, in a sense, a hermetic mannerism. Thus he became the champion of postmodern architecture in Japan.

Twenty-five years later Isozaki seems to be returning to his early dream of experimenting with large-scale urban planning, as seen in "Haishi." This project, which we first presented at the Anywise conference, is an artificial island to be located in Zhuhai City near Macao [see *Anywise* (MIT Press, 1996), 24–31]. In a sense, it looks like an old-time metabolist utopia; all of the forms, including the island itself, are obviously biomorphic. It is even reminiscent of "Tokyo Plan: 1960" in that it is a city of landfill in the sea, it has a central axis, and so on. On the other hand, these patterns are only a tentative pretext for the interactive design. Isozaki has invited architects from all over the world to design the whole or parts of the prototype. Furthermore, he has organized an experiment in which some patterns of the city are self-organized, beginning from a random distribution of points via various programs, such as cellular automation. While these design processes proceed simultaneously on different levels, the intervention – sometimes even viral – of outsiders via the Internet constantly transforms the total pattern. It is far from the methodology that imposes a homogeneous tree structure. It follows that, if we still dare to call it metabolism at all, it is not the molar metabolism of the organic holistic model but a new metabolism formed of informatics – it is molecular.

Should a manifesto of molecular metabolism be proposed here? This is not possible yet, or ever. From the beginning, molecular metabolism is not a vision to be imposed from above. It is therefore flickering like a mirage beyond the ongoing Haishi project.

I-2

The Haishi project proposes to construct a city as an island on the real South China Sea. Although it was conceived as a project that could be realized directly, it was also intended as an imaginary vision constructed over a site plan, as indicated by the Chinese metaphor *haishi*, which means both "ocean city" and "mirage."

"Island" became a practical concept with which to conduct a hypothetical experiment, based on the assumption that the world will be an archipelago after the present border lines disappear. Under the prerequisite that the information network be globalized to the limit, the archipelago assumes a basic scheme: every individual community is central but not the center, its boundary, that is, the coastal line, being open to the infinitely continuous body of the ocean. The unit is the "island" (*shima* in Japanese), with its ambiguous connotation: either the island as a geographically continuous land or as a zoning map of the invisible territoriality claimed by the

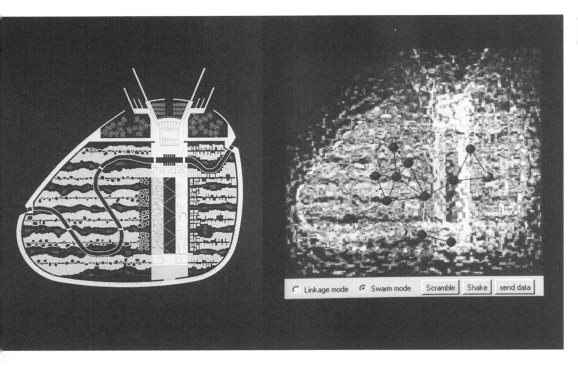

Arata Isozaki, Plan of
Haishi Jimua (Mirage City),
Computer Graphic, 1996.

Japanese outlaw societies. That is, an island can be an enclosed homogeneous unit or a network of mutually related places.

Haishi was first conceptualized within real geographic space, which then became the prototype. Then, for three months before and after the Anyhow conference, we conducted an experiment in transposing topology: the island went through a morphological transformation on the Internet, and we documented and exhibited the processes through which the four islands with isomorphic coastlines were metamorphosed by different functional agents.

1. Prototype: Via the intrusion of a computer virus – or a violent act – the pre-installed program of Haishi undergoes a morphological transformation.

2. Signature: Piranesi's Campo Marzio is cut into the shape of Haishi. Within the zone, 48 building sites are chosen and assigned to 48 cities. Forty-eight architects who live in or are in some way connected to the cities are asked to propose architecture, objects, or systems with their signatures. *Shimas* – islands or zoning maps – scattered all over the world are reconnected and gathered into a single *shima* via the frame of historical time (Piranesi's grand Rome). This patchwork of signatures is knit together through fax and e-mail.

3. Visitors: Twelve architects and artists who work with digital means in turn visit the exhibition space each week. Each is to propose his/her idea in relation to the previous visitor's idea – develop or oppose, succeed or destroy. This method can be likened to

Arata Isozaki, Haishi
Jimua (Mirage City),
Computer Graphic, 1997.
Top: Negative image of the
street pattern creates urban
blocks. Bottom: A study
of automatic generation of
web generated network
simulates a street pattern.

AKIRA ASADA IS ASSISTANT
PROFESSOR AT THE KYOTO
INSTITUTE OF ECONOMIC
RESEARCH AND EDITOR
OF THE JOURNAL CRITICAL
SPACE. HIS BOOKS INCLUDE
KOZOTO CHIKARA (STRUC-
TURE AND POWER) AND
HERUMESU NO ONGAKU
(MUSIC AND HERMES).

ARATA ISOZAKI IS AN
ARCHITECT IN TOKYO. HIS
PROJECTS INCLUDE THE
MUSEUM OF CONTEMPO-
RARY ART IN LOS ANGELES,
TEAM DISNEY BUILDING
IN FLORIDA, THE MUSEUM
OF MODERN ART IN GUNMA,
THE KYOTO CONCERT
HALL IN KYOTO, THE SANT
JORDI SPORTS HALL IN
BARCELONA, AND LA CASA
DEL HOMBRE IN LA CORUÑA.

that of Japanese *renga* (verse linking), in which poets gather to produce linked *waka* or *haiku* poetry. In this particular experiment, each participant's work was performed one after another in the continuity of one space, and the originary features disappeared, superseded little by little, except for an enormous record.

4. Internet: Any participant could send any idea through the Internet. In order to edit the automatic accumulation of information, we produced and combined several auto-generative, self-organizational programs.

The ongoing events of the four models were also accessible through the Internet. They gradually came into existence, flickering like a mirage during the web site interaction. I intended to organize here the process through which a citylike event (I dare to call it this, rather than city) comes into existence. In this process the interventions of multiple others — with or without signatures — are both inevitable and indispensable. The point is that for intervention, control in the traditional sense is impossible, therefore it is necessary to establish a new subject that involves others. In this precise sense, are not the problematics of uncertainty and undecidability taken up in the 1960s still streaming like subterranean water?

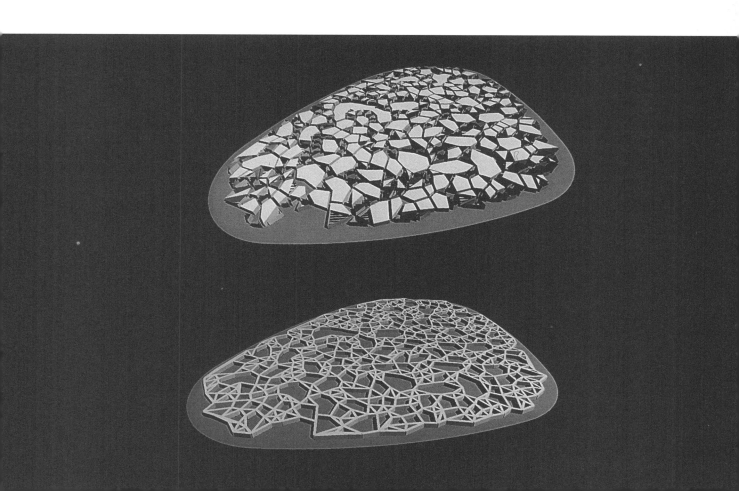

Francesca Hughes

"How" is here

Faking it: Pregnant Pauses
and Other Constructions of Delay

In the first few hours of the Anyhow conference the words *pregnancy* and *pregnant* came up several times. This was not some weird harbinger of the paper I was about to deliver, but a typical (normal even) symptom of the latent metaphors at work in architecture. "Pregnancy" and "pregnant" lay strewn on the ground with all of the other words issued forth and fast accumulating into unmanageable snowdrifts of words around the speakers. But for me at least, these two words did not melt away at quite the same temperature as the rest.

Pregnancy has long provided a metaphoric model for architectural production.[1] The building as baby recurs, in varying degrees of explicitness and implicitness, through the history of the fiction-making of architecture-making. Architecture is (still) obsessed with

1 As indeed it has for many other forms of production.

momentum from sketch to building."[2] But the staging of the concept sketch as already existing, let alone at some original position, and the faking of a chronology extruded from it, are currently under stress (more than the usual stress that accompanies lying), the stress of extreme distortion. The faking, always a distortion anyway, is now stretched so thin that it is almost transparent, and when lies are transparent, they no longer work. They are no longer convincing, and it is no longer even important to be convinced. That is, not only are you no longer even momentarily convinced by the faking of the making, you no longer even

2 "The Strange Time of the Sketch," a paper given at the "Time & Image" conference, (London), June 29, 1997, by Mark Wigley, to whom I am here indebted for his wonderful rendition of the staging and restaging of this chronology in the work of Enrique Miralles, among others, via the making and remaking of concept sketches.

interpreted as the local infrastructure of production within the space of our studio, where

pregnancy. But is this model of the production of architecture itself (still) pregnant?

The origin of the architect's progeny is the concept drawing, the register of the supposed temporal location of conception: that thing which must always be at the very beginning or must at least be *staged* as being at the very beginning and whose authorship, whose genealogy, is never in any doubt. The teleological trajectory originating in the concept has conventionally structured at least the *representation* of architectural practice and production. The genealogical authenticity of the final product, the building – drawn up and constructed by many – can be established by its likeness to the concept sketch or model – made only by one and unsigned because it is itself the signature. The fiction is in the faking of the linearity of this process, the reassertion of this uninterrupted trajectory from conception to construction, the "relentless

bother to fake belief back. Consequently, going through the motions of this newly meaningless action (the annunciation of the fiction) starts to take on the absurdity of the redundant. Like Bruce Nauman's clown that jumps up and down interminably shouting "No!" at the camera[3] or Man Ray's iron with nails protruding from its base,[4] form and function are split both physically and psychically, and the resulting enigmatic property is the suspension of sense itself.

3 Bruce Nauman, *Double No*, 1988, video, Froehlich Collection, Stuttgart.

4 Man Ray, *Cadeau*, 1921, mixed media: iron and tacks (original lost; existing photograph by the artist).

But what exactly brought about the redundancy of this age-old fiction? In other words, what has happened to the infrastructure of production to test and contort its current representation so? In what is termed the post-medium age, relations governing structure and media in practice are themselves transformed and consequently transform the infrastructure, specifically the temporal infrastructure, of production. As in much of current art practice, there is no longer a clearly dominant medium or even a clear *sequence* of media in the making of architecture: medium is no longer structuring production. Structure is no longer even informed by media, let alone medium specific – there are too many, and they change too fast. To suggest that an artist who paints is necessarily a painter no longer makes sense – medium and structure have strayed from each other. As a corollary, media now no longer lend identity to (or even locate) their users; instead the user's identity, as if mimicking the media, is also only transitional. Practice that is a matrix of media and users (identities, not necessarily individuals) must seek, in the absence of a medium that

both the proper sense of authentic discovery and the improper sense of false origin, of identity faked; faking per se is not gone. This invented structure of practice is wholly indifferent to medium such that work and medium at times slide past each other, slipping in and out of phase, overlapping. At any given moment structure might slide from detail design to an editing decision, without any warning, leaving no trace. The inherent promiscuity of a structure that is almost mediumlike is such that the faked and the real are indistinguishable, interchangeable; process need no longer come before product. The staging of a smooth transition from concept to object would require such contortion that it is no longer possible; the conditions of production have strayed too far. The camouflaging function of practice framed to support this teleology has collapsed, and the

infrastructure (physical and conceptual), process (how), and product (what) merge and become

might provide coherence or continuity, a working structure that *behaves* like a medium but that is not a medium, a structure that emerges from the crisis of medium and structure relations, that is itself neither truly structural nor mediate.

In our practice we paint, write, edit, teach, design, make, curate, lecture, build – all of these inform each other. All activities collectively constitute our practice. All detritus collectively constitutes our product. There is no origin, no concept sketch, no signature, and next to no discernible likeness among products; all are bastard progeny. And when the structure of work must become mediumlike, medium becomes the (banal) structure: there are teaching days, designing days, painting days, and paperwork. A structure with mediate tendencies is exactly the condition we are struggling to invent as a way to organize both work and relations between works. *Invention* crucially incorporates

faking must be reconfigured. Other fictions must be faked. The alternative option, of course, is to tell the truth. But this option is always already foreclosed, as the truth, even if it could be excavated, or recognized, or iterated, would be by definition too complicated. Instead, the making of faking and the faking of making present a rich territory for practice. Faking *is* the creative process that, like all good fictions, actually changes the truth – the making of work.

Being a child or, more specifically, a teenager of the Thatcher era, I am too young to remember engagement with infrastructure that is coherent and connected. In abstraction, infrastructure promises a ubiquitous condition, always everywhere and always everywhere equally. But, like the stripped and (apparently arbitrarily) fragmented infrastructure that was transport, education, health care, utilities, and prison services (the list goes on), we find that the conceptual infrastructure of architecture no longer works, has lost its meaning. Coherence is lost structurally: it is fragmented, elements are isolated and broken off from the rest. Or, more curiously, coherence is there structurally but not conceptually: like a journey on the the U-Bahn lines that ran under the wall into East Berlin then back into the West, we pass through spaces (empty, dimly lit stations) that appear to make sense, but the train does not stop there. Even if it did, the spaces are sealed underground, isolated from the potential coherence of connecting to the city above.[5]

5 I am thinking in particular of the (then ironically named) Stadtmitte "center of the city" stop on line 6.

Train and city, time and space slide past each other, split both physically and conceptually. In our practice, medium and structure no longer coincide in a way that makes clear sense. As they slip past each other not only do oppor-

this irreversibility. When we look at the concept sketch we find that though it disciplines the construction drawings (prevents them from straying from likeness and introducing genealogical doubt), it is itself disciplined by them (they make it stand up, both physically and conceptually). Without a clear chronology of production it would become increasingly ambiguous whether the later media are being disciplined by earlier ones or earlier by later, or the structure is disciplining medium or medium, structure. In other words, what or who is disciplining what and where. Clearly genealogy relies on chronology (a strictly linear construction) to maintain sequence and rank; the disciplining action, this enforcing of chronology, is itself symptomatic of genealogical anxiety. A strict maintenance of chronology is crucial

camouflaged against the surface of practice. The images of the studio attempt, literally, to

tunities for other logics emerge, but curious pockets of work, like the Stadtmitte U-Bahn stop, are trapped. These pockets whose meaning is not quite lost but newly disturbing, newly provocative, are above all enigmatic. Structure and medium are in suspension; any possibility of their precipitation into sense is deferred, delayed. These resistant pockets are important as they constitute territories generated uniquely by this media/structure crisis, and it is on them that we focus — not to force a precipitation of sense but more to gape at its suspended state, to read what other infrastructures for production (temporal, spatial) might be suggested.

Returning to the metaphor of pregnancy, its surface likeness (but, as we shall see, even this is unfaithful) to the *temporal* structure of architectural production is crucial to its viability. Conception is followed by a state of irreversible delay. But already the concept sketch questions

to the assertion of origin and authorship: who was at the scene of the crime when. But if practice is fragmented by the use of multiple media that fail, in their shifts, to coincide with shifts in structural modes, then the urge to discipline can only be frustrated, can only fail to fulfill the criteria conventionally associated with it: establishing and sustaining at all costs a single story about the origin of a piece of work, whether true or false. Indeed, "true or false" becomes so irrelevant that the distinction is quite lost in the process.

In the production of work, heat is given off. But the friction, here between structure and medium, refers to coitus not interruptus but deferred — delayed and in suspension. The space of this suspension is the space of practice, the space of the invented structure that carries, as if in suspended belief, the product of the friction or *frottage* between structure and medium.

But if we look at the work we find that not only the register of structure in the work, but the register of work in the structure is delayed. This moment is pregnant (itself a construction of delay), a pregnant moment that is "promising, rich, fruitful" or "a construction, rhetorical, in which more is implied than is said or seems."[6] This pregnancy might not only be illegitimate, it might be phantom, or worse, faked.

6 *Webster's New Twentieth Century Dictionary*, unabridged 2nd ed., s.v. "pregnant."

In the Annunciation a pregnancy is given name, but the term *annunciation* remains ambiguous as to whether it refers to a previous, existing, or imminent condition. The many images of the moment of annunciation present a virgin (possibly even already pregnant) and Gabriel there, and the Holy Spirit or dove just arriving (Figs. 1–2).

plete set of bedroom furnishings.) (Fig. 6) Chronology, genealogy, discipline: "Who got there first?" or more accurately, "Who *came* first?" Clearly a chronology, immaculate or not, is being faked, and when a chronology is being faked so too, we might suspect, is a genealogy. Who exactly precipitated this conception? How many were there? Alexander Pushkin's poem *Gavriiliada* would have it three. The Devil in the morning, hence the "Virgin" might be already pregnant at the moment of annunciation:

> He offers a small flower with one hand.
> The other in her plain dress is a fumble
> And quickly up inside her vestments steals
> And playfully a gentle finger feels
> In there for secret pleasures. Mary reels.[8]

Gabriel in the evening:

> Dearly she wanted to love heaven's master
> Whose words have given her a pleasant thrill,

portray this mottled surface in which the "hows" and the "whats" appear like the wood in

(Figs. 1–6, left to right) Piero della Francesca (1415/20–92), **The Legend of the True Cross: The Annunciation**, 1452–66, 329 x 193 cm, fresco, The Church of San Francesco: Arezzo. From Guillaud Jacqueline and Maurice, **Piero della Francesca: Poète de la Forme, les Fresques de San Francesco** (Paris: Editions Guillaud, 1988); 65; Duccio (c.1278–1318/19), **The Annunciation**, 1311, 43 x 44cm, egg (identified) on poplar. Courtesy of the Trustees, The National Gallery: London, NG 1139; Sandro Botticelli (c.1445– 1510), **The Annunciation**, date unknown, 49.5 x 61.9cm, tempera

Or the Holy Spirit already there touching a Virgin's forehead and a flustered Gabriel rushing in the door or asking directions outside (Figs. 3–4).

Or Gabriel there, no sign of the Holy Spirit, and Gabriel looking rather amorous (Fig. 5).

The order in which Gabriel and the Holy Spirit arrive is ambiguous, to say the least. Several fictions are current, but all ask: *Who* got there first? If the Bible is clear that Gabriel arrived first – "The Holy Spirit *will* come upon you"[7] – then why in so many of these scenes is the Holy Spirit also almost there? What is the rush? Why is the Holy Spirit sometimes even ahead of Gabriel, there to witness the announcement of its own imminent arrival, checking up on Gabriel, so to speak? And what are all these beds doing, so beautifully made, waiting? (Surely immaculate conception with a dove does not require a com-

7 Luke 35 [my emphasis].

> In reverence to Him no one surpassed her,
> But Gabriel, thought she, was nicer still.[9]

And the Holy Spirit that night, after which:

> A weary Mary as he flew away,
> Thought 'Ah what fun and games I've had today!
> That's – one, two, three. They're really not too bad!
> I've weathered it, I think I can record.
> Together in a single day I've had
> The devil, one Archangel and the Lord.[10]

When chronology collapses, so too does simple, singular genealogy. In place other, more complex genealogies emerge that in turn require more complex temporal constructs, temporalities potentially as multiple as the genealogies they describe. The appeal of the metaphor of pregnancy to genealogically anxious architectural culture is all too understandable. There is this messy and murky problem of establishing legitimate conception in the beginning, but the period of delay that follows is reassuringly

8 Alexander Pushkin, *Gavriiliada*, trans. A. D. P. Briggs in *Alexander Pushkin*, ed. A. D. P. Briggs (London: Everyman, 1997), 75–90; 84, lines 327–31.

9 Ibid., 78, lines 93–96.

10 Ibid., 89, lines 511–16.

sealed: no one can intervene in the middle of the process and hijack the project. Indeed it is the impenetrability of the delay state that makes the stressful invisibility and undecidability of conception tolerable.

The construction of pregnant delay is not unlike the temporal construction of astronomical photography. The index left on the photographic plate is itself a trace of the past, of light (whose source may be presently expired) that is fixed, in the photographic process, by the light of the enlarger. Old light and young light combine and are indistinguishable. Past unimaginable, distant past, recent past, and present collapse, flattened by the photograph. The astronomical photograph is a complex register of the interface between present light and old light, of present traces and past traces, of elements that we can see and elements that we can't see and

at night or, in other words, objects invisible to the telescope.

With the camouflaging effect of the surrounding younger light removed, the old, distant light is exposed. The proverbial trees are removed and the wood cannot help but be seen. But CCD photography, unlike X-ray, reveals not only what is behind spatially but also what is behind temporally. The photograph effectively unfurls the space of delay by partially excavating the collapsed chronology. But the condition that CCD photographs depict is of course a fiction or at least remains ambiguous; we can't see it otherwise, so we have no means of verifying it.

When the camera that never lies shows us things that we cannot see by rearranging light (read time) in space, chronology as a means of underwriting a fiction becomes utterly redundant. Instead, the actual complexity of relations

the proverbial trees: they are right there, but you can't necessarily "see" them."

FIG. 3 FIG. 4 FIG. 5 FIG. 6

FRANCESCA HUGHES TEACHES DESIGN AND THEORY AT THE BARTLETT SCHOOL OF ARCHITECTURE IN LONDON. SHE HAS LECTURED WIDELY AND SERVED AS AN EXTERNAL EXAMINER IN THE U.S. AND EUROPE. SHE IS EDITOR OF THE ARCHITECT: RECONSTRUCTING HER PRACTICE AND COLLABORATES WITH JONATHAN MEYER IN A MULTIDISCIPLINARY PRACTICE, HUGHES MEYER STUDIO.

elements that we couldn't see anymore anyhow because they are gone. But this register asks to be read as other photographs are, as an instant condition, a "snapshot" where emission and reception are (still) perceived as simultaneous and not suspended by delay. After all, how is one to perceive delay if everything is equally arrived at the same moment for all to see?

However, in the wonderfully named charge-coupled-device photography the sealing of the space of delay is not quite so secure. In CCD photography ambient, young light can be subtracted so as to expose distant, old light. The technique, developed to allow astronomical photographs to be taken in areas of high light pollution, uses a silicon chip that counts the photons that fall on it. An ambient quota can be subtracted from its readout, revealing images of objects that are fainter than the night sky; that is, fainter than the reflected light of the earth

between time, space, and event, the "what" and the "how," become vivid and require the invention of different kinds of fictions.

When we look at the stars, we are looking at the past. The past that we see is not a simulacrum but a real thing delayed. When we photograph the stars we are precipitating a delay into a present register. When we talk about how work happens, we are talking about a past, a delay collapsed, a syncopation made continuous. It is a past that, more than the future perhaps, presents a space for invention, for fictions far more rich than the chronology conventionally faked. Much as when we stage the astronomical photograph as simply a snapshot, an instant, and not a delay, when we stage the making of work as simply obvious (a seamless, uninterrupted, autonomous progression) not only are we faking the wrong fiction, we are missing the point.

Ed Taverne

Havens in a H

TECHNOLOGICAL SYSTEM

The question of **how** technical innovations in the transportation of people, goods, and information are not only developed but function via all kinds of programming techniques is essentially a question about the significance of technique in contemporary culture.

Technique and technology manifest themselves in society and modify it through the construction of large-scale technical installations such as harbors, airports, and highways and in the development of networks of communications and distribution. These complex systems – at least until recently – have been sustained by exemplifying artifacts such as the telephone, the car, and the computer, which in turn function in a broader social environment. This social embedding is neither static nor linear: in the course of the development and application of new technologies, ever-changing links appear between the social and the technical elements.

Historians of technology like Thomas Hughes and Ruth Cowan refer to this coherence between technology and the daily environment as the "sociotechnical system," by which they mean the factors that connect people, buildings, and cities to each other, not just physically but socially. Of course, various answers, from numerous scientific disciplines, can be given to this and other questions about the working of the so-called large-scale sociotechnical sys-

eartless World

tems at this time. Here I refer to the history of technology and science, and All images Port of Rotterdam, 1997.
especially in recent years, to the social history of technology.

If John Brinckerhoff Jackson were with us today, he would certainly have reduced the
question posed at this Anyhow conference to the fundamental dilemma at the base of our
own contemporary culture, namely the complex and paradoxical relationship between the
technologies upon which our lives are grounded **and** the landscape or the environment in
which we work and live.

J. B. Jackson is one of the most important landscape historians of this century and a con-
noisseur par excellence of the modern American cultural landscape. Upon his death in
Santa Fe, New Mexico, in 1996 at the ripe old age of 91, an obituary appeared in **Design
Book Review:**

> His memory will live on for a long time in the design fields as he ingrained in several generations
> a new way of understanding the environment – of looking not **at** the landscape or for anything in
> particular but of looking more empathetically **into** the land. His view from the motorcycle during
> the course of several decades as he criss-crossed the country between semesters at Harvard and
> Berkeley inspired a different, more democratic mode of perception among his students, col-
> leagues, and readers. Like Walt Whitman, he elevated the common, the plural, the open, into a
> new motorized "song of the open road." In his academic pursuit of such details as barbed wire
> and mow lines, he demonstrated that the human capacity to interpret the land was commensu-
> rate with the urge to shape it.[1]

1 "Remembering J. B. Jackson (1909–1996)," Design Book Review 37/38 (Winter 1996–97): 48.

Jackson founded **Landscape** magazine, in which, from 1951 onward, and independent of
the artistic milieu of American pop art and the academic scene of social science and community architecture, the first chapters of a history of the technical and commercial culture of
the United States were written. Via **Landscape** he gave form to what he called "vernacular
landscape": the world of trailers, parking lots, trucks, loading docks, and suburban
garages. This world of mobility, proliferation, and improvisation contrasts in all aspects
with the "political landscape," the symbolic background of the establishment, developed
according to certain aesthetic rules. These concepts have recently been enriched with new
categories by the geographer Peirce Lewis by which the American landscape can be
indexed into "areas where standards of taste are routinely invoked and areas where they
are not" – thus, into two integrated reservations, one referred to as "tasteful," the other
as "taste-free."[2] 2 Robert L. Thayer, Jr., *Gray World, Green Heart: Technology, Nature, and Sustainable Landscape* (New York: Wiley, 1994), 108–9.

In Jackson's last book, **A Sense of Place, a Sense of Time** (1994), he commented that his interpretation of the American landscape as "collective indicator" of the technological meaning of American culture goes back to flights he made over the American continent in the 1920s. From a plane at 30,000 feet, the aesthetic and symbolic dimensions become rather vague, and only then does it become apparent how much the American landscape is a **reaction** to the normative values of industrial and technological expansion. In Jackson's view, the American or, in fact, Western landscape can no longer be regarded as a formal composition of precisely defined, individual spaces such as settlements, districts, or ecological regions but should be seen more as a system of force fields fed and controlled by streets, roads, and highways.

ROTTERDAM HARBOR

In the context of the history of architecture, Jackson's position is interesting because, situated on the interface between journalistic intuition and science, he made the thrust toward a theoretical framework for the mutual coherence of the perceptual, functional, and symbolic features of an environment saturated by science and technology. His oeuvre illustrates how the professional field of recalcitrant landscape architecture can contribute to the conceptual development of, for example, the politics of the environment and to ecological modernization.

It is striking that the technical sciences in general, and architecture in particular, contribute so little to the acquisition of knowledge concerning large-scale sociotechnical systems. We require knowledge of the physical infrastructure in which the route, structure, and atmosphere and the mobility generated by these factors radically influence the semantics of space. In the current Dutch context, this is a hot item with regard to the enormous investments involved in constructing and improving large-scale infrastructure. Here the aim is to consolidate and strengthen the international competitive position of both Amsterdam Schiphol Airport and the Rotterdam harbor. Today physical infrastructure in the Netherlands is high on the political agenda, but the extent to which the architectural discussion is lagging behind the political, economic, and geographical analyses of the physical planning of traffic and distribution, cultural geography, urban planning, and environmental issues is embarrassing. For architecture, too, complex technical systems are of great cognitive significance and require concepts and analyses. The didactic implications of Rotterdam harbor for education and research in architecture as a technical science is one example.

HARDWARE

The spatial and technological developments in harbors of a scale matching that of Rotterdam have long drawn the attention of numerous scientists, especially geographers. In 1996 the International Geographical Society devoted a major congress to the problems of location and competition that European harbors were experiencing.[3] For architecture, Rotter-

3 "European Ports," special issue on the occasion of the 28th International Geographical Congress, *Journal of Economic and Social Geography* 87 (1994): 4.

dam harbor has paradigmatic significance due to the infrastructure of knowledge that it has developed and the corresponding spatial infrastructure due to the morphology of the harbor area as a configuration of enclaves.

Rotterdam harbor, like Schiphol and the network of national highways, is an immense technical system demanding a great deal of design and functional coordination. Moreover, it is vulnerable in many respects. Historians of technique define such technical systems as a hard **structure** that supports all kinds of **facilities** that subsequently initiate activities that, in turn, require planning, management, and, in particular, coordination.

Accordingly, Rotterdam harbor can be described as a concentration of hardware in the form of sea links and an expanse of pools, basins, wharves, and jetties that, in conjunction with the infrastructure under, on, and above the ground, such as pipelines, railways, and cable networks, form the support for all kinds of techniques and installations for transshipment and communication. Furthermore, this agglomeration facilitates production and management and the realm of residential dwellings and recreation. Together these stimulate a complex of activities coordinated by a network of organizations, public authorities, and service industries.

This picture of Rotterdam harbor as a combination of transshipment and communication technique, physical artifact and service-providing sector, is not exceptional

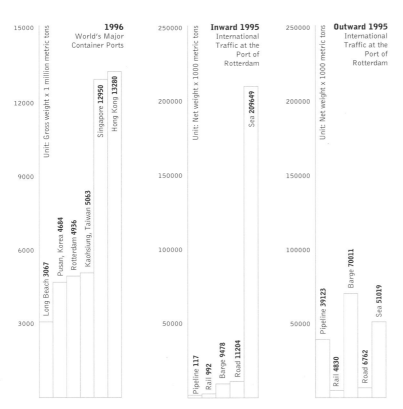

1996 World's Major Container Ports

Unit: Gross weight x 1 million metric tons

Long Beach **3067** — Pusan, Korea **4684** — Rotterdam **4936** — Kaohsiung, Taiwan **5063** — Singapore **12950** — Hong Kong **13280**

Inward 1995 International Traffic at the Port of Rotterdam

Unit: Net weight x 1000 metric tons

Pipeline **117** — Rail **992** — Barge **9478** — Road **11204** — Sea **209649**

Outward 1995 International Traffic at the Port of Rotterdam

Unit: Net weight x 1000 metric tons

Rail **4830** — Road **6762** — Pipeline **39123** — Sea **51019** — Barge **70011**

Left to right:
World's Major Container Ports. Source: Rotterdam Municipal Port Management
Ship Arrivals at the Port of Rotterdam. Source: Rotterdam Municipal Port Management
International Traffic at the Port of Rotterdam. Source: CB Sexcl

when compared to other technical systems. What makes harbors, and Rotterdam in particular, unique is the **nature** of the three systems mentioned. To an ever-increasing extent, this nature is becoming less fixed and more flexible so that the network of which they are a part, in both time and place, is becoming highly differentiated.

A second aspect that typifies Rotterdam is suggested by that phenomenon, namely its vulnerability and sensitivity to the economic climate. These issues form the effects of a new phase of internationalization (the globalization of the world economy), with the corresponding mobility of capital flows, technological innovations, and advanced production processes, and expansion strategies concocted by multi- and supranational enterprises. The globalizing effects of innovations in communications and distribution are demonstrated in Rotterdam harbor mainly by the way in which container transport has directed the structure and the dynamics of the harbor as a business since the 1960s. At the outset, the container was an innovation in transshipment that made handling piece goods as a form of bulk cargo in uniform containers possible. The effects of this new system were slow to manifest because the transshipment of containers required entirely new installations (in limited numbers initially), which, in turn, were also components of a normalized system of measurements, codes, and attachment systems. In the subsequent phases of container development, there was not only talk of all kinds of automation, scaling up, and integration, but also of computerization based on the design of communication networks and the development of new software (software engineering) for data processing to govern the contents, destination, attachment, and control of containers (Electronic Data Interchange). Together, globalization and computerization have led to the gradual creation of an **electronic harbor** of which the most prominent elements are the traffic guidance system and simulation.

Rotterdam harbor has become a technical laboratory for architecture not only because of the unique structure of expertise but also because it has a material infrastructure that is neither urban nor pastoral; instead, it is amorphous and "taste-free." Moreover, in the electronic harbor the distinction between virtual and real surfaces, between electronic and structural networks, is no longer relevant.

Partly as a result of developments in container transportation, Rotterdam harbor has been transformed into a largely silent and invisible operating environment. As a successful, local configuration of one of the many forms of a global economy, Rotterdam harbor has an ever-changing impact on both the region and the city of Rotterdam. Until recently, this relationship was clear geographically: the harbor was a rapidly expanding area in which activities took place that were directly related to the surroundings. The harbor produced noises and smells and, in addition, it had a fascinating skyline: it was a city of unrestrained form, detached from any form of urban intimacy (urban planning). The relationship between the harbor and the city was unilaterally determined by laws of annexation and colonization. Each time the harbor was enlarged, a centuries-old relief of villages, dikes, roads, and canals was simply ironed flat by a hard technical infrastructure.

If, until recently, there was mention of a hard confrontation between two spatial systems sharply opposed to one another, the legislation governing physical planning and environmental protection in addition to a general mobilization toward environmental protection and relaxed living situations has ensured soft transitions and extensive thresholds in the form of recreation areas and green buffers. These, in turn, offer space for numerous unprogrammed forms of leisure-time activities and recreation, activities for the city dweller individualized by consumerism and self-service.

It would appear that the time has come for the city to profit from the cohabitation of opposing conditions created by the harbor. However, the reverse seems to be happening: the Rotterdam harbor region, like so many similar locations in the world, seems to be the object of a conventional and routine urban planning process. Its hard substance is being landscaped, its high but invisible density of pipelines, sound contours, highways, and fiberglass cables is being degraded into requisites for a new theme park. The importance of Rotterdam harbor for architecture lies neither in embalming it in an unreal and romanticized way as a large-scale technical system nor in integrating it into urban society. Rather, it lies in investigating it as an object of expertise and in discovering what it has to offer in terms of new techniques, figures, combinations, and possibilities.

TECHNOLOGY AND ARCHITECTURE

In the economic world dealing in knowledge, the secret of success is the combination of different types of expertise in a productive manner. This is where the primary importance of Rotterdam harbor lies for the technical sciences and for architecture. Where in the past Rotterdam harbor was a commissioning agent for artifacts and, consequently, an important stimulation for architectonic renewal,[4] today the harbor is primarily significant as an

4 See work built in the Rotterdam harbor since the 1920s by Van Tijen; Brinkman & Van der Vlugt; Van den Broek & Bakema.

abstract and synthetic environment. Force and energy fields are at work that, in combination, break with existing concepts of time, space, mass, and behavior. As such, technological systems like Rotterdam harbor carry many levels of cultural meaning. As Cowan argues, "those meanings can sometimes be more potent to people than the social and economic functions those objects and technologies were designed to perform."[5] In gauging this large-scale

5 Ruth Schwartz Cowan, *A Social History of American Technology* (New York: Oxford University Press, 1997), 3.

industrial settlement, our observations and conjectures need to become familiar with new notions of architecture, of technology, and of the shape these will take in the "post-Ford" city. At the same time, we need new disciplinary tools in order to develop a "broad and critical perspective on our current technological society, which might affect a new relation with architecture and urban design."[6] But how?

6 Arie Graafland, "Closing the Gap: The Critical Landscape Conference (Some Backgrounds)," in Michael Speaks, ed., *The Critical Landscape* (Rotterdam: 010 Publishers, 1996), 12–29.

This question ultimately leads to the consideration of the largely one-dimensional character of education and research in architecture as a technical science. A transformation of the traditional polytechnic studies at universities has occurred in the United Kingdom and in the Netherlands in recent years. But does this automatically guarantee a better correlation with, for example, the cognitive sciences of a multidimensional business practice? The Politecnico of Turin, under the leadership of Carlo Olmo, has initiated a project to establish the Istituto Superiore di Scienze Umane del Politecnico. Without going into detail about the program, I must remark that the positioning of the new education and research institute in the economic culture of the city is extremely interesting. This is based on the idea that technological innovation is chiefly a social activity and that a technical university with an acquiescent and multidisciplinary orientation provides an important democratic function in the critical acceptance and social embedding of the many products of technical innovation. Furthermore, Turin reveals a high commitment to the formation of the architect and the engineer; this formation is directed toward the cultivation of, to quote Sanford Kwinter, "new intensities, alternative off-line forms of culture and attention"[7] by means of early confrontations with other disciplines and patterns

7 Sanford Kwinter, "Virtual City, or the Wiring and Waning of the World," in *Assemblage* 29 (1996): 86–101.

of thought. These include programs and seminars covering economic, linguistic, and organizational systems, biotechnology, various modes of conveyance of technical know-how and expertise, and techniques of operations research. With this goal, one should also investigate the diverse relations between space, with its many histories and associations, and all kinds of technological expansion. The ultimate objective is to answer questions concerning the possible content and substance of a contemporary technological culture – questions that, in addition to the endless and exhausting debate on the necessary reconfiguration, recycling, and revision of an architectonic avant-garde, belong at the center of architectural discussion at the end of the millennium.

ED TAVERNE IS PROFESSOR IN THE DEPARTMENT FOR THE HISTORY OF ART AND ARCHITECTURE AT THE UNIVERSITY OF GRONINGEN.

Ben van Berkel

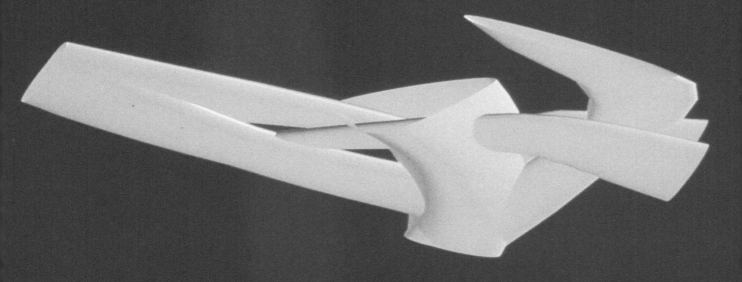

Basically (for now) Three Topics

Arnhem Transfer Hall, 1997–2010. Top: Organization of distribution of density. Bottom: Intertwining public spaces and program.

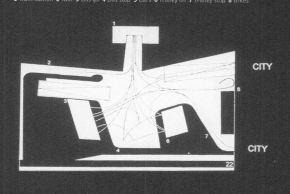

1 Train station **2** Taxi **3** Bus go **4** Bus stop **5** Cars **6** Trolley on **7** Trolley stop **8** Bikes

CITY

CITY

Transportation **1** Bus **2** Car **3** Trolley **4** 1–2 min: at bus stop, at trolley stop, at bike parking **5** 2–4 min: walking for connection (elevator) **6** 4–10 min: waiting for the bus, waiting for the trolley **7** 5–15 min: delivery **8** 10–30 min: waiting for the train

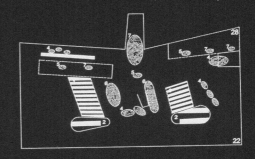

1 Train station **2** Taxi **3** People coming to the city **4** Bus stop **5** Cars **6** Trolley stop **7** Bikes **8** People going to the city

1 Train station **2** Taxi **3** Bus go **4** Bus stop **5** Cars **6** Trolley on **7** Trolley stop **8** Bikes

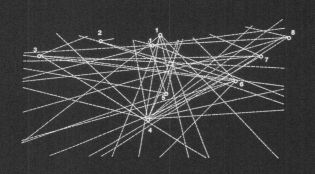

CITY

CITY

(clockwise from top left) Area for pedestrian flow; Residence of time for groups of people; Organization of the movements between the transportation systems; Visual orientation between transportation systems.

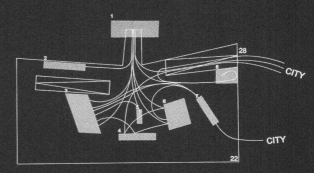

THE NEW SOCIAL CONSCIENCE

We should start by acknowledging that all architecture is deeply rooted in the public field. The question of new techniques and strategies in contemporary architecture, however, is more often considered in light of a formalization of Deleuzian theory than in the context of concrete social and economic transitions. I want to propose that the search for new techniques is a response to new public, economic, and political conditions. The basis for the work that we produce lies in those conditions.

The globalization of social and economic activity has been related to the compartmentalization of experience. Economist Anthony Giddens has observed how in the modern era internally referential social systems have emerged. This development is associated with the orientation of modernity toward surveillance and control. With the maturation of modernity, abstract systems play an increasingly pervasive role in coordinating the various contexts of day-to-day life. Among the arenas of sequestration are sickness, sexuality, crime, and nature. If we objectify and extend Giddens's psychological perspective to our own field, it seems inevitable that architecture will not only reflect this growing sequestration of experience but materially confirm it.

The sheer measurability of the internally referential systems of modern society encourages the sequestering of ever more separate processes or discontinuities, each with its own architectural conditions. Airports, shopping centers, and train and bus stations, for instance, are increasingly perceived and treated as distinctive and enclosed trajectories.

TEXTURE, FIELDS, AND TECHNIQUES

In this context, how do we instrumentalize such new social conditions? Are there techniques that can help us inventory, intuit, and imagine these conditions as architectural entities? And how do we correlate this with the decoding of public space caused by the intensive cross-cultural rituals and communication systems of contemporary transportation systems and infrastructures? A workable answer can be found in an emerging articulation of a policy of mobility and the incorporation of aspects of time into architecture. New computational techniques make it possible to lay bare the multiplicitous layering of experiences and activate this knowledge in new ways.

When mapping movement patterns, the time-program relationship is not compartmentalized but is a reflection of synchronic, continuous time. Infrastructural layers may be classified, calculated, and tested individually, then interwoven to achieve both effective flux and effective interaction. In this way temporal conditions are connected to programmatic themes in a simulation of the nonsegmented manner in which time flows in a real situation.

INCLUSIVENESS

The individual project, with its clearly delineated edges and purpose, is not obviously embedded in the interpretation of organizational structure as seen in deterritorialized mobility diagrams and process modeling — unlike the large-scale urban reanimation proposals that are fast becoming a staple of contemporary architecture. Can a building low in movement-generated instability be subject to a transformative strategy? Or should, for instance, the single-family house be treated as an iconic typology determined in local conventions? In response to the ambiguous status of the more limited, localized unit we have developed an approach to inclusiveness in our work that connects neither to the notion of the *Gesamtkunstwerk* nor to notions of phenomenological totality. This form of inclusiveness pertains to an intensive coherence in the design approach, an integration of construction, circulation, and the distribution of program. In an architectural ensemble of this sort there is no structural core around which program and circulation are organized. Circulation and the distribution of program organize the substance and construction in one integral gesture. As a result such a project presents an identity without solidity, a multiple identity, like a complex icon.

The inclusiveness of the architectural organization complies with a notion of consistency within which fragmentation and difference occur. This is in contrast to architecture based on techniques of fragmentation and collage, which imply coherence in the organization itself.

An image indicative of the contemporary acceptance of the simultaneous existence of different identities within one cohesive organization is that of the Manimal. A computer image of the hybridization of a lion, a snake, and a human, this work provides another example of the capacity of endlessness. The Manimal's identity is so loosely defined that it divulges no information about the original component parts. All traces of the previous

Images: Courtesy van Berkel & Bos, Amsterdam unless otherwise noted

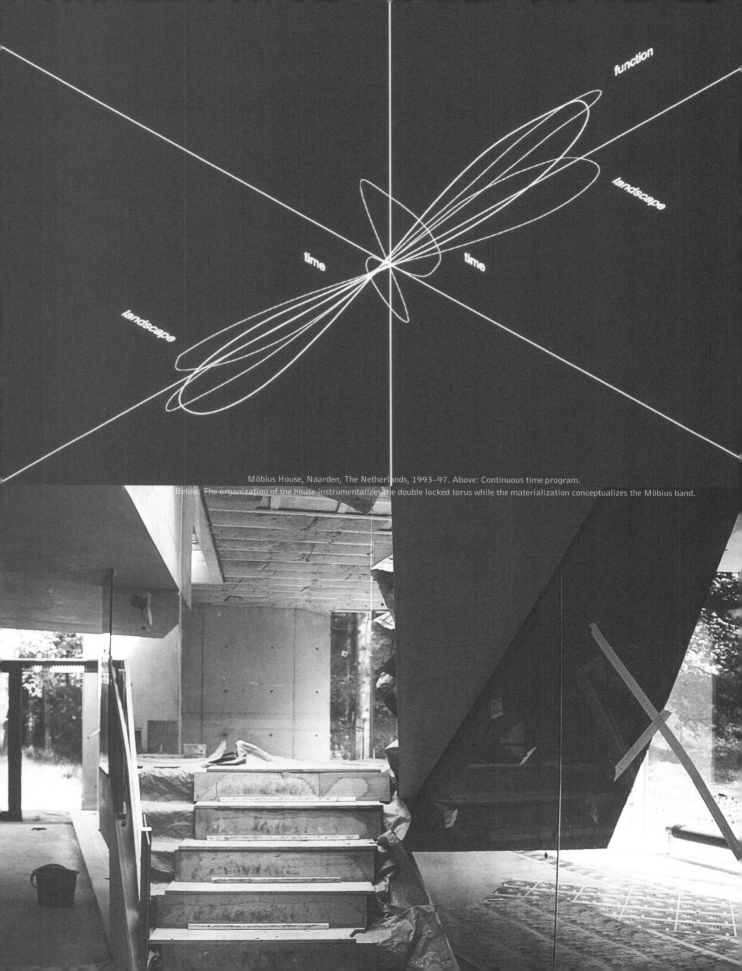

Möbius House, Naarden, The Netherlands, 1993–97. Above: Continuous time program.
Below: The organization of the house instrumentalizes the double locked torus while the materialization conceptualizes the Möbius band.

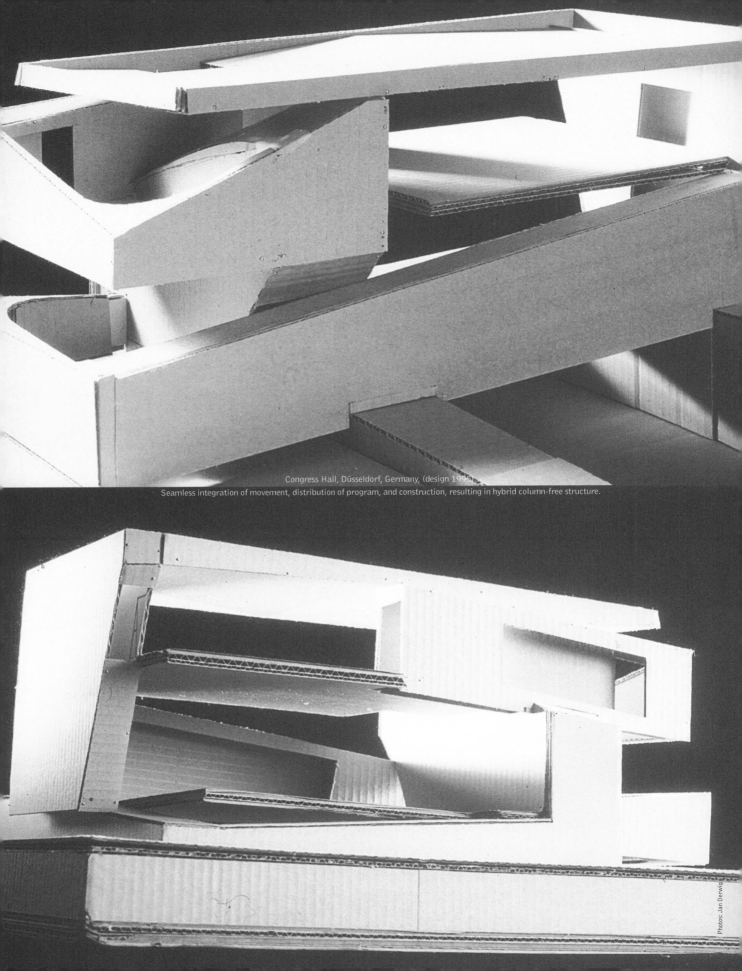

Congress Hall, Düsseldorf, Germany, (design 1995)
Seamless integration of movement, distribution of program, and construction, resulting in hybrid column-free structure.

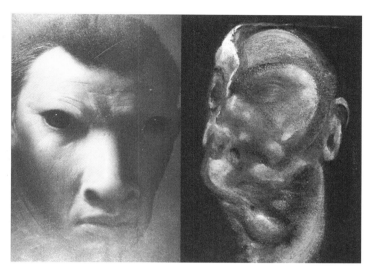

Left: Seamless computation
of different species. [Daniel
Lee, Manimal, 1993.]

Right: Smearing technique.
[Francis Bacon, Study for
Three Heads, 1962, detail,
right panel of triptych, oil
on canvas, 14 x 12 in. Collection William S. Paley,
New York.]

BEN VAN BERKEL IS
PRINCIPAL OF VAN BERKEL
& BOS IN AMSTERDAM AND
CRITIC AND UNIT MASTER
AT THE ARCHITECTURAL
ASSOCIATION. HIS WORKS
INCLUDE THE KARBOUW
OFFICE AND WORKSHOP,
AND THE REMU ELECTRICAL
SUBSTATION, BOTH IN
AMERSFOORT, AND THE ERAS-
MUS BRIDGE IN ROTTERDAM.
TOGETHER WITH CAROLINE
BOS HE IS THE AUTHOR
OF DELINQUENT VISIONAR-
IES AND MOBILE FORCES.

identities have been seamlessly absorbed within the image. Architecturally, the Manimal could be read as an amalgamation of several different structures that generate a new notion of scale and identity. The process that has generated the image is at least as potentially interesting as its effect. The seamless, decontextualizing, dehistoricizing combination of discordant systems of information can be instrumentalized architecturally. Understood as an effect, the image makes one wonder how something like this would translate spatially. As a technique it excites because it has been produced in a manner that is radically different from all pictorial techniques previously employed by artists.

Research, technique, and effect are the three steps central to architecture. When the imagination is stimulated by something exterior to architecture, techniques will begin to be developed to realize that effect in architectural substance. In our architecture we acknowledge the fact that space may be subject to evolution, expansion, inversion, and other contortions and manipulations that go beyond the generic space that was the ideal and ultimate achievement of modernist

architecture. New mediation and computational techniques now at our disposal enable the deepest understanding of endlessness ever possible. The tantalizing new spatial conditions suggested on every computer screen result in a general familiarity with the potential of a multidimensional spatial experience. Generic space – which used to be an expression of the *summum* of spatial conceptualization – seems rigid, static, and limited compared with the potential of spatial arrangements that follow the diving, swooping, zooming, slicing, folding motions that take place on computer screens. Special effects in films, silly cartoons, even screen savers express a delight in explorative spatial conditions and lead to a rapid increase in the capacity for spatial conceptualization that architecture should absorb.

The freedom to assume different identities is an achievement of the condition of endlessness. We seek to apply this capacity for endlessness in such a way that a structure could incorporate all aspects of a building – time, the distribution of program, construction – into one single gesture. Frederick Kiesler first conceptualized an endless architecture. Kiesler's capacity for endlessness in his projects is only exceeded by that conveyed in a series of photographs of him: Kiesler as surrealist, as a Minotaur, as Willem De Kooning, as a chess player, as Mies van der Rohe – these are just some of his incarnations. The message in those photographs is "Imagine, invent, express, pretend." With this variety of poses, the contemporary reading of Kiesler is one in which multiplicities constitute a cohesive identity. For us, the whole Kiesler is found in the wide-ranging series of Kieslers. Kiesler-as-Kiesler is a manifold, generating, proliferating, and projecting an infinite measure of possible identities.

Discussion 2

Rem Koolhaas Yesterday I would have forgiven you for having a sense of déjà vu or, as it is pronounced in America, "déjà voo," because it seemed, with minor modifications, that we have been having similar discussions year in and year out. It is almost inevitable that these yearly intervals give the impression of perceptible but slow changes, but if I look back six years to the first Any conference in Los Angeles and define the difference in tone – which is greater than the difference in subject matter – I would say that there was much stronger confidence then than there is now. I remember in Los Angeles a number of people really emanating a sense of how things could be done in a very adventurous and confident way and people very confidently proclaiming that certain inventions were possible in architecture. If we look at the recent manifestations of Any, I would say that that confidence maybe hasn't eroded, but it has become a lot less explicit and less visible, more discreet, more underground, as it was partly in Sanford Kwinter's announcement of an invisible manifesto.

Today we are dealing with infrastructure and distribution. For architects, infrastructure is a relatively new subject; it offers a domain of the inevitable that is extremely attractive to architects because it means that instead of merely worrying about being loved, architects can have a much stronger sensation of being needed. That is the incredible attraction for an engagement with infrastructure. It offers a domain of certainties, and it also allows architecture to be much less isolated in its own territory and to find a connection with subjects, dangerous and glamorous, like demographics, the incredible explosion of population. It therefore offers a perspective of a certain alignment with a reality that we rarely can find if we stay in the pure domain of architecture. Infrastructure is a very difficult project because as we saw and heard yesterday in a discussion about flows, there is an inherent paradox with regard to architecture's interest in flow. Essentially flow moves, and architecture fixes or attempts to define a moment. There is an inherent conflict between the tradition of architecture, what has been seen as the essence of our profession, and this interest in rapidly changing conditions. This very change might make our professional knowledge a very awkward way of dealing with the phenomena that we also find so fascinating. Instead of actually being about infrastructure or being part of infrastructure, we begin to represent infrastructure or flows and then we are back to all of our old problems. For instance yesterday, when Ignasi de Solà-Morales showed architectural designs for tunnel entrances, I had the sinking feeling that we are like King Midas in reverse; that the moment architecture begins to be interested in something, it almost means the death of that particular subject. Maybe the most interesting recent manifestation of this conflict between architecture and infrastructure was an enormous billboard that I saw about the conversion of Logan Airport in Boston, which read, "Closed 'til the 21st century for a world-class upgrade." That seems to suggest that airports are one of these things we know are inevitable. We are sitting at the table with Paul Andreu, one of the greatest authors of airports and maybe the person who has done the most to define the notion of the airport, but even for him, the airport is one infrastructure that represents a neck and neck race between our wish to define and the phenomenon that itself outruns our definition.

Francesca, I thought your presentation was incredibly suggestive, surprising, and effective, but why is it so important for you to dispel the myth of this linearity of the collective process, and what do we gain by assuming other mythologies?

Francesca Hughes I felt the ambition to dislodge the myth because it is a myth — it's not true, and it's not a very good myth. Maintaining that myth limits the scope of what practice might be and the idea that there is a more complex genealogy to the making of work. To limit that genealogy to a linear condition shuts down possibility.

Koolhaas Do you think that the myth is too simplified because it tends also to simplify the creative process?

Hughes Yes, it's partly ideological or political, that I don't like it as a set of ideas, but it's also only trying to produce a more complex body of work, not necessarily helping us to produce more interesting work.

Koolhaas Akira, I felt a strange sadness in your presentation because it seemed that you were extremely excited to show the early metabolism, even though you were also eloquent in identifying its fallacies. You became slightly more melancholy with the recent metabolism, even though it contained fewer fallacies. Can you explain this position?

Akira Asada It's partly psychological because I was in the difficult position of presenting Arata Isozaki's plan, about which I'm not totally convinced. You were right when you said that we were feeling a strange déjà vu. Everything **looked** as if it were somehow resuscitated from the ruins of the 1960s. But today we have to pay attention to more complicated conditions, hence a certain melancholy.

Koolhaas Ben, not only did you refer a number of times to some kind of immanent grouping and suggest that Jeff Kipnis might assume a kind of Giedion-like position in terms of eloquently formulating the diagrams and concepts according to which future architects may behave, you also presented a virtuoso demonstration of a project that explores an oval, an absolute continuity. I am also occasionally interested in similar continuities, but I find it slightly contradictory that the continuity indicates openness and freedom. If you compare your house to the Farnsworth House, there is an incredible amount of overdetermination. After seeing the incredible analyses of Arnhem and the ingenuousness of those manipulations – of the givens and of the data – I have to ask, what happens if any of that data changes, and to what extent does it then engender an erosion of plausibility? In a house, the program continuously mutates in terms of children growing up and leaving home. In terms of newness, your house is made of glass and concrete with no visible structure as a separate element. The Farnsworth House, made of steel and glass, also has no visible structure but it seemingly has an infinitely greater capacity to accommodate almost any potential scenario. How do you conceptually resolve the commitment to an incredible determinacy while researching fluidity and continuity?

Ben van Berkel I do not think that there is an incredible determination in the house. There is a specific articulation of details present in the house because it is for a client who wants to live his perfect life in this house. He wants to have a well-articulated jacket. In a certain way, when we talk about fluidity versus distribution of program versus construction, the idea is not so much to refine as to integrate fragmentation and determination in one plane, one surface that supplies difference. The same is happening in Arnhem where, although there are parking areas and two bus stations that do not change location, there is mobility in the central square. In the layering and the landscaping of this layering there is an enormous amount of actual difference and possible difference related to an enormous amount of intensive program and superficial program, all of which is interchangeable.

Asada Ben, I'd like to ask about the seeming discrepancy between the multiplicitous nature of your project and your insistence on what is called intensive coherence. On the one hand, your project for stations or bus terminals looks wonderful because it copes with the multilayered structure of traffic and communication. On the other, you insist on a so-called intensive coherence at the design level. It might be a very beautiful representation of the Deleuzian idea of **plan de consistance** [plane of consistency], but I don't see the clear connection between the multiplicitous action and the seeming coherence.

Koolhaas That may not be a matter of clarity but of criticism. It's not necessary for you to explain yourself more, but the notion that these two are in conflict could be a criticism or actually a defense that you accept, and therefore you believe in a certain fluidity and formlessness. At the same time, however, you find it interesting to create a cantilevered fireplace that also acts aggressively as a room divider.

Van Berkel Okay, I accept this criticism, but only in that it is true that there is a possible corporealization within the notion of intensive coherence. The reference to the Manimal shows that information is not being formed by classical montage, collage, or assemblage. The difference is intensified and organized so that it is not an incoherent structure. So you're right that there is incoherence in the work, a lot of difference, but this is actually part of the coherence.

Sanford Kwinter I think the criticism leveled at Ben is misdirected. What needs to be understood historically as well as theoretically is that there are extensive multiplicities that are generally separated and apparent. We have traversed a good 15 years if not longer of architectural history in which those things were rhetorically foregrounded in terms of a fragmentation aesthetics of deconstruction, deconstructivism, etc. Asada's ambivalence about Isozaki's project comes from the idea that multiplicities can be intensive as well and that our world has mutated to where the multiplicities that determine our reality are in fact intensive and now invisible and that there needs to be some kind of structure or project that engages those processes and is not obsessed with apparent multiplicity but rather with real multiplicity, which is very often intensive.

Asada I totally agree. But why should the virtual image of intensive multiplicities be directly turned into an actual image of continuity? There seems to be a discrepancy between perceiving the virtual coherence and trying to represent it or to express it with a coherent image.

Koolhaas On the whole, Sanford, I dislike any doubts, nevertheless I want to tell an anecdote that is significant here. It used to be that before Richard Meier had to lecture, he went to Peter Eisenman and locked himself in a room with him. Peter, who was smoking a cigar and had his feet on his desk, would brief Richard about the lecture he had to give. The next day you would go to the university to hear Richard Meier, who would speak perfectly adequately about German baroque architecture and German baroque churches and their special qualities and then seamlessly turn to a lecture of his own work. Then somebody in the audience would ask Meier, "What is the connection?" Then, as if bitten by a serpent, Eisenman — sitting in the first row — would stand up, turn to the audience, and say, "That's an unfair question!" Right now there is a similar condition. The Giedion metaphor – which is a paternal metaphor – of intellectuals and thinkers might consider individual architects as the illustrators of their theories. Therefore they suffer the agonies of having their theories badly explained or imperfectly illustrated.

Hughes Akira, you commented on Ben's use of representation and expression – on what the project and the infrastructure look like. This might address your problem with Isozaki's floating island project. Metabolism was uniquely figurative and molecular metabolism is still figurative – it looks like a cell. Can you comment on that?

Asada Frankly speaking, I share your suspicion. Yes, it's still too figurative.

Greg Lynn Perhaps the issue of the generic should become explicit here. It's clear that Ben's notion of a differential generic, which is a continuous series of rooms in a house in which there is no room, is a kind of sequenced generic condition. Rem's statement, however, about a neutral generic or the banal might be a way to talk about infrastructure. Is infrastructure necessarily banal, or could it be considered generic in a new way? This might be what Ben is proposing. It seems that any tension here is between the modernist notion of the generic as banal or extensive and a newer version of the generic as differenced and not about terminal conditions but continuities.

Koolhaas We are all willing to entertain the idea that there is a new generic and that there are new relationships between the new generic and the new specific, or the new intensity or the new coherence, but somehow we always expect that at the end of newness there is an escape from the inherent disappointment of design. For me, that's where the fireplaces are significant.

Lynn You can't design the generic?

Koolhaas No. In the end design is always like a shadow tracing these kinds of arguments, but design is the shadow that we cannot shake off.

Van Berkel This is the point where we have to refer to the notion of techniques. If you talk about your idea of intensive coherence or the particular aspect of program, construction and distribution of time could be introduced in a generic structure like an intensive coherent structure, then you should forget the word **design**. I think it is an organized structure, a dissipative system, as I called it.

Saskia Sassen My question is addressed primarily to Paul Andreu and Ed Taverne, though I'm thinking about the image of intensive coherence presented by Ben and also of Francesca's notion of the multiplicity of origins in the trajectory of production. It concerns digital space and a peculiar duality that one can find there in terms of some of the categories that have been set on the table between infrastructure and the other space that is not infrastructure. Digital space today in the context of the economy and of globalization – in other words, a specific instantiation of digital space – has an ambivalent role. It is infrastructure like the telephone or any other kind of infrastructure, but it has also become a space in its own right – I don't know if the term **generic** applies – and is now one of the spaces where an increasingly dematerialized economic process and accumulation take place. It's not only a service infrastructure but also something else. Second, when you look at the topography of private digital space, which is radically different from public digital space, or the Internet, which in many ways dominates our understanding of cyberspace, you see something that continuously weaves in and out of actual space. It lacks the self-containment possible on the Internet because private digital space is so interconnected to actual structures of economic power. From the perspective of intensive coherence or from the multiplicity of origins that Francesca described there is an interesting problematic: there is a continuous necessity to combine two very different instantiations of an economic process or, say, of an office space if we're thinking of work spaces. Is there something here about infrastructure becoming two things: infrastructure and non-infrastructure? Or about this continuous connection and rearticulation between two different instantiations of space, particularly economic space, both actual and digital, and how that is handled architecturally?

Ed Taverne I presented the Rotterdam harbor at this conference in relation to globalization. I wanted to point to a strategic site beyond architecture that has nothing to do with architecture. It is, in other words, a taste-free space. It deflects architecture from a status as object into a system that is more than just buildings. I wanted to intensify the topic of the harbor, yet in this morning's discussion, and as we heard yesterday,

I'm a little worried about returning to metabolism and the familiar models of Archigram because for me these are artistic inspirations, illustrated narratives that are interesting for art historians to study but have no real content because they are just illustrations. How can we not only represent mobility, represent flows, but go into the flow and create a new condition?

Koolhaas I would like to exploit the presence of Paul Andreu, because if anyone is an expert in flows, it is Paul Andreu. At first he was very serious and exhilarated about flows. He designed and conceived Charles de Gaulle Terminal One, which is an absolute masterpiece of architecture but also a revolutionary building. Anyone in this room is probably inspired by it daily and copying its parts, from its smoothness to the outrageous way the air-conditioning ducts are handled. It really is a stunning bible in a way. After that Paul became a more complex and less innocent person and discovered that there is something very interesting about flows, namely that they can take any form and can assume any trajectory. The hoped-**for** relation between flow and function is actually a hope**less** nonsense. If you look at most of those airports, their trajectories are completely absurd, and daily changes make them even more absurd. For instance, if you walk through Heathrow Terminal Four, you walk through spaces that are infinitely more complex than even Peter Eisenman has ever imagined in his wildest dreams. They are ugly spaces with no aesthetic except in terms of sheer complexity, in terms of the number of times that you have to go up and down, the number of times that you have to turn corners, the number of times that you find astonishing obstacles, and your incredible ability to handle them without any effort. This is one of the paradoxes of our discovery as architects of flow. There is still this old-fashioned architecture instinct that says that if we have flow, we have to create the best connection between A and B. It's still about a certain latent, bright, and functional adequacy about flow.

Paul Andreu I have had the very rare chance to work for 30 years at the same place, which doesn't normally happen to architects. It taught me that nothing happens as you forecast, nothing happens exactly as you design it, but there is continuity. If there is something true about metabolism, it is that there must always be two things in these kinds of big structures, the organization that all living animals and plants have and the possibility of evolution, of adaptation to changes. Unfortunately, we are victims of images. Looking at Isozaki's project, I was thinking, why do we have to see the full image? This is the wrong point. You want diversity, you want time, you want everything, but you want it instantly. You want to show it. You want to discuss images. I believe that there is a limit to what drawing images and things like that produce and that we should not draw everything and make so many virtual images. They don't lead anywhere.

Alejandro Zaera-Polo This denotes an incredibly Derridean attitude. Rem tells us that the Heathrow terminal doesn't work, but so what, we can still go through it. Where do you act as an architect? When you say we cannot give a better form to flows and we cannot propose a certain way of organizing these flows that will be better than Heathrow Terminal Four, basically you are abdicating your place as an architect.

Koolhaas It's not a matter of abdication because basically we are exploring whether engagements with other domains give us a new energy and a new legitimacy. I am questioning our understanding of those other domains and the way in which we are still programmed with a number of other archetypal programs, one of which is functional. Functionalism in some sick, forgotten, and debased way makes us proudly proclaim that we can organize, that we are experts of flow or circulation or organization, even though a real expert would analyze what is happening at Heathrow and analyze at least the evolution, or let's say the impossibility, of creating a single correct flow. We are confronted with programs and institutions that somehow forever resist the articulation of the ideal configuration of this. I am questioning whether we are still pretending that an ideal configuration is what we imagine, if not for A then at least for domain B.

Zaera-Polo You don't have to pretend that you are going to create the ideal configuration, but you have to claim that you are able to produce **a** configuration. This may be better or may be more interesting than whatever way you choose to define it down to ones that exist out there. Otherwise you have to give up your role as an architect.

Koolhaas That's your opinion, but I deeply disagree. We are surrounded by a parallel universe that can in the most blatant way contradict too many of the things that we are saying, and that is dangerous in terms of the vigor of our profession, so I totally support and sympathize with the ambition to extend our claims. Nevertheless I also want to confront them with other threatening and undermining realities of that claim.

Andreu When you do volumes for a terminal, you try to make them as clear as possible, but Rem is right, when it changes, you can do anything with the space. Something that is not functional but goes with function is pleasure, the pleasure you have to be in a volume. That is something we don't speak of very much, and why? Function is very often an incentive to prepare happiness and pleasure.

Zaera-Polo Pleasure is a function. If you are able to define pleasure as a function, then maybe you are able to claim that you can make the spaces pleasurable.

Audience With regard to your critique that Ben thought that flow has one form, is the relation of flow to form totally arbitrary? I thought he was saying that if it is arbitrary, it is dangerous because then anything is possible.

Koolhaas That's true, and every architectural discussion is a horrible attempt to escape from that truth. Let me make it very clear that none of this is intended as criticism. It's only to clarify the issues.

Van Berkel The tricky and dangerous thing about the discussion is that you focus too much on the notion of the physicality of how flow could work. I think it is really about digital infrastructure and new ways of working with others. For instance, I am not working on the Arnhem station alone, there are 20 advisers at the table. As an architect you are part of an organizational process of a flow that is far more interestingly related to possible new ways of working in relation to new techniques, new ways of dealing with these forces. It's not the physical force, it's the instrumentalized force.

Andreu We should speak not of a flow but of flows of infrastructure. In an airport, a train station, or a parking lot there are the flows of planes, trains, and cars combined with the flows of the passengers, and all of them have very specific requirements. How the electron moves is really the simplest thing of all. The flow of electrons never caused me any problem. The others, yes.

Bernard Tschumi The difference between yesterday's session and today's can shed some light on this part of the discussion. Yesterday was all about culture; today seems to be all about infrastructure. Yesterday we heard names like Bramante, Palladio, Colin Rowe, and Yves Klein as a sort of preliminary experience to the understanding of our condition today. In this discussion there is a clear attempt to liberate oneself from that cultural baggage, and that is fascinating. Take for example the buildings of Paul Andreu. We often talk about the buildings of Mies, Palladio, or van Berkel, which we have occasionally seen in person but mostly know through photographs. I've only spent a few hours in buildings by Mies but I've spent approximately a thousand times that in Andreu's building in the last 25 years. I would even object to his point about pleasure. The greatest pleasure I had was once when I went from the taxi to the plane in two minutes in a major international airport. Congratulations to you; Palladio never gave me that! The fascination with diagrams, with the notion of flow, is the apparent abstraction that allows us to free ourselves from our cultural baggage. It's not about infrastructure but about infraculture, and if we can reach that level of objectivity, then maybe we can move to some other image. I get worried when I see the sign of culture coming back, when I recognize in Ben van Berkel a certain cultural coda in the fireplace, for example. But fortunately the flows take everything away with it, right? How can we get to that absolute objectivity, the objectification of no culture?

Hubert Damisch I totally disagree with this remark. I had the opposite impression. We are entering the domain of culture but we have to define what culture is. Although I don't like to discuss this, yesterday we were speaking about certain aspects of the media culture. Today we are trying to reach infrastructure in the domain of architecture. Is it possible — using the ingredients, the ways of thinking, and the substance of fluidity of infrastructure — to incorporate this in our own culture? When you say we are leaving the domain of culture and going to another, I think we are doing just the opposite. This is my plea for a new culture of technology. Culture in the real sense of a culture that reaches different parts and levels of our society.

Tschumi You worry me enormously because you are talking about fetishizing complex technology in order to turn it into culture.

Damisch No, no! Absolutely not.

Tschumi The moment you turn flow into culture, you do exactly what people did 20 years ago when they took semiotic models and turned them into architecture. Taking them out of the cultural model is interesting only if you don't turn them into new cultural models.

Damisch We are turning it into architecture. We are confronting architecture with new domains. That's the point and that is a cultural impression, from my point of view.

Andreu I may be one of the very few pupils who had Deleuze as a professor of philosophy. He spoke very much of Lewis Carroll because he thought that was our level. I'm not sure that citing Deleuze or citing René Thom is making culture or speaking of culture. When we speak of flows, we speak also of a subject that Michel Serres, for example, would develop in books. Are Serres and Thom less representative of culture than Deleuze and Guattari? That's a fight I would not begin.

Hughes Bernard, can you explain to me how I was not talking about culture?

Tschumi I hope you were not talking about culture. I hope that you resorted to those wonderful pictures as a way of explaining a diagram, not as a way of announcing a cultural relationship.

Hughes I'm certainly not saying that culture is a Renaissance image or that if you haul those pictures in or haul in the word **romantic**, for example, you're suddenly hauling in culture. I was talking about the culture of the manifestation of the practice of architecture and the culture of the production of architecture and the way a kind of funny push-me/pull-you relationship between changes in the physical infrastructure has actually caused changes in the conceptual infrastructure of practice. There's a direct link between the physical work and how it affects culture and how culture then changes: how we make money or whether we choose to buy a drill press or a new computer. Perhaps we are using capital-**C** culture.

Tschumi Perhaps I was using a capital **C**. I'm interested in what you just said about process as an ideological dimension. There are certain processes that are better, newer, or different from others. For me, processes in architecture are entirely pragmatic. In other words, the process is related to the result you want to achieve and not the other way around. The process is not a repeated thing. It's always modified or even completely altered according to the circumstances. If you try to use a process in an ideological sense, it will work once but not a second time around.

Asada We are still too cultural, we are not savage enough. Saskia Sassen is right, today the digital network functions as an infrastructure, but it's an invisible structure; it's a really processual mechanism. On the other hand, there is still a remnant of image cultures, especially to use Greg Lynn's words, an image culture of adolescent techies that somehow tries to visualize what is supposed to be an invisible, endless process. I still see a discrepancy between the acultural machinic process and a certain, if not adolescent, too colorful representation of this process.

Van Berkel It would be interesting to clarify what process is.

Tschumi I would distinguish two processes: one is the process of making, the process of production; the second is the programmatic process, the process of change of use. The first one has had a whole history in architecture, from the series of variations made through tracing paper as you superimpose and modify every superposition, to certain processes that are entirely machinic and require the humanist cultural study of composition and proportion. This is a variety of processes that have no value assigned to them. I cannot see one as better than the other. They have simply changed over time, in part due to changes in technology. The more interesting question is, to what extent does the actual process of the series of problematic sequences contaminate and challenge the idea of the typology or the archetype of a bus station? The moment you start that programmatic process to challenge the received idea and values of a bus station, it becomes interesting.

Van Berkel Cross-programming or using cross-programming is a technique similar to computational techniques.

Lynn Francesca, you showed a series of images of an atelier. There is something you didn't speak about, even though it was your atelier, until you said it was **your** drill press and **your** computer. When you eliminate certain diagrammatic techniques for their authorial capacity to retroactively justify a project, doesn't something rush in the door, which is this series of photographs of a work space of a master architect? This was never addressed. As an unspoken aspect of your presentation, it made me a little uncomfortable.

Hughes It's not a rushing-in-the-door. It's what you've got left when you remove the retroactive diagrams or the "faking it," as it were. I was quite careful to frame the images so that if any work appeared, it pretty much just appeared in fragments.

Audience One of the big arguments at this table is, to what extent is infrastructure becoming part of architecture and should we consider it part of architecture and hence design it as an integrated system? If I understood what Paul Andreu said, we neglect infrastructure because we don't attribute something other than functional value to it. We have to bring it into our culture in order to conceive of it in another way than, say, they did in 1960s modernism, which conceived of an urbanism that separated infrastructural systems and living conditions. Andreu said that the time of transit should be given a value if we want to integrate it as a living space and not as a space we want to get through as quickly as possible. You can misread this point in terms of the current economic systems, which would give it a value that would exploit the time of transit in the most profitable way. It might be that in order to give a value to this time of transit, we have to waste it. In concrete terms this might mean that we have to reinvent the journey as a programmatic activity that, according to people like Paul Virilio, we have forgotten because we don't depart for anywhere because everything arrives to us. The space of transit might help us understand the cultural condition of infrastructure, what Virilio calls **le trajet**, as opposed to the object and the subject. Maybe we need to consider infrastructure in terms of culture and to take it seriously as a living space.

Audience These sessions have proven eloquently that architects are experts in wasting time. When somebody just tries to deal with airports or just tries to describe the harbor, it is immediately seen as fetishization. I think this is a projection of a problem that these architects have themselves. I think that the only thing I saw yesterday and a lot of the things I heard today were fetishizations of their own design processes. There is a very strange arrogance in assuming that anybody would be interested in how you design.

Money, Market, Policy

Fredric Jameson

The Brick and the Balloon:

I want to think aloud today about a fundamental theoretical problem – the relationship between urbanism and architecture – which, alongside its own intrinsic interest and urgency, raises a number of theoretical issues of significance to me, although not necessarily to all of you. But I need to ask for some provisional interest in those issues, and in my own work in relationship to them, to formulate some more general urban and architectural problems. For instance, an investigation of the dynamics of abstraction in postmodern cultural production, in particular the radical difference between the structural role of abstraction in postmodernism and the kinds of abstractions at work in what we now call modernism or, if you prefer, in the various modernisms, has led me to reexamine the money form – the fundamental source of all abstraction – and to ask whether the very structure of money and its mode of circulation have not been substantially modified in recent years, during the still brief period some of us refer to as postmodernity. That is, of course, to raise again the problem of finance capital and its importance in our own time and to raise questions about the relationships between its peculiar and specialized formal abstractions and those found in cultural texts. I think everyone will agree that finance capital, along with globalization, is one of the distinctive features of late capitalism, that is, of the distinctive state of things today.

Precisely this line of inquiry, reoriented in the direction of architecture itself, suggests the further development I want to pursue. For in the realm of the spatial there does seem to exist something like the equivalent of finance capital, indeed a phenomenon intimately related to it, and that is land speculation: something that may have found its field of endeavor in the countryside in years gone by – in the seizure of Native American lands, in the acquisition of immense tracts by the railroads, in the development of suburban areas, and in the extraction of natural resources – but that in our time is a preeminently urban phenomenon (not least because everything is becoming urban) and has returned to the big cities, or to what is left of them, to seek its fortunes. What then is the relationship, if any, between the distinctive form that land speculation has taken today and those equally distinctive forms found in postmodern architecture (to use that term in a general, chronological, and hopefully rather neutral sense)?

It has often been observed that the emblematic significance of architecture today and its formal originality lie in its immediacy to the social, in the "seam it shares with the economic." This is a rather different immediacy than that experienced by other expensive art forms, such as cinema and theater, which also certainly depend on investment. But this very immediacy presents theoretical dangers that are themselves fairly well-known. It does not seem preposterous to assert, for example, that land speculation and the new demand for increased construction opens a space in which a new architectural style can emerge. But to use the time-honored epithet, it seems "reductive" to explain the new style in terms of the new kinds of investment. This kind of reductionism supposedly fails to respect the specificity, the autonomy or semiautonomy of the aesthetic level and its intrinsic dynamics. Some would indeed object that bald assertions of this kind never descend into the detail of the styles that they thereby stigmatize; they are able to neglect formal analysis, having discredited its very principle in advance.

One might then attempt to enrich and complexify this interpretation (of "the origins of postmodernism") by introducing the matter of new technologies and showing how they dictated a new style at the same time that they responded more adequately to the aims of the investments. This inserts a level of "mediation" between the economic and the aesthetic and can begin to suggest why, for the immediacy of an assertion about economic determination, we would do better to elaborate a series of mediations between the economic and the aesthetic or, in other words, why we need a revitalized conception of the mediation as such. This concept of mediation is based on the existence of what I have referred to as a "level," or in other words (those of Niklas Luhmann) a differentiated social function, a realm or zone within the social that has developed to the point at which it is governed internally by its own intrinsic laws and dynamics. I want to call such a realm "semiautonomous" because it is still somehow part of the social totality, as the term function suggests. My own term is deliberately ambiguous or ambivalent in order to suggest a two-way street in which one can either emphasize the relative independence, the relative autonomy of the area in question, or else, the other way around, insist on its functionality and ultimately its place in the whole (at least by way of its consequences for the whole) if not its "function" understood as a kind of material interest and slavish or subservient motivation. So, to use a few of Luhmann's more obvious examples, the political is a distinct "level" because, since Machiavelli and the emergence of the modern state under Richelieu, politics is a semiautonomous realm in modern societies with its own mechanisms and procedures, its own personnel, its own history and traditions (or "precedents"), and so forth. This does not imply that the political level does not have manifold consequences for what lies outside it. The same can be said for the realm of law, the legal or juridical level, which is in many ways the model and exemplar of just such a specialized and semiautonomous domain. Those of us who do cultural work will no doubt also want to insist on a certain semiautonomy of the aesthetic or the cultural (even though today the relationship between those two alternate formulations is once again a very contested topic indeed). The laws of storytelling, even for a television series, are surely not immediately reducible to the institutions of parliamentary democracy, let alone the operations of the stock market.

And what about that: the stock market itself? The emergence of the market, and of the theory of the market, from the 18th century onward has established the economy as a semiautonomous level, if it was not one before. Money and land are precisely the phenomena that will concern us today and will allow us to test the usefulness of the concept

Architecture, Idealism, and Land Speculation

of mediation and its related idea, the semiautonomous instance or level, it being understood in advance that neither money nor land can constitute such a level in its own right since each is clearly a functional element within the more fundamental system or subsystem that is the market and the economic.

Any discussion of money as a mediation must confront the work of Georg Simmel, whose massive *Philosophy of Money* (1900) pioneered what we would today call a phenomenological analysis of this peculiar reality. Simmel's subterranean influence on a variety of 20th-century thought currents is incalculable, partly because he resisted coining his complex thinking into an identifiable system; meanwhile, the complicated articulations of what is essentially a non-Hegelian or decentered dialectic are often smothered by his heavy prose. A new account of this life work would be an indispensable preliminary stage in the discussion I want to stage here.[1] To be sure, Simmel bracketed the economic structures themselves, but his work suggests the ways in which the phenomenological and essential, as well as the cultural, effects of finance capital might be described and explored. This is not the moment for any such full-dress study, so I will limit myself to a few remarks on his seminal essay "Metropolis and Mental Life," in which money also plays a central role.[2]

That text is fundamentally an account of the increasing abstraction of modern life and in particular of urban life (in the Berlin of the late 19th century). Abstraction is precisely my topic and still very much with us, sometimes under different names (Anthony Giddens's key term *disembedding*, for example, says very much the same thing at the same time that it directs us to other features of the process). In Simmel's essay, abstraction takes on a remarkable multiplicity of forms, from the experience of time to some new distance in personal relations, from what he calls "intellectualism" to new kinds of freedom, from indifference and the "blasé" to new anxieties, value crises, and those big-city crowds so dear to Charles Baudelaire and Walter Benjamin. It would be an oversimplification to conclude that for Simmel money is the cause of all of these new phenomena: not only does the big city triangulate this matter, but in our present context surely the concept of mediation is more satisfactory than the fact of money in general. In any case, Simmel's essay places us on the threshold of a theory of modern aesthetic forms and their abstraction from older logics of perception and production. It also places us on the threshold of the emergence of abstraction within money itself, namely what we now call finance capital.[3] Within the collage of phenomena that make up the essay's texture we also find the following fateful sentence. Discussing the new internal dynamics of abstraction, the way in which, like capital itself, it begins to expand under its own moment, Simmel writes: "This may be illustrated by the fact that within the city the 'unearned increment' of ground rent, through a mere increase in traffic, brings to its owner profits which are self-generating."[4] It is enough; these are the semiautonomous connections we have been seeking. Now let us retrace our steps and begin again with the possible kinships between modern or postmodern architectural form and the self-multiplying exploitations of the space of the great industrial cities.

I have been particularly interested, in this respect, in a badly organized and repetitive book that, like a good detective story, has an exciting narrative to tell and has all of the excitement of discovery and revelation. *The Assassination of New York*, by Robert Fitch, offers the occasion not merely to confront the urban with the architectural but also to assess the function of land speculation and to compare the explanatory value of various theories (and the place of mediations in them). Put baldly, as Fitch himself does fairly often, he conceives of the "assassination" of New York as the process whereby – deliberately – production is driven out of the city in order to make way for business office space (finance, insurance, real estate). The policy is supposed to revitalize the city and promote

1 For a more comprehensive discussion, see my forthcoming essay, "The Theoretical Hesitation: Benjamin's Sociological Predecessor." I also want to signal the related projects of Richard Dienst on debt as a postmodern phenomenon, for example, "The Futures Market," in *Reading and the Shape of the World*, ed. H. Schwarz and R. Dienst (Boulder, Colorado: Westview, 1996); and also that of Christopher Newfield on corporate culture today, for example his essays in *Social Text* 44 and 51, Fall 1995 and Summer 1997.

2 Translated in Georg Simmel, *On Individuality and Social Forms*, ed. Donald Levine (Chicago: University of Chicago Press, 1971), 324–39.

3 See my essay, "Culture and Finance Capital," in *The Cultural Mutation* (London, forthcoming).

4 Simmel, *On Individuality and Social Forms*, 334. To which I would like to append the following: "The flexibility of money, as with so many of its qualities, is most clearly and emphatically expressed in the stock exchange, in which the money economy is crystallized as an independent structure just as political organization is crystallized in the state. The fluctuations in exchange prices frequently indicate subjective-psychological motivations, which, in their crudeness and independent movements, are totally out of proportion in relation to objective factors. It would certainly be superficial, however, to explain this by pointing out that price fluctuations correspond only rarely to real changes in the quality that the stock represents. For the significance of this quality for the market lies not only in the inner qualities of the State or the brewery, the mine or the bank, but in the relationship of these to all other stocks on the market and their conditions. Therefore, it does not affect their actual basis if, for instance, large insolvencies in Argentina depress the price of Chinese bonds, although the security of such bonds is no more affected by that event than by something that happens on the moon. For the value of these stocks, for all their external stability, none the less depends on the overall situation of the market, the fluctuations of which, at any one point, may for example make the further utilization of those returns less profitable. Over and above these stock market fluctuations, which even though they presuppose the synthesis of the single object with others are still objectively produced, there exists one factor that originates in speculation itself. These wagers on the future quoted price of one stock *themselves have the most considerable influence on such a price*. For instance, as soon as a powerful financial group, for reasons that have nothing to do with the quality of the stock, becomes interested in it, its quoted price will increase; conversely, a bearish group is able to bring about a fall in the quoted price by mere manipulation. Here the real value of the object appears to be the irrelevant substratum above which the movement of market values rises only because it has to be attached to some substance, or rather to some name. The relation between the real and final value of the object and its representation by a bond has lost all stability. This clearly shows the absolute flexibility of this form of value, a form that the objects have gained through money and which has completely detached them from their real basis. Now value follows, almost without resistance, the psychological impulses of the temper, of greed, of unfounded opinion, and it does this in such a striking manner since objective circumstances exist that could provide exact standards of valuation. But value in terms of the money form has made itself independent of its own roots and foundation in order to surrender itself completely to subjective energies. Here, where speculation itself may determine the fate of the object of speculation, the permeability and flexibility of the money form of values has found its most triumphant expression through subjectivity in its strictest sense." Simmel, *The Philosophy of Money*, trans. David Frisby and Tom Bottomore (London: Routledge and Kegan Paul, 1978), 325–26.

new growth, and its failure is documented by the astonishing percentage of floor space left vacant and unrented (so-called "see-through" buildings). Fitch's theoretical authority here seems to be Jane Jacobs, whose doctrine about the relationship of small business to the flourishing neighborhood he enhances by positing the equally necessary relationship between small business (shops and the like) and small industry (of the garment district type). His radical rather than Marxian analysis aims to promote activism and partisanship. He therefore lashes out at a variety of theoretical targets, which include certain Marxisms and certain postmodernisms along with the official ideologies of the city planners themselves, and these polemics (or rather, these denunciations) will mainly interest us here. Making allowance for a characteristically American anti-intellectualism and antiacademic stance, Fitch's primary theoretical target is the doctrine of historical inevitability, in whatever form, no doubt on the grounds that it demoralizes and depoliticizes those who begin believing in it and makes political mobilization and resistance much more difficult, if not altogether impossible. This is a plausible and pertinent position, but in the end all conceptions of long-range trends and of a meaningful logic of capitalism become identified with this "inevitabilist" ideology, and this in turn rebounds onto the very forms of praxis that Fitch wishes to promote, as we shall see.

Let's begin all over again at the beginning. Not only has New York undergone a massive restructuring in which 750,000 manufacturing jobs disappeared and in which the ratio of manufacturing to office work (Fitch's acronym FIRE: finance, insurance, real estate) has gone from 2:1 before the war to 1:2 today;[5] this change (not inevitable! not in the "logic of capital!") was the result of a deliberate policy on the part of New York's power structure. It was, in other words, the result of what is today widely and loosely called "conspiracy," something for which the evidence is very suggestive indeed. The "proof" lies in the absolute congruence between the unrealized 1982 zoning plan for the metropolitan area and the current state of things: the removal of manufacturing posited there has been realized here, the implantation of office buildings foreseen there has here come to pass; Fitch supplements all of this with lavish quotes from the planners of yesteryear and those of the recent past. For example, from an influential businessman and political figure of the 1920s:

5 Robert Fitch, *The Assassination of New York* (London: Verso 1996), 40.

> Some of the poorest people live in conveniently located slums on high-priced land. On patrician Fifth Avenue, Tiffany and Woolworth, cheek by jowl, offer jewels and jimcracks from substantially identical sites. Childs' restaurants thrive and multiply where Delmonico's withered and died. A stone's throw from the stock exchange the air is filled with the aroma of roasting coffee; a few hundred feet from Times Square with the stench of slaughter houses. In the very heart of this "commercial" city, on Manhattan Island south of 59th Street, the inspectors in 1922 found nearly 420,000 workers employed in factories. Such a situation outrages one's sense of order. Everything seems misplaced. One yearns to rearrange things to put things where they belong.[6]

6 Ibid., 60.

Such statements clearly reinforce the proposition that getting rid of the garment district and the port of New York was a conscious aim elaborated through a number of strategies that were finally, over the 50-year period between the late 1920s and the 1980s, successful and that in the process entailed the deterioration of the city into its present form. One need not argue about the particulars of the result, but the motivation behind this "conspiracy" does need to be set in place. Not surprisingly it has to do with land speculation and the stunning appreciation of land values that result from the "liberation" of real estate from its occupancy by various kinds of small businesses and manufacture. "There is a nearly 1000 percent spread between the rent received for factory space and the rent landlords get for class A office space. Simply by changing the land use, one's capital could increase in value many times. Presently, a long-term U.S. bond yields something on the order of 6 percent."[7]

7 Ibid., xii.

Behind this more general "conspiratorial" explanation lies a more specific and local conspiracy whose investigators will be named in time. But this explanation, at this level of generality, confirms a more properly Marxian notion of the "logic of capital" and in particular of the causal relationship of such immediate real-estate developments to a (relatively cyclical) notion of the moment of finance capital that interests me in the present context. Save for one exception, which I will touch on later, Fitch is not interested in the cultural level of these developments or in the kind of architecture or architectural style that might accompany a deployment of finance capital. These are presumably superstructural epiphenomena, which such analyses tend to see as a kind of cultural and ideological smokescreen for the real processes (in other words, an implicit apology for them). I will come back to this central problem of the relationship between art or culture and the economy later on.

Concepts of "trends" and the inevitability of the logic of capital do not give a complete or even an adequate picture of the Marxian view of these processes: missing is the crucial idea of contradiction. For the very notion of trends in investment, capital flight, the movement of finance capital away from manufacturing and into land speculation, is inseparable from both the contradictions that produce these uneven investment possibilities across the field and, above all, from the impossibility of resolving them. This is exactly what Fitch shows with his impressive statistics about vacancy rates in the speculative construction of white-collar office buildings: the redeployment of investments in that direction solves nothing, having destroyed the viable city fabric that would have produced new returns (and increasing employment) in those spaces in the first place. There could obviously be a narrative satisfaction in this outcome ("the wages of sin"), but from Fitch's point of view, the prospect of inevitable contradiction – which might advance a rather different conception of the possibility of political action – is equally incompatible with the kind of activism he has in mind.

At this stage, we already face several levels of abstraction: at the most rarefied end, a conception of the preponderance of finance capital today, which Giovanni Arrighi has usefully redefined for us as a moment in the historical development of capital as such.[8]

8 In Giovanni Arrighi, The Long Twentieth Century (London: Verso, 1994). For more on this work see the essay referenced in note 3.

Arrighi posits three stages: first the investment-seeking implantation of capital in a new region, then the productive development of industry and manufacture in that region, and finally a deterritorialization of the capital in heavy industry in order to seek its reproduction and multiplication in financial speculation – after which this same capital takes flight to a new region and the cycle begins again. Arrighi finds his point of departure in a sentence of Fernand Braudel, "The stage of financial expansion is always a sign of autumn," and thus inscribes his analysis of finance capital on a spiral, rather than in some static and structural fashion, as a permanent and relatively stable feature of "capitalism" everywhere. To think otherwise is to relegate the most striking economic developments of the Reagan-Thatcher era (developments which are also cultural) to the realm of sheer illusion and epiphenomena or to consider them, as Fitch seems to do here, as the most noxious by-products of a conspiracy whose conditions of possibility remain unexplained. The shift from investments in production to speculation on the stock market, the globalization of finance, and — what especially concerns us here — the new level of frenzied engagement with real estate values are realities with fundamental consequences for social life today (as the rest of Fitch's book so dramatically demonstrates for the admittedly very special case of New York City); and the effort to theorize those new developments is far from an academic matter.

With this in mind we turn to Fitch's other basic polemic target, which he tends to associate with Daniel Bell's old idea of a "postindustrial" society, a social order in which the classic dynamics of capitalism have been displaced, perhaps even replaced, by the primacy of science and technology, which now offers a different explanation of the alleged shift from a production to a service economy. The critique here focuses on two, not necessarily related hypotheses. The one posits a well-nigh structural mutation of the economy away from heavy industry and toward an unaccountably massive service sector and thereby offers ideological support to the elite New York planners who wish to deindustrialize New York and find aid and comfort in the notion of the historical inevitability of the "end" of production in its older sense. But the commodification of services can also be accounted for in a Marxian framework (and was so explained, prophetically, as long ago as 1974 in Harry Braverman's great book, *Labor and Monopoly Capital*); I won't pursue that point any further today, particularly since the development Fitch has in mind specifically concerns office workers in business high-rises more than service industries.

The second idea he associates with Bell's putative "postindustrial society" has to do with globalization and the cybernetic revolution, in the process taking sideswipes at some very eminent contemporary accounts of the new global or informational city (by Manuel Castells and Saskia Sassen in particular).[9] Surely an emphasis on new communications technologies need not imply a commitment to Bell's notorious hypothesis of a change in the mode of production itself. The replacement of water power by gas and later on by electricity involved momentous mutations in the spatial dynamics of capitalism as well as in the nature of daily life, the structure of the labor process, and the very constitution of the social fabric. Nevertheless, the system remained capitalist. It is true that a whole variegated ideology of the communicational and the cybernetic has emerged in recent years that merits theoretical challenge, ideological analysis and critique, and sometimes even outright deconstruction. On the other hand, the account of capital developed by Marx and by so many others since his day can perfectly well accommodate the changes in question; indeed the dialectic itself has as its most vital philosophical function the coordination of two aspects or faces of history that we otherwise seem ill-equipped to think: namely identity and difference, the way in which a thing can both change and remain the same, can undergo the most astonishing mutations and expansions and still constitute the operation of some basic and persistent structure. One can argue, as some have,[10] that the contemporary period, which includes all of these spatial and technological

9 Both descriptions specify the causal relationship between the informational and financial developments they analyze and increasing structural unemployment and the ghettoization of the contemporary city. See Manuel Castells, *The Informational City* (New York: B. Blackwell, 1989), 228; or Saskia Sassen, *The Global City* (Princeton, N.J.: Princeton University Press, 1991), 186.

10 Most notably Ernest Mandel, in *Late Capitalism* (London: Verso, 1975).

innovations, may approximate Marx's abstract model more satisfactorily than the still semi-industrial and semiagricultural societies of Marx's day. More modestly, however, I simply want to suggest that whatever the historical truth of the hypothesis about the cybernetic revolution, it is enough to register a widespread belief in it and in its effects, not merely on the part of elites but also in the general populations of the first-world states. Such a belief constitutes a social fact of the greatest importance that cannot be dismissed as sheer error. One must also see Fitch's work dialectically, as an effort to restore the other part of the famous sentence and to remind us that people still make this history, even if they make it "in circumstances not of their own choosing."

We must therefore look a little more closely into this question of the people who have made the spatial history of New York, and this brings us to the inner or more concrete conspiracy that Fitch dramatically wishes to disclose to us, complete with the names of the perpetrators and an account of their activities. We have already noted one level of this operation – that of New York's planners, who are also part of the circle of New York's financial and business elite – and Fitch certainly names names and gives brief accounts of some of their careers. In general, though, his narrative unfolds at a still relatively collective level, in which these very real people still represent a general class dynamic. It seems fair to invoke the dialectic one more time by observing that, insofar as Fitch wishes to appeal to the activism of individuals in his political program for the regeneration of New York, he is also obliged to identify specific individuals on the other side and to validate his claim that individuals can still accomplish things in history by demonstrating that individuals have already done so and have brought us to this sorry state by way of their agency as private people (and not as disembodied classes).

Ironically, and Fitch himself points out the irony, there is a precedent for such an account of a specifically individual conspiracy against the city. This lies in the identification of Robert Moses as the fundamental agent and villain in New York's transformations, an account we owe to Robert Caro's extraordinary biography, *The Powerbroker*. In a moment we will see why Fitch needs to resist this particular account, suggesting that its function is to make Moses into the scapegoat for these developments: "In retrospect it will turn out that Moses' greatest civic accomplishment was not the Coliseum or Jones Beach but taking the rap for two generations of New York City planning failures."[11] Fair enough. Every causal level invites deeper digging for another one and sends us back another step, to construct a more fundamental "causal level" behind. Was Moses really a world-historical actor, was he really acting on his own, etc.? It is true that behind the richness of Caro's variegated accounts there eventually looms a purely psychological dimension: Moses wanted power and activity, was genial enough to see the possibilities, and so forth. Fitch's implicit critique is, however, more telling (and it tells against his own ultimate version of the narrative as well): the private individual Moses cannot bear the whole weight of the story, which demands an agent who is both individual and representative of collectivity.

Enter Nelson Rockefeller. For it is he, or rather the Rockefeller family as a group of individuals, who will offer the key to the mystery and serve as the center of Fitch's new version of the tale. I will quickly summarize this interesting new story. It begins with a

11 Fitch, *The Assassination of New York*, 149.

disastrous mistake on the part of the Rockefeller family or, more particularly, of John D. Rockefeller, Jr., which was to take out a 21-year lease from Columbia University on the midtown plot of land on which Rockefeller Center now stands. From 1928, Fitch tells us, "to 1988 when they flip Rockefeller Center to the Japanese, understanding what the Rockefellers want is prerequisite to grasping what the city becomes."[12] We need to ground this understanding in two facts: first, Rockefeller Center was initially a failure. Occupancy rates in the 1930s ranged only from "30 percent to 60 percent"[13] owing to its eccentric position in midtown; many of the tenants were peers whom the Rockefellers had made special arrangements to attract (or to coerce, as the case may be). "It was Nelson who had digested the results of the transit study which the family had commissioned to find out why Rockefeller Center was empty. The principal reason, the consultants explained, was that Rockefeller Center lacked access to mass transit. It was too far from Times Square. Too far from Grand Central. Mass transit was the key to healthy office development. The automobile was killing it."[14] The motivation behind a development of this kind lies in the fabulous appreciation in value of the developed property; but given the twin circumstances of massive vacancies and the rental obligations to Columbia, the Rockefellers were unable to make good on these future prospects.

The second crucial fact, according to Fitch, is documented in Richardson Dillworth's testimony at Nelson Rockefeller's vice-presidential confirmation hearing in 1974, which revealed not only "that by far the bulk of the family's $1.3 billion wealth came from midtown – the equity in Rockefeller Center" but also the degree to which the family fortune had at that point "dwindled spectacularly" and indeed, by the mid-1970s "shrunk by two-thirds."[15] This particular real-estate investment thus marked a desperate crisis in the Rockefeller fortunes, a crisis that could only be surmounted in four ways: either the lease with Columbia was modified in their favor (understandably enough, the university was unwilling to comply); or it was abandoned altogether, with disastrous losses; or the area immediately surrounding the center was favorably developed by the Rockefellers themselves, a solution that in effect meant pouring more good money in after bad. "Other obstacles seemed insuperable without changing the structure of the city, but this is precisely what the family now proceeded to do. Ultimately, the city officials proved far easier to manipulate than the trustees of Columbia University or the thirties real estate market."[16] It was a breathtaking and Promethean proposition: to change the whole world in order to accommodate the self. Even Fitch is somewhat embarrassed at his own daring. "How could such a family [their civic and cultural achievements having been enumerated] be totally obsessed with such mean endeavors as driving hot dog sellers away from 42nd Street?" "An explanation relying on the behavior of one family, it must be conceded, seems less than robust. . . . Doctrinaire historical determinists will naturally insist that New York would be 'just the same' without the Rockefellers." "A focus on the family may annoy academic Marxists for whom the capitalist is only the personification of abstract capital and who believe, austerely, that any discussion of individuals in economic analysis represents a fatal concession to populism and empiricism."[17] Etc.

On the contrary, Fitch here gives us a textbook demonstration of the "logic of capital" and in particular of that Hegelian "ruse of Reason" or "ruse of History" whereby a collective process uses individuals for its own ends. The idea comes from Hegel's early study of Adam Smith and in fact transposes the latter's well-known identification of the "invisible hand" of the market. Discussions of Hegel's version mostly assume that the crucial distinction here runs between conscious action and unconscious meaning; I think it is better to posit a radical disjunction between the individual (and the meanings and motives of individual action) and the logic of the collective or of history, of the systemic.

12 Ibid., xvi–xvii.
13 Ibid., 86.
14 Ibid., 94.
15 Ibid., 189.
16 Ibid., 191.
17 Ibid., 189, 226, xvii.

From the family's point of view, and according to Fitch, the Rockefellers were very conscious of their project, which was completely rational. As for the systemic consequences, we are of course free to suppose that they could not foresee them or even that they did not care. But in the dialectical reading, those consequences are part and parcel of a systemic logic radically different from the logic of individual action with which it can only rarely, and with great effort, be held together within the problematic confines of a single thought.

I need briefly to digress on the philosophical positions at stake here. Hegel was very conscious of chance or, as we would call it today, contingency,[18] and a necessary contingency is always foreseen in his larger systemic narratives, which do not always insist on it explicitly, however, so that the casual reader may be forgiven for overlooking Hegel's own commitment to it. Yet at the level of chance and contingency, systemic processes are far from inevitable; they can be interrupted, nipped in the bud, deflected, slowed down, and so forth. Remember that Hegel's perspective is retrospective, seeking only to rediscover the necessity and the meaning of what has already happened: the famous owl of Minerva that flies at dusk. Perhaps, since contemporary historians have rediscovered the constitutive role of warfare in history with such gusto, a military analogy may be appropriate. The "conditions not of our own making" can be identified as the military situation, the terrain, the disposition of forces, and the like. The individual in the synthesis of perception organizes that data into a unified field in which the options and the opportunities become visible. This last is the realm of individual creativity with respect to history and, as we shall see later on, it holds for artistic and cultural creation as much as for the individual capitalists.[19] A collective movement of resistance plays out on a somewhat different level, even though famously there are moments in which individual leaders have just such strategic as well as tactical perceptions of possibility. But the ruse of history runs both ways, and if individual capitalists can sometimes be instrumental in working toward their own undoing (the deterioration of New York City is not a bad example), left movements also sometimes unwittingly promote the "cause" of their adversaries (in impelling them to new technological innovations, for example). A satisfactory conception of politics somehow coordinates both the systemic and the individual (or, if you prefer, to use a popular idea that Fitch often parodies, reconnects the global and the local).

We need now to move more rapidly in two directions at once (perhaps these are indeed some version of the systemic and the local). One road leads us toward the individual buildings themselves, the other toward a further interrogation of finance capital and land speculation that can be expected to bring us, in the end, to that knotty theoretical problem that the Marxian traditionally and quaintly designates as "ground rent." The building, or rather the complex of buildings, looms up first, and it is best to respect its unavoidability. It is of course Rockefeller Center — the stake in all of these maneuvers and the object of a good deal of interesting architectural analysis. Fitch seems relatively bemused by such discussions. "The modern architectural equivalent of a medieval cathedral," he quotes Carol Krinsky as saying, correcting this seemingly positive assessment with Douglas Haskell's perception of the center as "some giant burial place,"

18 See Dieter Henrich, "Hegels Theorie über den Zufall," in *Hegel im Kontext* (Frankfurt: Suhrkamp, 1971).

19 Proust's interest in military strategy is in this connection most revealing indeed: see for example the discussions on the visit to Saint-Loup, during the latter's military service at Doncières, in *Le Côté de Guermantes*.

before washing his own hands of the matter: "There is no way to confirm or disconfirm perceived symbolic values."[20] I think he is mistaken about this: there are certainly ways of analyzing such "perceived symbolic values" as social and historical facts (I don't know what "confirm" or "disconfirm" might mean here). Clearly, Fitch is not interested in doing that, and in terms of his own analysis the cultural icing has little enough to do with the ingredients out of which the cake has been baked (along with the availability of the ovens, etc.). Oddly, this disjunction of symbolic value and economic activity is also registered by the work of one of the subtlest and most complex contemporary architectural theorists, Manfredo Tafuri, who has devoted a whole monograph to the context in which Rockefeller Center is to be evaluated.

20 Fitch, *The Assassination of New York*, 186–87.

Tafuri's interpretive method can be described as follows: the premise is that, at least in this society (under capitalism), an individual building will always stand in contradiction with its urban context and its social function. The interesting buildings are those which try to resolve those contradictions through more or less ingenious formal and stylistic innovations. The resolutions are necessarily failures because they remain in an aesthetic realm disjoined from the social one from which such contradictions spring and also because social or systemic change would have to be total rather than piecemeal. Tafuri's analyses tend to be a litany of failures, and he often describes the "imaginary resolutions" at a high level of abstraction, giving the picture of an interplay of "isms" or disembodied styles that the reader is left to restore to concrete perception.

In the case of Rockefeller Center, however, we may well face a redoubling of this situation: for Tafuri and his colleagues, whose collective volume *The American City* I use here, also seem to think that the situation of the American city (and the buildings to be constructed in it) is somehow doubly contradictory. The absence of a past, waves of immigration, construction on a tabula rasa are certainly features that one would expect the Italian observer to stress. But the Americans are contradicted twice over and doubly doomed, so to speak, because their very formal raw materials are borrowed European styles, which they can only coordinate and amalgamate in various ways without seeming to be able to invent new ones. In other words, the invention of the new is already impossible and contradictory in the general context of capitalism, but the eclecticism of a play of those already impossible styles then replays that impossibility and those contradictions at one remove.

Tafuri's discussion of Rockefeller Center is embedded in a larger discussion of the symbolic value of the American skyscraper itself, which at the outset constitutes "an organism that, by its very nature, defies all rules of proportion"[21] and thus wishes to soar out of the city and against it as a "unique event." Yet as the industrial city and its corporate organization progress, "the skyscraper as an 'event,' as an 'anarchic individual' that, by projecting its image into the commercial center of the city, creates an unstable equilibrium between the independence of a single corporation and the organization of collective capital, no longer appear[s] to be a completely suitable structure."[22] As I follow the complex and detailed history that Tafuri then outlines (from the Chicago Tribune competition in 1922 to the construction of Rockefeller Center in the early 1930s), I seem to be reading a dialectical narrative in which the skyscraper evolves away from its status as "unique event" and toward a new conception of the enclave, within the city but apart from it, now reproducing something of the complexity of the city on a smaller scale. The "enchanted mountain," in its failure to engage the city fabric in some new and innovative way, is thus doomed to make itself over into a miniature city within the city and thus to abandon the fundamental contradiction it was called upon to resolve. Rockefeller Center serves as the climax of this development.

21 In Giorgio Ciucci et al., *The American City*, trans. Barbara Luigia La Penta (Cambridge: MIT Press, 1979), 389.

22 Ibid., 390.

In Rockefeller Center (1931–1940), the anticipatory ideas of Saarinen, the programs of the Regional Plan of New York, Ferriss's images, and Hood's various pursuits were finally brought into synthesis. This statement is true in spite of the fact that Rockefeller Center was completely divorced from any regionalist conception and that it thoroughly ignored any urban considerations beyond the three midtown lots on which the complex was to rise. It was, in fact, a selective synthesis, the significance of which lies precisely in its choices and rejections. From Saarinen's Chicago lakefront, Rockefeller Center drew only its amplified scale and the coordinated unity of a skyscraper complex related to an open space provided with services for the public. From the recently developed taste for the International Style, it accepted volumetric purity, without, however, renouncing the enrichments of Art Deco. From Adam's images of the new Manhattan, it extracted the concept of a contained and rational concentration, an oasis of order. Moreover, all the concepts accepted were stripped of any utopian character; Rockefeller Center in no way contested the established institutions or the current dynamics of the city. Indeed, it took its place in Manhattan as an island of "equilibrated speculation" and emphasized in every way its character as a closed and circumscribed intervention, which nevertheless purported to serve as a model.[23]

23 Ibid., 461.

The allegorical interpretation becomes clearer; the center was "an attempt to celebrate the reconciliation of the trusts and the collectivity on an urban scale."[24] This, and not cultural window dressing, is the symbolic significance of the building and its eclectic play of styles — as superficial a decoration for Tafuri as for Fitch — and it has the function of signifying "collective culture" to its general public and of documenting the center's claim to address public concerns as much as to secure business and financial objectives.

24 Ibid., 483.

Before turning to another related and even more contemporary analysis of Rockefeller Center, however, it may be worth recalling the center's emblematic value for the modernist tradition itself. Indeed, it figures prominently in what was surely for many years the fundamental text and ideological statement of architectural modernism, namely Sigfried Giedion's *Space, Time and Architecture*, which, promoting a new space-time aesthetic in the wake of Le Corbusier, in order to invent a viable contemporary alternative for the baroque tradition of city planning, saw the 14 associated buildings of the center as a unique attempt to implant a new conception of urban design within the (to him intolerable) construction of Manhattan's grid. The original 14 buildings occupied "an area of almost three city blocks (around twelve acres) . . . cut out from New York's checkerboard grid." These buildings of variable height, and the RCA building, a skyscraper slab some 70 stories tall, "are freely disposed in space and enclose an open area, the Rockefeller Plaza, which is used as an ice-skating rink throughout the winter."[25]

25 Sigfried Giedion, *Space, Time and Architecture* (Cambridge: Harvard University Press, 1982, originally 1941), 845. I am grateful to Charles Jencks for reminding me of this basic text.

In light of what has been said, it is appropriate to characterize Giedion's space-time concept, at least in an American context, as a Robert Moses aesthetic insofar as his principal examples are the first great parkways, brand-new in that period, about which he celebrates the kinetic experience: "Riding up and down the long sweeping grades produced an exhilarating dual feeling, one of being connected with the soil and yet of hovering just above it, a feeling like nothing else so much as sliding swiftly on skis through untouched snow down the sides of high mountains."[26]

26 Ibid., 825.

The bleakness of Tafuri's readings always stemmed from the principled absence in his work of any possible future aesthetic, any fantasized solution to the dilemmas of the capitalist city, any avant-garde path by which art might hope to contribute to a world transformation that could for him only be economic and political. Obviously the modern movement itself meant precisely all these things; and Giedion's space-time concept, now so distant from us and so redolent of a bygone age, was an influential attempt to synthesize its various tendencies. It implied a transcendence of individual experience that presumably also promised an expansion of it, in the world of the automobile and the airplane. Thus, of Rockefeller Center Giedion asserts:

> Nothing new or significant can be observed in looking over a map of the site. The ground plan reveals nothing. . . . The actual arrangement and disposition of the buildings can be seen and

grasped only from the air. An air-view picture reveals that the various high buildings are spread out in an open arrangement . . . like the vanes of a windmill, the different volumes so placed that their shadows fall as little as possible upon one another. . . . Moving in the midst of the buildings through Rockefeller Plaza. . . one becomes conscious of new and unaccustomed interrelations between them. They cannot be grasped from any single position or embraced in any single view. . . . [This produces] an extraordinary new effect, somewhat like that of a rotating sphere of mirrored facets in a ballroom when the facets reflect whirling spots of light in all directions and in every dimension.[27]

27 Ibid., 849–51.

This is not the place to evaluate the modernist aesthetic more comprehensively, but rather to observe that whatever the value of Giedion's aesthetic enthusiasm, it seems to have been wiped out by the proliferation of such buildings and spaces across Manhattan altogether. Or perhaps one should say this negatively and suggest that the modernist euphoria depended on the relative scarcity of such new projects, spaces, and constructions: Rockefeller Center was for the 1930s, and for Giedion at that moment, a *novum*, something it no longer is for us.

When this space is utterly overbuilt, then, as it is today, the need arises for a rather different kind of aesthetic, which, as we have seen, Tafuri refuses to provide. But what Tafuri deplores and Giedion does not yet anticipate – a chaos of overbuilding and congestion – Rem Koolhaas has the originality to celebrate and to embrace. *Delirious New York* enthusiastically welcomes the contradictions that Tafuri denounced and makes of this resolute embrace of the irresolvable a new aesthetic very different from Giedion's, an aesthetic for which, however, Rockefeller Center again stands as a peculiarly central lesson.

Koolhaas's reading of the center is of course embedded in his more general proposition about the enabling structure of the Manhattan grid, but I want to underscore the specificity with which he is able to endow Tafuri's still very abstract formulation of the fundamental contradiction (the two discussions, as far as I can see, taking place completely independently of each other and without cross-reference). For now it becomes Raymond Hood's inner "schizophrenia" (as expressed, for example, in his impertinent combination of an immense parking garage with the solemnity of an enormous house of prayer in Columbus, Ohio), which makes him the fittest Hegelian instrument for Manhattan's "ruse of Reason," allowing him "simultaneously to derive energy and inspiration from Manhattan as irrational fantasy *and* to establish its unprecedented theorems in a series of strictly rational steps."[28] Or, to take a slightly different approach, to produce an artifact (in this case, the McGraw-Hill Building) that "looks like a fire raging inside an iceberg: the fire of Manhattanism inside the iceberg of Modernism."[29]

28 Rem Koolhaas, *Delirious New York* (New York: Oxford University Press, 1978), 144.

29 Ibid., 142.

But the more definitive account of the opposition will posit the term *congestion*, along with its novel solution in Hood's "city within a city," namely to "solve congestion by creating more congestion"[30] and to interiorize it within the building complex itself. The concept of congestion now condenses several different meanings: use and consumption, both urban and market exploitation of land parcels, traffic along with ground rent, but also the foregrounding of the collective or popular, populist appeal. Congestion itself is the mediator between these hitherto distinct features of the phenomenon and the problem; just as Koolhaas's more general specification mediates between Tafuri's abstractions and a consideration of the concrete building complex in either architectural or commercial terms. The other term of the antithesis is less definitively formulated, probably because it runs the danger of endorsing the center's taste or aesthetic. Some-

30 Ibid., 149.

times in Koolhaas's account it is simply "beauty" ("the paradox of maximum congestion combined with maximum beauty")[31] just as in Tafuri it is often simply "spirituality." But clearly enough this gesture toward the cultural realm and its function as a Barthesian "sign" or connotation can itself be prolonged and incrementally specified. The crucial operation is the establishment of a mediation capable of translation in either direction: able to characterize of the economic determinants of this construction within the city as much as it offers directions for aesthetic analysis and cultural interpretation.

31 Ibid., 163.

Put another way, these analyses seem both to demand and to evade the traditional academic question about the aesthetic, namely that of value. As a work of art, how is Rockefeller Center to be judged — indeed, does this question have any relevance at all in the present context? Both Tafuri and Koolhaas center their discussions on the acts of the architect himself, on what he confronts, let alone the raw materials and forms, on the deeper contradictions that he must somehow resolve in order to build something, and in particular on the tension between the urban fabric or totality and the individual building or monument (in this case the peculiar role and structure of the skyscraper). This analysis can cut either way, as in the now time-honored formula of imaginary toads in real gardens; or, as Kenneth Burke liked to put it, the interesting peculiarity of the slogan "symbolic act" is that you can and must choose your emphasis in a binary way. The work may turn out to be a symbolic *act*, a real form of praxis in the symbolic realm; but it also might prove to be a merely *symbolic* act, an attempt to act in a realm in which action is impossible and does not exist as such. I have the feeling that for Tafuri, Rockefeller Center is the latter — a merely symbolic act that necessarily fails to resolve its contradictions; whereas for Koolhaas the fact of creative and productive action within the symbolic is the source of aesthetic excitement. But, perhaps on both accounts, the problem is simply that we have to make do with a bad or, at the least, a mediocre set of buildings, so the question of value is then out of place and excluded from the outset. Yet in this context, in which the individual building seeks somehow to secure its place within the urban and within a real city that already exists, is it possible that all buildings are bad, or at least failures, in this sense? Or is the aesthetic of the individual building to be radically disjoined from the problem of the urban in such a way that the problems raised by each belong and remain in separate compartments (or I dare say in separate departments)?

I want to turn briefly to the other basic issue, ground rent, before making some hypotheses about the relationship between architecture and finance capital today. The problem of the value of land posed well-nigh insuperable difficulties for the classical political economy of the 18th and early 19th centuries, not least because in that period the process whereby traditional and often collective holdings were being commodified and privatized as Western capitalism developed was substantially incomplete. This included the basic historical and structural tendency toward the commodification of farm labor, or in other words the transformation of peasants into agricultural workers, a process far more complete today than it was even at the time of Marx, let alone that of David Ricardo. But the elimination of the peasantry as a feudal class or caste is not the same as the elimination of the problem of land values and ground rent. I must pay tribute here to David Harvey's *The Limits to Capital*, which is not only one of the most lucid and satisfying recent attempts to outline Marx's economic thought but also perhaps the only one to tackle the thorny problem of ground rent in Marx, whose own analysis was cut short by his death, its posthumous publication cobbled together by Friedrich Engels. I don't want to get into the theory, but I can report that, according to Harvey's magisterial review and retheorization (he offers a plausible account of the more complicated scheme that Marx might have elaborated had he lived), ground rent and land value are both essential to the dynamic of capitalism and also a source of contradiction for it. If too much investment is immobilized in land, there are problems; if investment in land is out of the picture, there are equally grave problems in another direction. So the moment of ground rent and the moment of finance capital that organizes around it are permanent structural elements of the system, sometimes taking a secondary role and sinking into insignificance, sometimes, as in our own period, coming to the fore as though they were the principal locus of capitalist accumulation.

I mainly want to appeal to Harvey for his account of the nature of value in land. If land has a value, it cannot be explained by a labor theory of value. Labor can add value in the form of improvements, but labor cannot possibly be the source of land value as it is for the value of industrial production. But land has value nonetheless. How to explain this paradox? Harvey suggests that for Marx the value of land is something like a structurally necessary fiction. Indeed he speaks of "fictitious capital" – "a flow of money capital not backed by any commodity transaction."[32] This is possible only because fictitious capital is oriented toward the expectation of future value, and thus with one stroke land value is revealed to be intimately related to the credit system, the stock market, and finance capital generally: "Under such conditions the land is treated as a pure financial asset which is bought and sold according to the rent it yields. Like all such forms of fictitious capital, what is traded is a claim upon future revenues, which means a claim upon future profits from the sue of the land or, more directly, a claim upon future labor."[33] Now our series of mediations is complete, or at least more complete than it was: time and a new relationship to the future as space of necessary expectation of revenue and capital accumulation or, in other words, the structural reorganization of time itself into a kind of futures market. This is the final link in the chain leading from finance capital through land speculation to aesthetics and cultural production itself, in our context, to architecture. Historians of ideas tell us tirelessly about the way in which, in modernity, the emergence of the modality of various future tenses not only displaces the older sense of the past and of tradition but structures our form of historicity. The effects are palpable in the history of ideas and also more immediately in the structure of narrative itself. Can this be theorized in its effects on the architectural and spatial field? As far as I know, only Tafuri and his philosophical collaborator Massimo Cacciari have evoked a "planification of the future," although their discussion is limited to Keynesianism, to liberal capital and social democracy. We have posited this new colonization of the future as a fundamental tendency in capitalism itself and the source of the recrudescence of finance capital and land speculation. One can certainly begin a properly aesthetic exploration of these issues with a question about the way in which specific "futures" – now in the financial as well as the temporal sense – come to be structural features of the newer architecture: something like planned obsolescence in the certainty that the building will no longer have an aura of permanence but will bear in its very raw materials the impending certainty of its own future demolition.

I need to make at least a gesture toward fulfilling my initial program – setting in place the chain of mediations that might lead from infrastructure (land speculation, finance

32 David Harvey, *The Limits to Capital* (Chicago: B. Blackwell, 1982), 265.

33 Ibid., 347.

capital) to superstructure (aesthetic form). I will take the shortcut of cannibalizing Charles Jencks's wonderful descriptions of what he calls "late modernity" (a distinction that will not particularly concern us in the present context). Jencks first allows us to see the way not to do this, that of thematic self-reference, as when Anthony Lumsden's Branch Bank project in Bumi Daya "alludes to the silver standard and an area of investment where the bank's money is possibly headed."[34] Jencks also identifies at least two features (and very fundamental ones at that) that might well illustrate the formal overtones proper to a late finance capitalism. That these are, as he argues, extreme developments of the features of the modern, energetic distortions that end up turning this work against the very spirit of the modern only reinforces the general argument: modernism to the second power no longer looks like modernism at all, but some other space altogether.

The two features I have in mind are "extreme isometric space"[35] and, no doubt even more predictably, not just the glass skin but its "enclosed skin volumes."[36] Isometric space, however much it derived from the modernist "free plan," becomes the very element of delirious equivalence itself in which not even the monetary medium remains and not only the contents but also the frames are now freed to endless metamorphosis: "Mies' endless, universal space was becoming a reality, where ephemeral functions could come and go without messing up the absolute architecture above and below."[37] The "enclosed skin volumes" then illustrate another aspect of late-capitalist abstraction, the way in which it dematerializes without signifying in any traditional way spirituality "breaking down the apparent mass, density, weight of a fifty storey building," as Jencks puts it.[38] The evolution of the curtain wall "decreases the mass and weight while enhancing the volume and the contour – the difference between brick and a balloon."[39] Both principles – features of the modern projected into new and original spatial worlds – no longer operate according to the older modern binary oppositions. Weight or embodiment, in its progressive attenuation, no longer posits the non-body or the spirit as an opposite; in the same way, where the free plan canceled older bourgeois space, the infinite new isometric kind cancels nothing but simply develops under its own momentum like a new dimension. Without wishing to belabor the point, I believe that the abstract dimension or materialist sublimation of finance capital enjoys something of the same semiautonomy as cyberspace.

"To the second power." This is more or less the formula in terms of which we have been imagining some new cultural logic beyond the modern one, and the formula can be specified in any number of ways: Barthesian connotation, for example, or reflection about reflection – provided only that it is not construed as increasing the magnitude of the "first power" as in mathematical progressions. Simmel's comparison with voyeurism[40] does not quite do the trick, particularly since it pertains to "first" or "normal" finance capitalism only and not to the heightened forms of abstraction produced by our current variety, from which even those objects susceptible of voyeuristic pleasure seem to have disappeared. Whence, no doubt, the resurgence of ancient theories of the simulacrum as some abstraction from beyond the already abstracted image. Jean Baudrillard's work is surely the most inventive exploration of the paradoxes and afterimages of this new dimension of things, which he does not yet, I think, identify with finance capital; and I have already mentioned cyberspace, a rather different representational version of what cannot be represented and yet is more concrete — at least in cyberpunk science fiction like that of William Gibson — than the old modernist abstractions of cubism or classical science fiction.

34. Charles Jencks, *The New Moderns: From Late to Neo-Modernism* (New York: Rizzoli, 1990), 85.

35. Ibid., 81.

36. Ibid., 86.

37. Ibid., 81.

38. Ibid., 86.

39. Ibid., 85.

40. "Money thus provides a unique extension of the personality which does not seek to adorn itself with the possession of goods. Such a personality is indifferent to control over objects; it is satisfied with that momentary power over them, and while it appears as if this avoidance of any qualitative relationship to objects would not offer any extension and satisfaction to the person, the very act of buying is experienced as such a satisfaction, because the objects are absolutely obedient to money. Because of the completeness with which money and objects as money-values follows the impulses of the person, he is satisfied by a symbol of his domination over them which is otherwise obtained only through actual ownership. The enjoyment of this mere symbol of enjoyment may come close to the pathological, as in the following case related by a French novelist. An Englishman was a member of a bohemian group whose enjoyment in life consisted of his sponsorship of the wildest orgies, though he himself never joined in but always only paid for everybody – he appeared, said nothing, did nothing, paid for everything and disappeared. The one side of these dubious events – paying for them – must, in this man's experience, have stood for everything. One may readily assume that here is a case of one of those perverse satisfactions that has recently become the subject of sexual pathology. In comparison with ordinary extravagance, which stops at the first stage of possession and enjoyment and the mere squandering of money, the behaviour of this man is particularly eccentric because the enjoyments, represented here by their money equivalent, are so close and directly tempting to him. The absence of a positive owning and using of things on the one hand, and the fact on the other that the mere act of buying is experienced as a relationship between the person and the objects and as a personal satisfaction, can be explained by the expansion that the mere act of spending money affords to the person. Money builds a bridge between such people and objects. In crossing this bridge, the mind experiences the attraction of their possession even if it does in fact not attain it." Simmel, *The Philosophy of Money*, 327.

Yet as we are certainly haunted by this particular specter, perhaps in the ghost story itself – and particularly its postmodern variants – some very provisional analogy can be sought in conclusion. The ghost story is virtually the architectural genre par excellence, wedded as it is to rooms and buildings ineradicably stained with the memory of gruesome events, material structures in which the past literally "weighs like a nightmare on the brain of the living." Yet just as the sense of the past and of history followed the extended family into oblivion, lacking those whose storytelling alone could inscribe it as sheer event into the listening minds of later generations, so also urban renewal seems everywhere in the process of sanitizing the ancient corridors and bedrooms to which a ghost might cling. (The haunting of open-air sites such as a gallows hill or a sacred burial ground presents an earlier, premodern situation.)

Yet the time is still "out of joint," and Jacques Derrida has restored to the ghost story and the matter of haunting a new and actual philosophical dignity it perhaps never had before, proposing to substitute for the ontology of Martin Heidegger (who cites these same words of Hamlet for his own purposes) a "hauntology," the barely perceptible agitations in the air of a past abolished socially and collectively, yet still attempting to be reborn. (Significantly, Derrida includes the future among spectralities.)[41]

How is this hauntology to be imagined? We scarcely associate ghosts with high-rise buildings, even though I have heard of multistoried apartment structures in Hong Kong that are said to be haunted.[42] Perhaps the more fundamental narrative of a ghost story "to the second power," of a properly postmodern ghost story, ordered by finance-capital spectralities rather than the old and more tangible kind, demands a narrative of the very search for a building to haunt in the first place. Stanley Kwan's *Rouge*[43] certainly preserves the classical ghost story's historical content: the confrontation of the present with the past, even in this instance the confrontation of the contemporary mode of production – the offices and the businesses of Hong Kong today (or rather yesterday, before 1997) – with what is still an *ancien régime* (if not a downright feudalism) of wealthy slackers and sophisticated establishments of hetairai, replete with gaming and sumptuary feasts, as well as erotic connoisseurship. In this pointed juxtaposition, the moderns – bureaucrats and secretaries – are well aware of their bourgeois inferiority; nor does the suicide for love stand in any fundamental narrative tension with the decadence of the romantic 1930s – save perhaps by accident, for the playboy fails to die and is finally unwilling to follow his glamorous partner into an eternal afterlife. He does not wish, so to speak, to be haunted; indeed, as a derelict old man in the present, he can scarcely be located in the first place. The traditional ghost story did not, surely, require mutual consent for a visitation. Here it seems to; and the success or failure of the haunting never depended quite so much, as in present-day Hong Kong, on the mediation of present-day observers. To wish to be haunted, to long for the great passions that now exist only in the past, indeed, to survive in a bourgeois present as exotic cosmetics and costumes alone, as sheer postmodern "nostalgia" trappings, as optional content within a stereotypical yet empty form: some first, "classical" nostalgia as abstraction from the concrete object, the second or "postmodern" one as a nostalgia for nostalgia, a longing for the situation in which the process of abstraction might itself once again be possible, whence the feeling that the newer moment is a return to realism – plots, agreeable buildings, decoration, melodies, etc. – when in fact it is only a replay of the empty stereotypes of all of those things and a vague memory of their fullness on the tip of the tongue.

41 See my discussion in "Marx's Purloined Letter," *New Left Review* 209, no. 4 (1995): 86–120.

42 An unpublished paper by Kevin Heller explores the even more complex analogies in *Gremlins 2* (1990), not coincidentally filmed in Donald Trump's Trump Tower.

43 Stanley Kwan, dir., *Rouge* (Hong Kong: Jackie Chan, 1987). I am indebted to Rey Chow for suggesting this reference.

FREDRIC JAMESON IS DIRECTOR OF THE GRADUATE PROGRAM IN LITERATURE AT DUKE UNIVERSITY. HIS BOOKS INCLUDE LATE MARXISM; POSTMODERNISM, OR, THE CULTURAL LOGIC OF LATE CAPITALISM; THE SEEDS OF TIME, AND THE FORTHCOMING BRECHT AND METHOD.

Alejandro Zaera-Polo

New Platforms

Approaching the question of instrumentality in an architectural practice implies a reconsideration of the limits of the discipline in order to question its relationships with domains originally external to it, such as the themes proposed by this panel: money, market, policy. I would like to suggest two oppositions that may identify ways of understanding how we produce architecture and the relationship between the nature of the processes that we use and the products that result from them. These categories will hopefully suggest a position for architectural practice with respect to discussions about language and determinism, subjects common to many of the Anyhow panels.

The processes we use to produce work can be external or internal to the resulting product. We can use processes driven by the search for effects or by the object's internal constitution. This opposition is exemplified in the classic tension between the marketing and the engineering departments of a corporate structure. While the marketing techniques target a product's integration into a system external to its own material production – the market – the engineering techniques aim at controlling the manufacturing processes and the relationships between components. Very often, the respective determinations of the product differ radically.

The second category relates to the products of a practice. These can be internal or external to the applicable field of production. This dichotomy has a long tradition in the history of aesthetics: *Baukunst* versus *Kunstwollen* in the Gottfried Semper/Alois Riegl discussion; "what" and "how" in Mies van der Rohe's terms. Riegl describes this opposition between the "internal coherence" of a work of art – when the productive requirements of a piece are sufficient to complete the product – and "external coherence" – when a product can only be understood and completed within an assemblage that exceeds its pure production, whether as a form of expressive authorship or through a functional purpose.

Colin Rowe's description of "composition" and "character" as two distinct aesthetic qualities of architecture illustrates this opposition: while an architecture determined by compositional requirements focuses on the construction of the piece and the relationships between components, an architecture of "character" is concerned with its capacity to fit within an assemblage of social uses, representations, and types external to the product. Another good example is the opposition between "pure" and "applied" research in the production of knowledge. Pure research – such as investigations in quantum physics, logic, and advanced mathematics – primarily affects a particular field of existing knowledge, that is, the internal forms of a scientific discipline. Applied research – such as medical or engineering research – attempts to produce effects beyond a particular disciplinary domain by targeting objectives external to a certain body of knowledge.

While there is a link between an "internal" disciplinary instrumentality and the delivery of products of "internal coherence" and between using "external" techniques and making works of "external coherence," this is not necessarily the rule, and it is useful to consider the coordinates that a certain practice may take in the field defined by these oppositions. We can anticipate four basic modes of practice: the first involves operating within the limits of the discipline, both on the level of the processes used and with respect to the effects sought. We include here all speculative practices that attempt to produce effects primarily on the structure of the discipline through the operation with disciplinary processes, such as with some forms of historicism, formalisms, and deconstructive or metalinguistic experiments. The second mode operates beyond the limits of the discipline on both levels, aiming at producing effects beyond the discipline's borders and borrowing techniques from outside the discipline, as in commercially oriented practices, participative design processes, and direct action. In a third case the operation seeks to go beyond disciplinary boundaries to effect the disciplinary field, such as with some forms of regionalism, symbolic manipulation, and "pop" practices that incorporate images, rituals, and idiosyncrasies. The fourth mode requires operation within the disciplinary boundary but draws programs, constraints, and determinations from outside. This mode is composed of what could be defined as pragmatic, operational, or functional practices. Perhaps we could recover the "functional" mode by describing it as the construction of "functions" – that is, relations between two different domains or parameters.

Below is a chart of these possible states.

	Targets Outside	Targets Inside
Instruments Outside	Commercial Practices Direct Action Participative Design Processes	Regionalism Pop Symbolism
Instruments Inside	Pragmatism Functionalism	Formalism Linguistic Technological

Neither of the two first options will help us to draw links between the practice of architecture and the processes occurring beyond its disciplinary domain and, therefore, will not be able to throw much light on the potential relationships between concepts such as those framing this session and the processes that we use to produce architecture. Moreover, and without entirely negating their potentials, both have limited ability to produce "positive" affirmative statements about the project while allowing the disciplinary openness needed to innovate. In other words, the only opportunity for the first two modes of practice is to produce innovation by adopting a "negative," critical attitude toward existing disciplinary, political, and economic bodies. Without constructing random "negative" processes, these single-domain practices remain imprisoned in their own logic, confined in a tautological mode. Hybrid modes of practice, on the other hand, facilitate "positive" determinations on either side of the disciplinary boundary, producing unforeseen effects on the other side and enabling an openness for innovation.

The fourth mode of practice, determined or constrained by "external" processes – such as money, market, policy – but open as a disciplinary structure, can become more innovative and can open substantial extensions within the disciplinary body. This claim in favor of an operational, "functional" mode of practice can provide an alternative and a reply to some of the proposals made in this forum. On the one hand, it opposes the proposition that only indetermination can grant the necessary openness to allow for innovation: a pragmatic or "functional" approach does not preclude mutations within the disciplinary body, or in the nature of the products, yet it requires determinations and constraints in terms of its effects on the "outside." It is at once positive, affirmative, yet inconclusive and open. On the other hand, it may also offer an alternative to the need for a dialectical relationship with either history or architectural language in order to make "new figures" significant in a certain domain. It does not matter whether a mutation in a mode of practice is meaningful within the history of the architecture or the current structure of the discipline, as it becomes relevant beyond that domain on the "outside." "New figures" can be produced through a truly productive or poetic practice instead of through a rhetorical operation.

The mutations that the nature of the architectural ground suffers as a result of changing

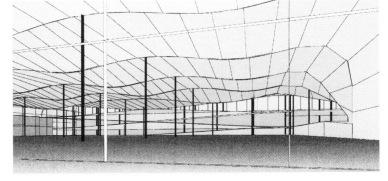

Below: Glass Centre, Newcastle, United Kingdom, competition entry, October 1994. Previous page and right: Welding test inside cardboard structure of Yokohama International Port Terminal, Yokohama, Japan, projected completion, 2003.

conditions on the "outside" is perhaps one of the most remarkable examples of these functional processes. As increasingly mobile resources and investment and flexible temporal and spatial organizations have come to characterize economic integration, the very nature of the grounds – physical, political, economic, or cultural – where we operate is

determination and of a public or infrastructural nature. Our selection depended on the pertinence of the projects to the processes that we had identified as relevant and, obviously, on their availability. Only recently have we started to gain awareness of the precise relationships between our original theoretical agenda and the architectural research that

also becoming increasingly unstable and fluctuating, rendering "new figures" of the ground as an architectural element. This will be an attempt to frame momentarily the emergence of these figures, illustrated through some architectural projects. Although we are conscious of the limitations and methodological problems implied in fixing these figures, an alternative approach to contributing positively to the development of a body of knowledge seems unlikely.

When we started Foreign Office Architects five years ago, we had a relatively precise agenda vis-à-vis some of the fields or opportunities that we were aiming to address in the practice. We defined these not within the discipline of architecture but as emerging processes of production and economic integration that seemed increasingly to determine all contemporary practices beyond their disciplinary categorization. In the constant spatial reconfiguration characteristic of the current economic regimes we foresaw unprecedented possibilities for new techniques and processes with which to construct architecture.

The subsequent operations within our practice aim at identifying opportunities within relatively large-scale projects of atypological

followed. The process by which we came to propose an alternative model of the architectural ground is by no means a direct path from our original theoretical agenda, but is, on the contrary, heavily mediated by the nature of our commissions and by certain intuitions that we are now able to explain more cohesively.

This process started to take shape in a 1994 competition entry for a building to host a glass factory and glass museum on a steep site in suburban Newcastle (ground level drops 10.5 meters). The idea of a shedlike structure arose almost immediately due to the industrial program and the required integration of work and leisure. The manipulation of the ground was driven by the topography of the site and the museum circulation and access. Blending programmatic requirements to produce alternative programmatic structures and integrating the different inputs into a coherent whole, we started working with a hybridization of the two topographic structures: the ground and the envelope.

Another important decision in the process of formalizing this project was to couple the openings in the enveloping surface with the structure needed to support the roof. The roof-lighting openings in the shed were made by cutting and deforming rather than piercing the surface. Oriented to capture light from the north, the eye-shaped openings correspond to trusses that increase their depth proportionally to the bending moment. This was our first attempt to operate with an enveloping ground, where structural stresses are handled through singularities of the surface itself. In this case, however, the singularities were produced more as a hybridization of existing "types" – the shed and the "Belfast" truss – than as a differentiation of a system.

In the competition for the Yokohama International Port Terminal, we formulated many concepts initiated in the Sunderland Glass Centre project more clearly. The identification of the ground and the enveloping surfaces became more consistent, partly because we were simply carrying forward existing research on using surfaces as structural devices, partly because the program, a transportation facility, was suited to the exploration of a shifting, unstable construction of the ground.

The structural qualities of the ground in this project come much closer to the idea of a hollowed ground where loads are not distributed by gravitational force through columns, as in the Glass Centre, but by displacing stresses through the surface of the shell. This shell-like structure also became a potential solution to the lateral loads that seismic movements frequently produce in Japan. The particular condition of the Japanese ground, where nongravitational stresses are often more problematic than gravity, became instrumental in this development. The relationship in the Yokohama project between the topography of this ground and the areas of structural strength produced by its folds differs from the system used in the Glass Centre. The main zones of structural rigidity appear here parallel to the direction of the folds, rather than to the edges of the cuts.

The circulatory flow that shapes the building occurs along the longitudinal direction, suggesting the removal of the structure away from the cuts, the bifurcations of the surface, to produce points of physical access. But beyond the functional requirements, this shift also meant a higher degree of integration between the surface and its static properties. These were produced as true singularities of the shell rather than as structural elements embedded in its accidents. From a hybridization of types, the crucial step here was to move to a strategy of differentiation of a tectonic system: the folded surface.

In the headquarters for the Korean Catholic Church in downtown Seoul, we faced a much denser topographic, urbanistic, and cultural domain than we did in Yokohama. The program required the manipulation of a very fragmented collection of buildings into a coherent complex and the reintegration of those buildings into the surrounding fabric. Our first decision was to eliminate the classical distinction between the project and its frame. By making the limits of our operation coincide with the property boundary, the project became the construction of a new ground for the whole complex, instead of introducing another figure into the already crowded field. The frame is one of the most persistent

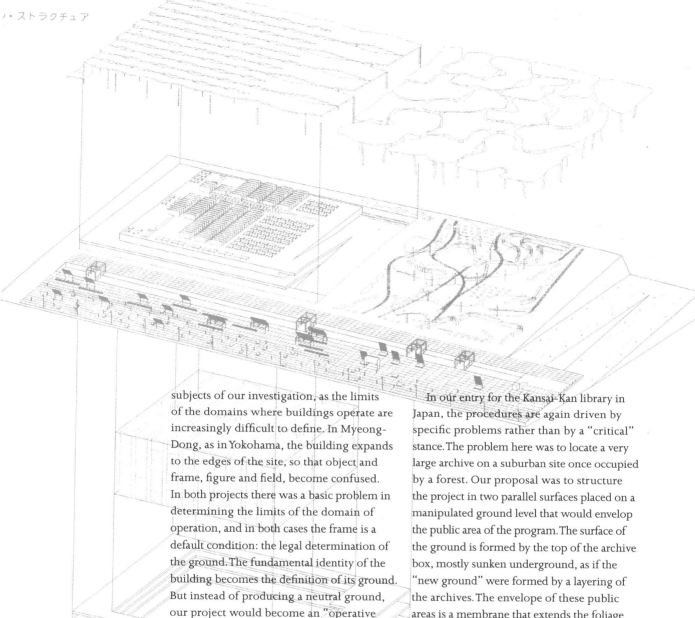

Left: Myeong-Dong, Korean
Catholic Church, Seoul,
Korea, competition entry,
March 1996. Above:
Kansai-Kan library, Kansai
Science City, Japan, compe-
tition entry, July 1996.

subjects of our investigation, as the limits of the domains where buildings operate are increasingly difficult to define. In Myeong-Dong, as in Yokohama, the building expands to the edges of the site, so that object and frame, figure and field, become confused. In both projects there was a basic problem in determining the limits of the domain of operation, and in both cases the frame is a default condition: the legal determination of the ground. The fundamental identity of the building becomes the definition of its ground. But instead of producing a neutral ground, our project would become an "operative system" for the complex: a focal organization enforces the congregational quality of the space implied in the design brief.

Structurally, this project was conceived as a kind of underground half-torus acting as a retaining wall and enclosure for the series of auditoriums to be placed under the new ground as a "sunken stadium." The geometry of the torus was produced by a complex curve determined by the corresponding radii of the different-size auditoriums. Circulation and access were organized by radial cuts in the torus's surface to avoid interrupting the structural membrane, which was itself radially organized.

In our entry for the Kansai-Kan library in Japan, the procedures are again driven by specific problems rather than by a "critical" stance. The problem here was to locate a very large archive on a suburban site once occupied by a forest. Our proposal was to structure the project in two parallel surfaces placed on a manipulated ground level that would envelop the public area of the program. The surface of the ground is formed by the top of the archive box, mostly sunken underground, as if the "new ground" were formed by a layering of the archives. The envelope of these public areas is a membrane that extends the foliage of the existing forest. This single layer of program combines two fields formed as gradients of proximity to the two access roads. The resulting graded field is mirrored by a differentiation in the pattern of cuts on the roof membrane to produce varied lighting conditions on the ground plane. In the Kansai project, the "framing" is an equipotential extension – the most efficient form to preserve a highly controlled environment – of the orthogonal structure of the conventional book-stacking system: a square envelope placed on the existing ground at a position determined by the aforementioned access fields. Although the envelope had to assume a regular form, the solution of the joint between the building's grounds and the existing slope blurs this functional delimitation, as does the mullion-free glass membrane that forms the building's envelope. But perhaps the most interesting consequence of the graded ground on the roof system was the opportunity to revisit the roof system used in the Glass Centre, now used as a differentiated pattern. It is perhaps peripheral to the main argument about the ground, but the solution we adopted here regarding the placement of the columns under the deepest area of the cut, allowing for a gravitational drainage system, was also an important moment in what became a sort of typological development. It is also an example of the construction of a form by the successive addition of new conditions toward higher levels of complexity across different projects.

The following project was a design consultation for a large multi-modal transportation hub in Pusan, Korea. The connection between the city and the developing waterfront, over the railroad tracks, was the main object. The scale of intervention – a 120,000-square-meter high-speed rail terminal plus bus station and associated parking – was a perfect opportunity for Pusan City to cross over the existing infrastructure of tracks and highways to connect to the new developments on the waterfront.

The spatial structure of the tracks became crucial as the need to keep the station operative during the construction of the new terminal forced us to incorporate these traces into our project. We turned the station into a new public space that will connect the ground level with the station concourse at 8.50 meters above grade and with a whole new city – with an area of 800,000 square meters – built over the tracks at 15.00 meters, the new building dissolves into a new plaza and the road infrastructure serving the complex. The dissolution of the building into the infrastructural elements that project beyond the "frame" of the site became the most remarkable development with respect to the construction of a new ground, formally and functionally blending building and ground. The "frame" thereby extends even beyond the limits of the legal ground, melting topographic and programmatic conditions between the project and frame. This moves one step beyond Myeong-Dong in the relations between figure and the ground.

The topography we proposed is a shredded surface that would connect the different levels by weaving undulating bands to provide access, light, and ventilation to the concourse and platforms. The structure of the bands is a series of arches and catenaries whose geometries determine the undulations of the ground/envelope.

Finally, a speculative competition for a "Virtual House" (see *ANY* 19/20) allowed us to test the same set of ideas on an entirely

Left: Pusan High-Speed Railway Complex, Pusan, Korea, competition entry, October 1996, view of plaza. Above: Interior view.

ALEJANDRO ZAERA-POLO IS AN ARCHITECT IN LONDON AND A TUTOR AT THE ARCHITECTURAL ASSOCIATION. HE IS A PARTNER WITH FARSHID MOUSSAVI IN FOREIGN OFFICE ARCHITECTS LTD., WHICH WON THE GRAND PRIZE IN 1994 FOR THE YOKOHAMA INTERNATIONAL PORT TERMINAL IN YOKOHAMA, JAPAN.

different scale. The idea here was to operate with an abstracted band of ground – a band of "disruptive pattern material" – to produce alternative organizations to the conventional compartmentalization of domestic space. The manipulation of the ground in this project differs from the previous cases. While in previous experiments we maintained the orientation of the surface with respect to gravity, in the Virtual House that relationship keeps reversing, every face of the surface shifting constantly between a "lining" and a "wrapping" condition. A diagonal shift in the plan increased the spatial complexity of this structure in comparison with previous projects, making possible the stacking of different units that enable the unlimited proliferation of the body of the house. In this project, the hollow ground that we have been developing acquires a more paradigmatic state, where the possibility of proliferating the structure offers an alternative to the "unframed" quality of the ground that we had previously explored.

The development that we have presented here was obviously possible only with respect to certain conditions with which we were involved during the brief history of our practice and the instruments and techniques used to produce these projects. It is not a direct exploration of a theorization of contemporary structures of money and market: we did not know the form of ground we were seeking, and only now can we identify a certain type

of ground that embodies our early agenda. We believe that we may thus produce a development of the disciplinary body.

To summarize the qualities of these "new grounds" we point to their fundamentally active, operative nature; these emerging grounds are closer to the contemporary conception of "platforms" as "operative systems" than to the classical concept of a "platform" – pediments, bases – aimed at framing, neutralization, and erasure of the field of operation to produce an ideal background for architecture to become a readable figure. These new grounds also move toward determining the condition of "site" as a kind of natural condition. New grounds derive from a proliferation of the fields of affiliation that we decide to construct within or beyond the site to exploit certain opportunities. These grounds have specific characteristics: (1) they are not natural – physically or culturally – but artificially constructed; (2) they are neither abstract nor neutral and homogeneous but concrete and differentiated; they are neither figures nor backgrounds but operative systems; (3) they have uncertain frames, as the field in which they exist is not a fragment but a differentiated domain affiliated with external processes; they are not separable from the operation we produce on them; (4) they are neither a datum nor a reference; (5) they are neither solid nor structured by gravity; they are hollow and "diagonally" structured.

Saskia Sassen

Hong Kong

Strategic Site / New Frontier

The global economy needs to be implemented, serviced, coordinated. We cannot take it for granted, as a given or a background. A cross-border network of some 30 to 40 cities is one of the key scaffoldings for the management, coordination, and servicing of the global economy. The cities in this network are strategic sites for the valorization of new forms of global corporate capital. Some of these cities are clearly more strategic than others, but perhaps the overriding feature is that the network itself matters: there is no such thing as a single global city, and this distinguishes today's global cities from the capitals of former empires. Hong Kong, along with New York and London, is one of the top cities in this network. One question being asked over and over again is whether it will remain as part of the network after its return to China.

These cities are also strategic sites for disadvantaged people who, while powerless, gain presence and hence the possibility of a new kind of politics/culture. Insofar as immigrants and political refugees are part of the disadvantaged, the global city is also a site for postcolonial history. Hong Kong has long been a place for the displaced of all sorts – from Shanghai businessmen in the late 1940s to Vietnamese boatpeople in the 1970s and Chinese human rights activists in the 1990s. Hong Kong has also long had its own disadvantaged – poor dockworkers, factory workers, servants. They can become present to each other and to the wider world in a way they cannot in a small town that operates in a local context. In this regard, global cities –

New York, London, Hong Kong – are a new frontier, where the top sectors of global capital encounter their necessary others in an engagement that becomes both political and cultural, because these others can gain presence even when they cannot have direct power.

The distinction between the global and the local needs to be rethought, as do established notions of membership, or of the necessity of proximity in the constitution of the "local." For example, both the new international professional class and the immigrant workforce operate in contexts that are both local and global; they are members of a cross-border culture that is in many ways "local." This holds even for such international financial centers as London, New York, Zurich, Amsterdam, Frankfurt: they all are part of an international yet very localized work subculture. We see here both proximity and deterritorialization. The experience of globalization and its impact on localities is partial; it is never an all-encompassing umbrella. It installs itself in very specific structures. We need to study this specificity, along with the macro processes, and to develop particular categories of analysis for it.

In order to understand whether Hong Kong will remain as one of the strategic sites for global capital after its return to China, we need to understand something about the inner workings of the current global economic system. Further, to understand whether Hong Kong will remain a space of a certain type of contestation – a new frontier – with the kind of political and cultural operations that come with it, we need to

understand what this space of the new frontier is.

FROM COMPRADORS TO SPECIALIZED SERVICE FIRMS

The story of Hong Kong today is partly embedded in the specifics of devolution (the return to China) and partly in the dynamics of the global economic system. It has been said that the strength of Hong Kong and its utility to China lie precisely in its difference from China. Hong Kong is today one of the major centers for the global exchange of capital.[1] What exactly does this mean in an era of instantaneous transmission around the globe and the ascendance of finance – a dematerialized economic output that travels in the form of light pulses? Why do we have a place like Hong Kong today, in an era of globalization and telecommunications? Why does its concentration of specialized financial, legal, and accounting services matter? If we can see why it matters vis-à-vis the global economy, we can also begin to see why keeping Hong Kong as it is might be the best for China's efforts to participate in the global economy. The answer for me is the story of the global city.

Three features of today's global economy explain why the network of 30 to 40 cities matters. First, the global economy is not simply a market; it is a system that needs to be implemented, coordinated, managed, serviced. Much of this specialized work is concentrated in cities and materializes in specific institutions and processes. Second, the privatization of public-sector firms and the deregulation of a growing number of activities have

1 David Meyer, Social Networks of Capital: Hong Kong as a Global Metropolis (Providence, R.I.: Department of Sociology, Brown University, 1997), forthcoming.

Photos: Damon Rich

brought with them a privatizing of governance functions, that is, a shift of such functions from the world of government to the corporate world. The work of governing the private economic system largely gets done in cities – in the form of various legal, accounting, and managerial tasks, through business associations, etc. Indeed, one of the key, though rarely recognized, features of the global economy today is the formation of an intermediary institutionalized world of high-level financial, legal, and accounting firms that have emerged as strategic agents often performing some of the functions fulfilled by national governments before privatization and deregulation. Third, the digitization of a growing sector of the economy has underlined the importance of access to the appropriate infrastructure; for leading sectors it has to be state-of-the-art infrastructure. Leading economic sectors will find what they need in the major international business centers that have enormous concentrations of such infrastructure. The importance of this infrastructure can be deduced from the orders of magnitude characterizing the financial markets. The global capital market is estimated by *The Economist* to have reached U.S.$75 trillion. A good part of this is not money or capital as we usually think of them: it is a set of electronic transactions that never leaves digital space.

Hong Kong today concentrates a variety of these functions and resources. It is the major center for specialized servicing in Southeast Asia and handles activities and flows that have to do not only with China but also with other Asian countries that

are internationalizing their economies. Whether it is international finance proper or international trade, a lot of specialized servicing is required, and not all countries in the region have it, even though they may be deregulating their economies, raising their international trade, and receiving more and more foreign investment. Hong Kong has the specialized lawyers, accountants, and financiers to handle the most complex transactions.

Hong Kong has a long history as a strategic center for intermediary functions – from the 19th-century compradors to today's specialized corporate services. In the 19th century, the British merchant houses in Hong Kong such as Jardine, Matheson and Company and Dent and Company, along with other Western merchant houses, controlled the import of opium into China. In an extraordinary new book on Hong Kong, David Meyer describes an important literature that reveals how British merchant houses hired Chinese managers known as compradors to operate from the treaty ports and negotiate with local and interior merchants to sell opium to British manufacturers and to buy tea and silk from China. The compradors carried out a variety of intermediary functions: at the most elementary level these often simple transactions consisted in knowing the languages and the norms involved on both sides; more complicated were the arrangements of payments through local banks and the supply of market intelligence to the merchant houses. Yet another aspect of this story was the role of Hong Kong vis-à-vis

the vast number of dispersed overseas Chinese communities and their entrepreneurial cores. Through Chinese compradors, Hong Kong emerged as the central nexus of the trade and information network in the Far East that bound these dispersed Chinese communities. Hong Kong's compradors controlled a growing share of a growing two-way trade: the export of goods to China and the supply of Chinese specialty goods to burgeoning Chinese communities throughout the Far East.

A key service provided by Hong Kong from the beginning was banking and finance. Foreign banks, starting with one from India, established operations in the mid-19th century. At the center of their operations were activities that supported the trading companies: taking deposits, giving credit, and buying and selling currencies, bullion, and bills of exchange. An international consortium of trading firms from Britain, Germany, Norway, and the U.S., which had major operations in Asia, joined forces with merchant firms based in Hong Kong to create the Hong Kong & Shanghai Bank in 1865. While the company offices were in both cities, Hong Kong served as the headquarters and the bank operated as an exchange bank to finance Hong Kong trade. Soon the bank added branches and agents throughout Asia, and by the end of the 19th century it was a global bank with control over Asia and strong access to European capital markets. Today, Hong Kong is host to a massive concentration of large global banks from Western Europe, North America, and Asia, including

2 The information about contemporary Hong Kong presented throughout this paper comes from the Hong Kong Trade Development Council (Government Information Services).

3 Meyer, *Social Networks of Capital.*

4 In this context it may be worth noting that on September 3, 1991, after a long dispute, China and Britain signed an agreement on construction of the new Hong Kong airport, a very expensive state-of-the-art project that brings Hong Kong to the cutting edge of airports. Besides the economic issue, this event for the first time gave China a voice in Hong Kong affairs.

5 Saskia Sassen, *Losing Control? Sovereignty in an Age of Globalization,* the 1995 Schoff Memorial Lectures (New York: Columbia University Press, 1996).

nearly fifty Japanese banks.

In the last few decades Hong Kong has become an important Asian center for re-exporting manufactured goods made elsewhere, reminiscent of the earlier 19th-century entrepôt function. While the number of manufacturing employees in Hong Kong went from 870,000 in 1979 to 380,000 in 1997, manufacturing employees producing for Hong Kong firms reached five million in 1997,[2] but they are located in China. This is Hong Kong's offshore proletariat. Much of this production is for reexport to the world. North America and Europe now receive increasing shares of manufacturing exports via Hong Kong traders, as do several Asian countries.

Hong Kong has the largest concentration of telematic capacity in the whole Asian region. It has the greatest complex of fiber-optic international cables of any city in Asia, and its satellites provide global access. A communications center in Hong Kong serves as the switching node for 3,500 international leased circuits and local extension lines, and Hong Kong operates as the largest teleport in Asia.[3] This enormous development of the telecommunications infrastructure is driven by the effective demands and needs of Hong Kong's specialized services firms with global operations.[4] Many of the global transactions in which Hong Kong's firms deal require advanced infrastructure and, indeed, significant concentrations of specialized personnel and firms. This combination is not easy to replicate in any city and the costs are enormous.

I have focused on Hong Kong's role as a center for specialized servicing of global operations. It would seem that China can only benefit from ensuring the ongoing vitality and state of the art conditions that give Hong Kong this powerful role. International trade and investment require expert servicing. Indeed, as China opened its doors to both and became active in global markets, the government and emerging private sector bought these services from the large international North American and European firms. There is no way around this world of intermediary specialists that can negotiate the border-crossings of trade and capital between different accounting, legal, and managerial cultures.[5] For instance, in 1996 China's government decided to sell a 100-year bond (that is to say, paper representing Chinese government debt to be cashed in the year 2096) and wanted to sell this bond not in Shanghai but in Hong Kong and New York. To do this the Chinese government did not have to go to Washington. It went to J. P. Morgan. (And it was a successful operation on Wall Street!) What also underlines the role of this intermediary world is the fact that China's government did not have to deal with the U.S. government – it just dealt with financial services firms, the new strategic intermediaries. For global capital, Hong Kong represents a strategic concentration of this intermediary world. Hong Kong will only continue to work this way if it can keep its enormous mix of foreign and national firms with global operations and state of the art expertise.

While Hong Kong is an international servicing center for trade and investment, it has an especially strong role in handling these functions for China. This role was there in its origins, and it returned in full force with the economic opening of China to foreign investment and foreign trade and Deng Xiaoping's 1978 decision to implement it. In 1997 Hong Kong accounted for 59 percent of all direct foreign investment in China. That makes Hong Kong the leading investor in China, and China is the third largest investor in Hong Kong. Hong Kong handles half of China's exports; one third of Hong Kong's reexports goes to China; and almost 58 percent of Hong Kong's reexports originates in China. There are 1,756 Chinese companies registered in Hong Kong, and 53,000 people employed by Chinese enterprises in Hong Kong. Hong Kong contributes one third of China's total foreign-exchange reserves. The total Hong Kong–China trade rose from U.S.$3.4 billion in 1979 to U.S.$134.6 billion in 1996.

One way of thinking about Hong Kong after its return to China is as an enormously powerful concentration of resources pulled between its role as a strategic agent in the new global economic system and its role as a strategic agent for China vis-à-vis that global system. It is power pulled and power of the in-between.

TOWARD A NEW NARRATIVE: RECOVERING PLACE IN THE GLOBAL ECONOMY

These economic details about Hong Kong illustrate a broader story about place and hypermobile global capital. The exclusive focus of mainstream accounts on hypermobility and the neutralization of geography cannot explain Hong Kong's story and would foresee a sad future for it and other such cities. Here it becomes necessary to tell the more abstract version of the story about place and globalization. As I have tried to show in detail elsewhere, place is central to the multiple circuits through which economic globalization is constituted.

professional. This account privileges the capability for global transmission over the material infrastructure that makes such transmission possible; privileges information outputs over the workers producing those outputs, from specialists to secretaries; and puts the new transnational corporate culture over the multiplicity of work cultures, including the immi-

the spatial dispersal of economic activities at the metropolitan, national, and global levels that we associate with globalization have contributed to a demand for new forms of territorial centralization of top-level management and control operations because this dispersal is happening under conditions of concentration in control, ownership, and profit appropriation.

Total Freight Movement In and Out of the Port of Hong Kong

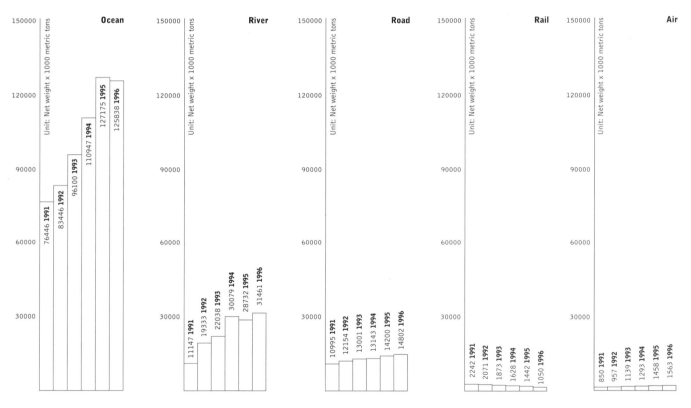

I think of the mainstream account of economic globalization as a narrative of eviction. Key concepts in that account — globalization, information economy, and telematics — suggest that place no longer matters and that the only type of worker that matters is the highly educated

grant cultures within which many of the "other" jobs of the global information economy take place. In brief, the dominant narrative concerns itself with the upper circuits of capital, and particularly with the hypermobility of capital rather than with that which is place-bound.

The massive trends toward

National and global markets as well as globally integrated organizations require central places where the work of globalization gets done. Further, information industries require a vast physical infrastructure containing strategic nodes with a hyperconcentration of facilities; we must distinguish between the capacity

Left to right:
Ocean. Source: Port of Hong Kong, Census & Statistics Department
River. Source: Port of Hong Kong, Census & Statistics Department
Road. Source: Port of Hong Kong, Customs & Excise Department
Rail. Source: Kowloon Canton Railway Corporation
Air. Source: Port of Hong Kong, Civil Aviation Department

for global transmission/communication and the material conditions that make this possible. Finally, even the most advanced information industries have a work process that is at least partly place-bound because of the combination of resources required, even when the outputs are hypermobile.

This type of emphasis allows us to see cities as production sites for the leading information industries of our time and to recover the infrastructure of activities, firms, and jobs necessary to run the advanced corporate economy.[6] Advanced information industries are typically conceptualized in terms of the hypermobility of their outputs and the high levels of expertise of their professionals rather than in terms of the work process involved and the requisite infrastructure of facilities and nonexpert jobs that are also part of these industries.

A central proposition here is that we cannot take the existence of a global economic system as a given but rather need to examine the particular ways in which the conditions for economic globalization are produced. This requires examining not only communication capacities and the power of multinationals but also the infrastructure of facilities and work processes necessary for the implementation of global economic systems, including the production of those inputs that constitute the capability for global control and the infrastructure of jobs involved in this production. The emphasis shifts to the practice of global control: the work of producing and reproducing the organization and management of a global production system

and a global marketplace for finance, both under conditions of economic concentration. The recovery of place and production also implies that global processes can be studied in great empirical detail.

The specific forms assumed by globalization over the last decade have created particular organizational requirements. The emergence of global markets for finance and specialized services and the growth of investment as a major type of international transaction have contributed to the expansion of command functions and the demand for specialized services for firms. Much of the new global economic activity is not encompassed by the organizational form of the transnational corporation or bank. Nor is much of this activity encompassed by the power of such firms, a power often invoked to explain the fact of economic globalization. The spatial and organizational forms assumed by globalization and the actual work of running transnational operations have made cities one type of strategic place and producer services a strategic input. Introducing cities in an analysis of economic globalization allows us to reconceptualize processes of economic globalization as concrete economic complexes situated in specific places. A focus on cities decomposes the nation-state into a variety of subnational components, some of which are profoundly articulated with the global economy and others not. It also signals the declining significance of the national economy as a unitary category in the global economy.

Why is it important to recover place in analyses of the global

economy, particularly place as constituted in major cities? Because it allows us to see the multiplicity of economies and work cultures in which the global information economy is embedded. It also allows us to recover the concrete, localized processes through which globalization exists and to argue that much of the multiculturalism in large cities is as much a part of globalization as is international finance. Finally, focusing on cities allows us to specify a geography of strategic places at the global scale, places bound to each other by the dynamics of economic globalization.

In brief, the combination of geographic dispersal of economic activities and system integration that lies at the heart of the current economic era has contributed to new or expanded central functions, and the complexity of transactions has raised firms' demands for highly specialized services. Rather than becoming obsolete due to the dispersal made possible by information technologies, cities: (1) concentrate command functions; (2) are postindustrial production sites for the leading industries of this period, finance and specialized services; and (3) are transnational marketplaces where firms and governments can buy financial instruments and specialized services.

I refer to this as a new geography of centrality. This geography cuts across the old North-South divide: it includes not only the major centers of economic power in the highly developed countries but also the corporate world of places such as São Paulo and Buenos Aires, Bombay and Bangalore. Alongside this new

6 Methodologically speaking, this is one way of addressing the question of the unit of analysis in studies of contemporary economic processes. "National economy" is a problematic category when there are high levels of internationalization, and "world economy" is a problematic category because of the impossibility of engaging in detailed empirical study at that scale. Highly internationalized cities such as New York, Hong Kong, and London offer the possibility of examining globalization processes in great detail, within a bounded setting and with all of their multiple, often contradictory aspects.

geography of centrality is a new geography of marginality. This too cuts across the North-South divide and includes the disadvantages of New York City and Paris as well as those of São Paulo and Bombay. The notion of such geographies engenders research agendas that can focus on questions of power and poverty in ways that combine the specificity of the local with broader cross-border dynamics, without losing some version of a "container." Only now the container is not "the nation" or "the city," but one that encompasses fragments of each in a cross-border space specified by systemic properties.

One question raised by such new cross-border geographies of centrality and marginality is whether they are also the space for a new transnational politics. For instance, insofar as an analysis of the global city recovers the broad array of jobs and work cultures that are part of the global economy, though typically not marked as such, one can examine the possibility of a new politics of traditionally disadvantaged actors operating in this new transnational economic geography. This politics arises out of the condition of economic participation in the global economy (albeit a participation based on employment in low-wage jobs, from factory workers in export processing zones to cleaners on Wall Street) and the fact that this is a shared condition among workers in many different places around the world – places integrated into the global system. Immigrant workers and women are among the strategic actors in this new transnational geography.

Such a focus allows us to conceive of globalization as con-

stituted through a global grid of strategic sites that emerges as a new geography of centrality. The global economy is a highly structured event, but while it extends across the world it is not the world.

CONTESTED SPACE

The global city concentrates diversity. Its spaces are inscribed with the dominant corporate culture but also with a multiplicity of other cultures and identities, notably through immigration, and in the case of Hong Kong, its own hybrid culture. The slippage is evident: the dominant corporate culture, which is now global, can encompass only part of the city. While corporate power inscribes noncorporate presences with "otherness," thereby devaluing them, they are present everywhere. The immigrant communities and informal economies evident in all major internationalized cities are but two instances. Hong Kong adds its own distinct identity, one different from Western forms.[7] Diverse cultures and ethnicities are especially strong in major cities with the largest concentrations of corporate power.

In this context it is important to remember that most residents of Hong Kong are not part of the global elite described earlier in this paper. This is also an old story. Most Chinese in Hong Kong during the 19th century worked as laborers on the docks, in the shipyards, in the warehouses; it was a small minority that operated as compradors.

Hong Kong has its own complex and charged immigration and refugee history. It is impossible to do justice to this history here; I can only mention a few

scattered items. In the 19th century and up to World War II, Hong Kong served as one of the important final embarkation points for Chinese migrants heading to Australia, other parts of Asia, and North America. After four years of Japanese occupation during World War II, Hong Kong's history is marked by several dramatic events in this regard. Between 1947 and 1949 major developments in China brought first a migration of businessmen, most importantly from Shanghai, and a migration of intellectuals and political refugees.[8] Although in 1950 Hong Kong abandoned its policy of free access and immigration from China and limited it to 50 a day, it received two million refugees from China in the ensuing decade. Hong Kong is overcrowded, has enormous housing shortages, and lacks necessary services. In the 1970s the saga of Indo-Chinese refugees and boat people began, marked in 1978 when 70,000 Vietnamese boat people arrived in Hong Kong. This story continued into the 1980s. In 1990 another marking event, the New Basic Law – Hong Kong's future constitution – was promulgated after approval by China's parliament. In response Britain granted full British passports with right of abode in the United Kingdom to 50,000 businessmen, administrators, and professionals and their families as worries about the future of Hong Kong increased.

There are other histories of those who lack power yet have presence. Perhaps most dramatic was the demonstration by one million people in early June 1989 protesting the murderous crackdown of the pro-democ-

7 Ackbar Abbas, Hong Kong: Culture and the Politics of Disappearance (Minneapolis: University of Minnesota Press, 1997).

8 The migration of some 100,000 Shanghai businessmen played an important role in Hong Kong as they succeeded in a broad range of enterprises. Tens of thousands came in this first wave from 1947 to 1949. Many were multimillionaires, many with dirty money. A second migration stream occurred from spring to October of 1949; immigration ended with the Communists' takeover in Canton. These immigrants brought enormous amounts of money to Hong Kong, which did not always stay but was transferred to other locations. They invested large amounts of capital in trade, manufacture, and infrastructure; they created jobs and improved manufacturing techniques. They were far more developed as a group than the local Hong Kong business community. It is worth noting that in a setting as mixed and international as Hong Kong, tensions developed between the local Cantonese and the "foreigners from North China," the name given to the immigrants from Shanghai.

9 See Yen-P'ing Hao, The Comprador in Nineteenth Century China: Bridge Between East and West (Cambridge, Mass.: Harvard University Press, 1970). Also, Hou Hanru, Hong Kong, exhib. cat. (South African Biennale, October 1997); and Roger Burbach, Globalization and its Discontents: The Rise of Postmodern Socialisms (Chicago: Pluto Press, 1997).

racy movement in Beijing and the most recent candlelight vigil commemorating that same event.

Then there are the histories that signal the joining of power across political lines and the depth of the contest between those who have it and those who do not. An illustration of this was the decision in the late 1980s to tear down the Walled City, an enclave of China in the middle of Hong Kong that is a home to the poor and is outside the bounds of law, hence drawing outlaws,

It invites us to see that globalization is not only constituted in terms of capital and the new international corporate culture (international finance, telecommunications, information flows) but also in terms of people and noncorporate cultures. A whole infrastructure of low-wage, nonprofessional jobs and activities constitutes a crucial part of the so-called corporate economy.

Large cities provide the terrain for a multiplicity of globalization processes to assume concrete, localized forms. The latter

cities have become a strategic terrain for a whole series of conflicts and contradictions. This joint presence happens in a context where the internationalization of the economy has grown sharply and cities have become increasingly strategic for global capital and where marginalized people have come into representation and are making claims on the city as well. This joint presence is further brought into focus by the sharpening of the distance between the two.

SASKIA SASSEN IS PROFESSOR OF URBAN PLANNING AT COLUMBIA UNIVERSITY'S GRADUATE SCHOOL OF ARCHITECTURE, PLANNING AND PRESERVATION. SHE HAS WRITTEN THE GLOBAL CITY: NEW YORK, LONDON, TOKYO, CITIES IN A WORLD ECONOMY AND IMMIGRANTS AND REFUGEES: A EUROPEAN DILEMMA. SHE RECENTLY COMPLETED IMMIGRATION POLICY IN A WORLD ECONOMY.

drug addicts, illegal immigrants, and unlicensed professionals of all sorts (for example, in 1987 there were 100 unlicensed dentists, accounting for 25 percent of Hong Kong's total). Hong Kong did not act on its own but got clearance from Beijing to destroy the Walled City and remove its 40,000 residents.

The story of Hong Kong brings to the fore the correspondence between great concentrations of corporate power and large concentrations of "others."

crete, localized forms. The latter are, in good part, what globalization is about. We can then think of cities also as the places where the contradictions of the internationalization of capital come to rest or to fight. If we consider, further, that large cities also concentrate a growing share of disadvantaged populations – immigrants in Europe and the U.S., African Americans and Latinos in the U.S., immigrants and refugees and local poor Chinese in Hong Kong – we can see that

The "center" now concentrates immense power, a power that rests on the capability for global control and the capability to produce super-profits. Marginality, notwithstanding little economic and political power, is an increasingly strong presence through the new politics of culture and identity. It is, in my reading, not only the strategic role of Hong Kong in the global economy but also its enormous diversity and hybrid culture that signal the limits of its being radically

Kojin Karatani

Architecture's Impurity

Although I am neither an architect nor an architectural theorist, for some time I have been thinking in the context of architecture. This is not necessarily because, as Plato put it, architecture is the *arché* of *techné* – the origin and master of all knowledge and technology – but rather because architecture is the most impure of the arts. Perhaps only film would be comparable with respect to this impurity. Or, to be more precise, it is not that film and architecture are particularly impure, but among all of the arts, they have the most difficulty suppressing their impurity.

From the most mundane building to the most symbolic, architecture is inextricably linked to politico-economic concerns. It is practical and scientific – rooted in the necessities of daily life – and aesthetic. A variety of dimensions converge on it, and the purely aesthetic dimension cannot simply be sifted out. This is the most crucial difference between architecture and fine art: fine art is not necessarily more pure, but one can appear to find purity constituted in it.

What's more, architecture, like filmmaking, is a collaborative practice, making it impossible to single out an author in a strict sense. Historically, buildings have been known by the name of the person who commissioned the architecture rather than by the name of the architect who designed it. By contrast, literary work is unequivocally attributed to one author. In literature, this understanding of authorship was established during the 19th century, which is to say that authorship, along with copyright, is a modern product. Following that precedent, authorship also emerged in architecture, although the residue of impurity could not be totally purged.

In literature it is easy to construct an illusion with respect to the autonomy of authorship: "I can write works alone with a pen (or a word processor), therefore I am the author who creates the work, independent of any direct politico-economic relations." The truth is that so-called creation is the product of reweaving various textures that have come before, and through that process the text assumes various meanings beyond the will of the author.

In the field of architecture, however, it has always been difficult to conceive of this kind of creative authorship in the same sense that there have always been legal difficulties surrounding copyright issues in filmmaking. For now, the authorship or authority of the film is ascribed to the director. But this dissolves the questions raised by this new form of art by imposing on it the 19th-century notion of authorship invented for modern literature; all in all, film is not conducive to single authorship. This is even more the case with architecture, which is only one part of an enormous industrial network. Architects cannot get along without clients, without a historical environmental context, and without the collaboration of various specialists. Architects face the other from beginning to end. My philosophical criticism has begun with architecture precisely because it resists the illusion of purity.

Since Plato, philosophers have regarded architecture as a model for philosophy. It is not more than a metaphor, yet it is this will to architecture that has driven Western philosophy. It could be said that poststructuralists have tried to think of philosophy using text(ure) instead of architecture as a metaphor: to consider things not as integrated by the author or the idea but as a texture of quotation or an interwoven network of various dimensions. This historical tendency notwithstanding, I insist on architecture as metaphor, with the proviso that the model I employ is a secular one that Plato despised in reality. I emphasize the term *secular* precisely because it is the secularity – namely, the social dimension – that text as metaphor abstracts to sanctify itself. Furthermore, to see things as a texture of various dimensions, a network without subject, results in abandoning the scrutiny of the problematic intrinsic to each domain.

From this viewpoint I wrote *Architecture as Metaphor: Language, Number, Money*, and with respect to issues of money per se, my analysis is fully presented there. I would like to talk here about the impurity that forms various domains. For, more than anything, it is the complicity with money that people find impure about architecture.

Thinking of purity and impurity, I want to go back to the Kantian categories for a moment. Following the traditional categories, Kant divided our relation to objects into three domains: (1) cognitive concerns of true or false; (2) ethical concerns of good or bad; and (3) concerns of taste, either pleasant or unpleasant. One of the points that distinguishes Kant from his predecessors is that he clarifies unhierarchically the three domains where different attitudes intervene. What does it mean? All of us respond to a given object in at least three domains at once. We receive it cognitively as true or false, ethically as good or bad, and according to taste as pleasant or unpleasant. In other words, these domains always appear as intermingled yet often contradictory sets. For this reason it so happens that an object can be pleasant even if it is illusory or evil and true even if it is unpleasant or boring.

According to Kant, the judgment of taste consists of the ability to see a given object with "disinterestedness," namely, to see it by bracketing cognitive and ethical concerns. Bracketing becomes necessary because it is impossible simply to discard these categories. This is not limited to the judgment of taste. The same is true in scientific recognition, where concerns of ethics and taste must be bracketed. For instance, it would not be recommended that a surgeon see his patient aesthetically or ethically while diagnosing or operating. On the other hand, when making ethical judgments – judgments of faith – the concerns of true or false and pleasant or unpleasant should be bracketed. This bracketing is inherent in modernity; scientific recognition was constituted by bracketing the previous stance toward nature, as religious signification or as a result of magical motivation, for example. Bracketing other domains is not the same as eradicating them. Modern aesthetics as conceived by Kant depends on this conscious method of bracketing.

According to Kant, beauty does not exist simply in sensual pleasure, but neither does it exist in simple indifference. Beauty is achieved by the conscious method of positively abandoning a direct "interest" in the object. In such cases, the more difficult the bracketing of interest, the more pleasurable the subject's effort to bracket. It is in this sense that the Kantian aesthetic is said to be "subjective." Kant existed in the transitional moment from classicism – which corresponded to the Enlightenment – to romanticism. The norm of the classicist aesthetic was based on the idea that beauty was located in the form of the object itself. In other words, whether it was beautiful or not was judged as objective form. Kant saw beauty in the "finality without end," which was not totally irrelevant to classicism. But the important break for him was the daring discovery that something could lack "classicist" finality. For instance, the imaginary reconstruction of symmetry (or finality) given a building that lacks symmetry presents a situation where the more difficult it is to bracket the interest, the more intense the pleasure of doing it.

We see the crux of Kant's aesthetic thinking in the theory of the sublime. The sublime is nothing other than the pleasure resulting from the subject's effort in going beyond the unpleasant object. According to Kant, the sublime does not exist in the object itself but in the infinity of reason that goes beyond the limitation of sensibility. To express this in reverse, the sublime is "self-alienation" in the act of discovering an infinity of reason in the object that is contradictory to the self.[1] It goes without saying that the sublime is not a manifestation of religious awe. An object that overpowers a human – lightning in the night sky, for instance – is deemed sublime only insofar as its cause is scientifically evident and the spectator is protected from its brutal force. If not, the lightning remains an object of religious awe or supernatural attributes, like a divine message. For this

1 The Feuerbachian notion that considers God as the self-alienation of man's generic essence is not a materialistic inversion of Hegel but rather derives from the Kantian theory of the sublime.

reason the sublime as an aesthetic judgment is connected, like the flip side of a coin, to the epistemology of modern science.

At this point, it is imperative to consider a realm that Kant did not scrutinize, a place where all differences are unconditionally bracketed: the monetary economy. This is where manifold use values and the practical labor that produces them are reduced to exchange value, or, in Marx's terms, "social and abstract labor." In the beginning of *Capital*, Marx wrote: "The commodity is, first of all, an external object, a thing which through its qualities satisfies human needs of whatever kind. The nature of these needs, whether they arise, for example, from the stomach, or the imagination, makes no difference. Nor does it matter here how the thing satisfies man's need, whether directly as a means of subsistence, i.e., an object of consumption, or indirectly as a means of production."[2] In other words, in the world of the commodity economy we find an attitude totally indifferent to the difference among things — their use value — and only concerned with one thing: interest.

Albert O. Hirshman points out that in the 18th century "interest" was introduced as a passion against passion; what suppresses passion is neither reason nor interdiction but passion that pursues "interest."[3] In the context of the commodity economy, Kantian "disinterestedness" is the act of rediscovering the difference of things by bracketing that "interest." For the romantics, then, Kantian disinterestedness functioned mainly to bracket economic interest, a practice that was manifest as "art for art's sake." More crucial in this context is that Kantian bracketing or, namely, purification of all domains is inseparable from the capitalist economy that nullifies differences of all domains. In fact, Kant attained the purified ethical domain by bracketing interrelated elements he called interest, usefulness, and happiness. He did not hierarchize the three precisely because the commodity economy reduces everything, equally, to interest. In *Critique of Judgment*, he attempted to bracket interest, although again, what made this thought possible was the commodity economy itself. Hence, ever since art came to be art it has been irrevocably connected to commodification like the flip side of a coin.[4] Disinterestedness as an aesthetic stance is made possible in the supremacy of economic interest, therefore, it is impossible to escape the latter by bracketing it.

With Kant it became clear that what makes art art is the subjective act of bracketing other concerns. This stance is not classical, but neither is it romantic. Kant did not reject classicism just to follow the path toward romanticism (as many others did). He dealt with the modern problematic of art lying beneath both, and this problematic is not yet obsolete. Clement Greenberg considered Kant to be the first modernist critic, and following him he defined "flatness" as what makes painting, painting as opposed to architecture or sculpture.[5] But the impetus of purification in modern art inexorably results in its self-destruction. Greenberg saw this in Piet Mondrian's making painting architectonic. This is nothing but a self-decomposition or an unbracketing from within that occurs at the moment when a pure domain, constituted by the manipulation of bracketing, is mistaken to be autonomous in and of itself.

2 Karl Marx, *Capital: A Critique of Political Economy*, intro. Ernest Mandel, trans. Ben Fowkes, vol. 1 (New York: Vintage Books, 1977), 125.

3 A. O. Hirshman, *The Passions and the Interests: Political Arguments for Capitalism before its Triumph* (Princeton, N.J.: Princeton University Press, 1977).

4 For instance, it is the most mundane and deceptive view simply to distinguish artistic value and commodity value. If a certain work is deemed truly valuable as art, it is valuable as commodity and sold to a collector or museum.

5 Clement Greenberg, "The Modernist Painting," in *The Collected Essays and Criticism: Modernism with a Vengeance, 1957–1969*, vol. 4 (Chicago: University of Chicago Press, 1993), 85.

It is possible to say, therefore, that Kant's reflection involves a modernist statement *and* its immanent critique. For instance, Marcel Duchamp exhibited a urinal with the title *Fountain*, and urged us to see it by bracketing our daily concerns. In this case, the signal "This is an artwork in an exhibition" demanded that we bracket it. An object seen in this context is no longer an object with use value but the material that constitutes the form of art. Duchamp showed that what makes art, art lies only in the signal "This is an artwork." To me this means, "Let's bracket it." Duchamp showed us that anything can be an art object, not only the objects customarily exhibited in museums and galleries, but this manipulation works only insofar as the convention – that being exhibited in museums and galleries guarantees the "artness" of the objects – is mutually understood.

Kant revealed that it is by bracketing that the domains of truth, good, and beauty can be established, and furthermore, that the bracketing must be removed when necessary. He refused to grant superiority to any one of these categories over any other; instead, he requested that we perform the most difficult task, that is, that we bracket and unbracket flexibly, whenever required. For instance, architecture, whether made for the bourgeoisie or the Nazis, can be assessed in and of itself as a work of art. This is possible only by bracketing the political and ethical concerns; in this commitment, it is difficult to bracket them and even more difficult to unbracket them.

We all live simultaneously in various dimensions and domains, and they can never be unified. For instance, priests and scholars both tend to think that they live in their own pure domains, but these are illusory constructs. Their jobs are part of the social division of labor. They might despise money in their illusion of pure autonomy only because they, as Marx said, "do this without being aware of it"[6] in the social division of labor mediated by money. Indeed the monetary economy enables us to ignore money and those social relations that are mediated by money.

While we live in a complex of cognitive, ethical, aesthetic, legal, political, and economic domains, we can neither separate them, synthesize them, nor determine the "last instance" among them. Never! According to my interpretation, the Kantian critique revealed that these domains can be identified only by bracketing others, illuminating the transcendental structure that functions unbeknown to us. In *Capital* Marx attempted to shed light on the autonomous category of the monetary economy by bracketing other domains. Thus Marx bracketed ethical responsibility:

> To prevent possible misunderstanding, let me say this. I do not by any means depict the capitalist and the landowner in rosy colors. But individuals are dealt with here only insofar as they are the personifications of economic categories, the bearers [*Träger*] of particular class-relations and interests. My standpoint, from which the development of the economic formation of society is viewed as a process of natural history, can less than any other make the individual responsible for relations whose creature he remains, socially speaking, however much he may subjectively raise himself above them.[7]

But again, we must always be prepared to unbracket social irresponsibility.

6 Marx, *Capital*, 166–67.

7 Ibid., 92.

Two points came to mind after the Anyhow conference. In *Architecture as Metaphor*, I presented the limits of formalization, the problematic I was scrutinizing in the late 1970s. I find it very strange that what I considered serious *aporia* then is now being taken up optimistically. This shift might be due to the significant increase in the calculating power of computers over the past 20 years; this development has enabled what was strictly formal thinking to become something visual. For example, the problem of the Koch curve (self-similarity) has been applied as fractal geometry, while what was once thought of as the paradox of self-referentiality has become the theory of self-organization, thereby totally inverting the problematic. However, none of these have posed ultimate solutions for the original problematic — whether or not formalization can produce becoming, and if not, why it is impossible. These new tendencies simply blind our eyes with the flash of calculation speed.

The "becoming" simulated in computers is, after all, "making" and not the actual becoming. No matter how many random elements are introduced, the programmed and simulated event is distinct from the actual event that derives from the social, that is, from communication with the other. The vision of architecture in computer graphics belongs to the realm of possible worlds, but when realized as architecture, it becomes something different. Self-proclaimed Deleuzians should remember that Deleuze distinguished virtuality from possibility; the former is equal to actuality itself and has nothing to do with the so-called virtual reality that belongs to possible worlds.

Secondly, while participating in the urbanization of contemporary China, Rem Koolhaas appreciates its bigness while rejecting the position that sees architecture as art. This denial of architecture as art functions only in this kind of conference, consisting of artistic architects. From the secular viewpoint, Koolhaas's position represents only a tiny end of the existing construction industry that in general flocks to any place where there is potential for gigantic profit; this is an enterprise that no one can see as art. What he calls dirty realism is a romantic irony that functions only among the circle of architects and architectural theorists who, in their nature, see architecture as art. It reminds us of Duchamp's urinal that becomes *Fountain* only in art exhibits, shocking mainly the group of artists and art theorists. After all, it is by his gesture of extinguishing the artness of architecture that Koolhaas tries to make architecture art in the most liminal sense. Earlier I touched upon Kantian "bracketing" or "transcendental reduction." Historically speaking, after Kant's analytic endeavors, romantic ironists such as the Schlegel brothers (August Wilhelm and Friedrich) attempted to remain in the free, i.e., the possible, worlds, precisely by their particular gesture of following the sensual/actual at the same time they despised it. If we remember the heyday of German romantics after Kant, we can see a repetition of the old paradigm in which Koolhaas and the self-proclaimed Deleuzians (or Bergsonians, in the strict sense) cooperate tacitly, despite their ostensible conflict.

KOJIN KARATANI IS PROFESSOR OF LITERATURE AT HOSEI UNIVERSITY IN JAPAN. HIS BOOKS INCLUDE TANKYU I (RESEARCH I), TANKYU II (RESEARCH II), ORIGINS OF MODERN JAPANESE LITERATURE, AND ARCHITECTURE AS METAPHOR, PUBLISHED IN ANYONE CORPORATION'S WRITING ARCHITECTURE SERIES WITH MIT PRESS (1995).

Ole Bouman

Don't Save Architecture

Spend It!

A famous one-liner goes: he who can, communicates; he who cannot, writes a theory about it. In other words, if you can't talk about *what* you do and *why* you do it, you can always fall back on talking about your methodology, about *how* you do it. Which soon comes to navel-gazing. I believe that "how" as an isolated question for fellow professionals is not so interesting for a millennial project like Any. But the question of the how related to what happens beyond architecture, the how that lets architecture transcend itself, seems to me to be the right ambition for such an endeavor. By architecture transcending itself, I don't just mean artistic transgression. Transcendence is beyond transgression. It's the next stage. Transgression presupposes a border to transgress and, as such, a territory to escape. Transgression is based on definition. After a while you become more and more involved in defining the territory you are leaving rather than in exploring the new frontier. As a transgressor, you become obsessed with borders and hence soon fall victim to the restrictions you set out to transgress. Transcendence is another thing altogether. It presupposes a much more relaxed relationship with the place you come from. You are ready to relativize or even to give up the law and order there. You are open to disorder. Eager. Hungry. Fearless. Transcendence is less about leaving things behind or endless, weepy good-bye rituals (without ever really leaving) than it is about getting on that

train and going west (or east, as some of us do these days).

Although some say that this period is characterized by undecidability and indeterminacy, I'm absolutely decisive and very determined to choose transcendence, to explore new lands. I'll take the past with me but I won't cultivate it, nor will I keep struggling with its ghost, even if I risk being rejected by a professional community. I believe the next stage will involve new kinds of communities, if any at all. Looking back at the different Any conferences I have attended and listening to different speakers at Anyhow, I feel a growing discomfort with the ongoing, subtle balance that has developed between asking new questions and reaffirming past achievements. This is a normal phenomenon and may be completely acceptable from a passive audience's point of view, but for someone who decisively prefers the questions, it is not attractive. The equally subtle engineering of consent, the neutralizing enumeration of private "hows," so to speak, may be instructive to the public, but it gradually undermines a conference as an intellectual project. I don't want a countdown to the millennium in the waiting room of the future; I want to count up a few things instead.

Not only me, actually. The first speaker of the conference was, in my opinion, capricious and convincing in his escape from endless self-reflection. He set the tone for a possible new Any tune to play, perhaps, for another three years. Trying to

get away from an object-oriented theory of architecture, or even a flow-oriented architecture, in which the discipline of building remains both a starting point and a predictable outcome, Sanford Kwinter made a plea for what he called a ridiculous effort to embark on a new project, a subtle coup, the "new organon." He may well have chosen another name because he was immediately tackled as a bad architectural historian by someone (Peter Eisenman) who took part in that history himself. Nevertheless, it is better to be a good thinker and a bad historian than the other way around. In Holland there are exceptionally good cliometricians who hardly ever think. Always beware of becoming a specialist in *wie es wirklich gewesen ist* (what really happened). Kwinter, picturing the new paradigm, talked about "territological deviations," "space and matter becoming indistinguishable," and "architecture in a transactional world," all according to a "computational paradigm." I agree with those who think that this is a peculiar language having to do with a certain responsibility to American academic discourse. I do not share this responsibility but I do agree almost completely with what Kwinter proposed: the dissolution of architecture as a separate, venerable, and distinguished discipline. Architecture offices of tomorrow will be offices for architecture-oriented actions. Or, after Nikolaus Pevsner's famous architectural dichotomy, since the death of God we don't need Lincoln

Cathedrals anymore. But if we continue to cultivate the inertia of MacWorld, we might not even need a bicycle shed. We'd just need built stuff. The question is what to do, what to think, what to feel in that stuff. I believe that architecture can still direct actions, thoughts, and feelings.

As I said, I *almost* agree with Kwinter. I'm certain of the prime importance of his observations. They are hallucinogenic in their cultural implications. But before adding a few things to what Kwinter said, I want to question his wishful thinking. Reflecting on cultural implications and trying to detect new freedoms for old disciplines are aspects of the same old paradigm he wants to kiss goodbye. Rem Koolhaas makes a career out of embracing new freedoms (in the plural). In my view this pursuit is rapidly becoming a kind of arts-and-crafts practice. The cultural implications and found freedoms are always homemade, are always ego-based. But if you take Kwinter's assertions seriously, there is no home, there is no ego anymore. There are just fields and impulses.

What I want to do here is to radicalize the "computational paradigm." This involves nothing less than a full anthropological, if not evolutionary shift. We shouldn't talk about a post-Cartesian world anymore. We'd do better to talk about a post-Deleuzian world. Although philosophically I am a great supporter of free will, I have great doubts about the noble volunteerism that is hidden in "more and more freedom in

matter," as Kwinter put it. We must accept that the freedom in this veiled notion of progress will not be able to make the shift to the digital realm. When Garry Kasparov lost all of his space on the chess board and walked away in despair about human civilization's loss of honor, IBM's Deep Blue was unfazed. For the computer, the decisive move was just another move. If you talk about computation, you'd better drop any pathos for freedom. Freedom is a Cartesian principle. A Deleuzian *bon goût*. But in post-Deleuzian terms it is a non-item. It's a matter of intellectual honesty.

I don't have a problem with manifestos. I do have one with historicism. I don't see why in a computational paradigm all honorable categories of the foundational worldview are shattered and overcome, while freedom retains its positive meaning. If more freedom comes in matter, it is the freedom of entropy, of the banal movement of particles. This has nothing to do with emancipation, with free speech, freedom of choice, or even with free enterprise. If we are strong enough to be honest, freedom should be removed from the discourse. It means too little.

Now I want to reconstruct the picture, but without the emancipatory rhetoric. In so doing, I adapt myself to the strong urge of the Any project to refrain from prescriptions and to give full voice to descriptions of what's really going on. *How* is life today? What do I mean by the anthro-

pological shift? Most of the discourse on the major changes under headings like "universal homogenization," "globalization," "modernization," and "the third wave" reduces to transformations of organizational processes and, of course, information technology. If we were to do an in-depth phenomenological study of social change, though, we would see that there is another factor: mentality. Mentality is much slower in adopting new challenges, as we all know, although in that regard, the Any participants are clearly among the fastest. Mentality has to do with our mind-set, our mental equipment, and that's why change is rather slow. On the other hand, we must accept that we do change incredibly, albeit unconsciously. (For example, Koolhaas would have been flogged at a conference 10 years ago if he had used the phrase "humanist sentimentalities," as he did here. Now we hardly notice.) So it's not just a matter of new media or new processes; it's not even a matter of new paradigms. It's a full-blown new stage of evolution. Another stage in the transcendence of matter. We are going to think differently – if we keep thinking at all.

The images that accompany this text are from an ongoing project called "RealSpace in QuickTimes" in which I explore different (paradoxical) aspects of the digitalization of architecture, one of the most influential factors in the aforementioned anthropological shift. Within the context of Anyhow, it occurs to me that one conclusion of these recent explorations is that the question of how, the great age-old question of pragmatism, is becoming obsolete. It is no longer an option. We don't instrumentalize anymore, we are instrumentalized. Instruments never ask how, they just do the job. "How" is a question for the Homo sapiens, which assumes a dubious degree of self-consciousness. We are leaving that guy, giving way to Homo transparens. Compatible man. Hyperwoman. For instance, money and market are no longer aspects of life and our mental framework. We *are* money. We *are* market. Politicians, intellectuals, architects, people still keep talking about new opportunities and new challenges. I believe, however, that these same opportunities and challenges have brought us beyond a point after which this discourse of the new is no longer accurate. The invention of the new becomes the engineering of the new. We don't use new media, we are new media. We don't use new technology, we are technology. We don't use infrastructure, we are infrastructure. In other words, we no longer penetrate the future, the future penetrates us.

For architecture, this assertion is even more radical than for the rest of the world, because no discipline and spatial art has been so ordered and hence moralized by time, program, and plan. The art of stasis. One can hardly imagine how an architecture that develops according to no plan, an architecture of endless mutations,

will look. How will it be produced? Who is the client? (Koolhaas has an idea about that: a Chinese guy who needs the stuff in three days.) Who talks about design? In the past, we have talked about double-coded architecture, about hybrid architecture, about teamwork and shared intelligence. One can also talk about an architecture of corruption. No integrity. Nevertheless, as always this architecture will have a creative dimension. That's something that will survive! But we will lose the final responsibility of a single author making single objects. We've heard that before, right? This time, however, he or she is not dead, because philosophy has neither the time nor the position to organize the funeral. The author just fades away.

Now, compare this de-moralization of architecture to the contemporary rhetoric of the millennium. What are we talking about? It occurs to me that these days culture is completely biased by the millennium. Individuals, institutions, firms, entire nations base their policies on the simple fact of a calendar jubilee. The whole discourse of power and establishment is centered around a vocabulary of completion. This is the fin de millennium. However, everyone knows that an arbitrary century shift doesn't guarantee new life. Creativity or clairvoyant insights can never rest on the simple fact of a few significant events some two thousand years ago. Architecture especially, a medium that interprets the world first in spatial terms,

has no need to cover our world clockwise. Much more important than rounding up time, however (returning to the anthropological shift), is the need immediately to begin detecting cultural promise. Before we are completely swallowed by a new mind-set, we can try to get a few important things focused. The first has to do with a philosophy of architecture; the other, with changed roles in a complex building process.

With the introduction of the postmodern worldview some two decades ago, the philosophy of architecture entered a new stage. After postmodernism and deconstructivism we now come to vitalism. The sequence is logical but it's far from new. It's just fresh. Vitalism is much older than classicism, but since classicism has been the leading force for centuries, it has hardly been presented as a genuine movement. Today, as classicism, anticlassicism, and postclassicism are really on the wane, vitalism is one remaining methodology that gives me the confidence to say that, yes, architecture has a great future, especially if we avoid the mistakes committed by vitalist thought in the past.

The most frequently quoted vitalist philosophers nowadays are G. W. Leibniz, Henri Bergson, and Gilles Deleuze. Such thinking started with Heraclitus, the pre-Socratic thinker of flux. Heraclitus is widely known for three incisive sound bites: the first is *Panta Rhei* (Everything goes), the postmodern mantra for more than a decade. The second is *Polemos pantoon pater* (War is the father of everything). This slogan is exclusively reserved for, to paraphrase Robert Kaplan, "the coming anarchy." Between these two is a third phrase: *Potamoi gar ouk estin embenai dis toi autoi* (One cannot step in the same river twice). Given that one cannot even step into the same river once, the way this basic insight is normally interpreted and applied in a metaphorical way is disappointing. Perhaps quoting any vitalist philosopher is like stepping into the same river twice: a contradictory act. But it could be worse. Taking a vitalist philosopher as one's intellectual starting-point is equivalent to stepping into that river thrice. Anyone who designs architecture as a metaphor for vitalist thinking doesn't distinguish between that river and the open sea. By which time one would certainly have drowned. The only genuine tribute to vitalistic philosophers and other baroque thinkers is to forget them: life is too beautiful and too full to file them away in memory as separate concepts or worshipped idols.

How are we to forget them? By getting back to work after reading. By making things. By sharing creativity, by joining forces with other professional fields. By exploring new mandates for architecture. The real potential of vitalist philosophy for architecture is to consider it not as a discipline but as a dimension of daily practice. Vitalism, far from a justification, is a great challenge to architecture. It implies new methods, new ways of thinking, and new

concepts. It rejuvenates architecture from within. And if architecture is bound to make the trip to the new anthropological paradigm, it could be an inevitable modality. But there is an even more active version of vitalism that accepts everyday life as the core of architectural thought. It inspires architecture from without, or rather, it inspires cultural debate with architecture. One can hardly think of a more rewarding role for architecture than as a host for culture, that is, the architectonic dimension of culture. If we have the courage, we can see the weightiest political problems as architectural problems. Homelessness, the aging of the baby-boom generation, changes in family structure, mass migration, the need for cultural and local identity, the reduction of meaning to signs, virtual communities, the ecological threat, the third world on our doorstep, the growing rift between rich and poor — the list is endless. Without architectural thinking, these will never be addressed properly. The choices that determine whether we will develop new typologies — whether the building brief will be radically extended, whether nature will be spared or tortured, whether houses will become bunkers — are all architectural choices.

In considering the opportunities for architecture in this late-capitalist age, I would suggest that we stop thinking of architecture as a fixed profession, a service industry, a trouble shooter, or a specialist of space that one might hire

sometime, somewhere, somehow in a given territorial and institutional context. We might even go beyond the idea of architecture as a generous host for other disciplines. The great future of architecture is to reconsider its mandate, to kill its darlings. Instead of talking of hosting, we had better think of infiltrating, of fighting an architectural guerrilla war. Since we are more and more aware of the architectural dimension of major cultural and social issues, we'd better stop complaining about the loss of architecture as a recognizable profession. More than ever one ought to redefine the big issues of our time as architectural issues. Instead of talking about context-specific architecture, as we have for centuries, or of context neutral architecture, as in those theories of autonomy, we might start thinking of architecture specific contexts. Instead of considering architecture as a passive adaptation to contextual circumstances or intellectual a prioris, we can develop new active modalities of architectural practice. To be found everywhere. This implies the only how for which the answer is indeterminate and undecidable. It's a risk, but well worth the effort. Architecture becomes an organizational art for possibly dirty hands.

In sum, the anthropological shift means transcendence. This time it is not the good guys who go to heaven but the smart ones. Don't save architecture. Spend it.

Stills from the multimedia program RealSpace in Quicktimes, Dutch entry to Milano Triennale.

OLE BOUMAN IS EDITOR OF ARCHIS, AN ARCHITECTURE MAGAZINE IN THE NETHERLANDS, AND AUTHOR OF THE BOOK REALSPACE IN QUICKTIMES.

Courtesy Ole Bouman and Harold Houdijk/BRS Premsela Vonk

A LIFE TO

MACHINE IN

WON'T OUR BODIES
HOWEVER PROSTHETISIZED
STILL RETAIN SUFFICIENT
EVOLUTIONARY DISADVANTAGES
TO MAKE ARCHITECTURE
NECESSARY
IN THE FUTURE ?

Discussion 3

Hans van Dijk I have a question for Fredric Jameson. You began by elaborating on Rockefeller Center, quoting both Manfredo Tafuri and Rem Koolhaas, and then you suggested that maybe it's not interesting at all, that it's just a mediocre building. The bracketing that Kojin Karatani talked about has already taken place with Rockefeller Center and other famous skyscrapers in Manhattan, but it may never take place in places like Seoul or São Paulo. Can you elaborate on Karatani's question of bracketing as a flip side of the development of a monetary commodity market?

Fredric Jameson The connection I wanted to make concerned the way in which certain practices of money generate their own kinds of categories, which are in effect new mental categories but also new formal categories. This has something to do with what I would call sublimation or dematerialization. The way in which Tafuri interprets Rockefeller Center in terms of signals of spirituality, by which he means spurious ideological promises of spirituality and popular culture, is very interesting. It is essentially based on the notion of dematerialization in which matter, the body, weight, heaviness, is still present but from which the spirit is then disengaged. The later descriptions I mentioned seemed to imply processes of sublimation that did not involve a sense of matter, a sense of weight, but rather some other realm. I would like to know whether Kojin feels that there have been shifts in the very way in which money is experienced and therefore in the way in which these new categories are generated — and whether the function of money today would generate radically new categories, formal and mental, different from the experience of money in the 19th-century city that Georg Simmel and, later, Walter Benjamin describe.

Kojin Karatani There's a general tendency to grasp the multiplicities of reality — the economic, political, aesthetic — as a lineup of many dimensions. This is important, but more important is the internal structure of those domains. I may collate the transcendent structure of the whole domain and also the limits of the domain and their internal relationship apart from empirical things. If you go to the empirical fact, you have to count many factors, put them together, and believe you've grasped a totality. Beauty, for example, is already a sublime; it already presupposes the origin of a monetary economy. In other words, money was made possible by money itself, so the relationship is made clear on a different level, not on the empirical level, which is already based upon those ideologies. When I talked about Immanuel Kant I said that he thought in this way, but that's not true; that's my understanding, but in a way I think I'm right. For example, Gilles Deleuze said in **Nietzsche and Philosophy** that Friedrich Nietzsche continued a Kantian critique. I think that Marx's **Capital: A Critique of Political Economy** is just the postcritique that Kant did not do. **A Critique of Political Economy** is not a **criticism** of the political economy, it's a **critique** in the Kantian sense. Nietzsche did the same thing on a different level.

Van Dijk We are not engaged in the same debate here because Kojin raises Kantian notions of beauty while Fred talks about symbolization and processes that take place in the metropolis and Saskia talks about recent and large-scale developments that surround us.

Saskia Sassen What Fred said is extremely important. On the one hand, money has always been virtual, but Fred points out that there is a material context. The kind of money that I was talking about, the $75 trillion in the global capital market, escapes that kind of dualization. This is no longer a matter of dematerialization. There is simply no material context. Money never leaves the certain space that makes it possible for it not to be engaged in the dematerialization discussion. On the other hand, this didn't just fall from the sky. This is a produced event that is extremely important and that reconnects with some questions of politics and power. For that $75 trillion to become some kind of reality, an enormous number of things had to be set in motion — innovations, inventions. Finance had to invent an autonomous circuit for circulation that made this kind of dematerialization possible. It is profoundly virtual, but that doesn't mean that a material context made this virtualization possible.

Audience It is important that we take mediation as a central issue in this discussion because it can connect the different discourses. I liked enormously Jameson's Theodor Adorno book, and it struck me that in talking today about mediation he referred to Tafuri and Koolhaas but did not address how Adorno would probably deal with such matters. I have interpreted his concept of mimesis as a possible vehicle for mediation that can also contain a critical moment. Do you think that when architecture is mediating these socioeconomic conditions, through mimesis for example, that a critical moment is possible in one way or another?

Jameson I was using mediation in terms of the analysis of these objects or texts and what one would have to do to connect different levels of analysis. There seem to be three ways to connect these objects with their situations. The first would be to look at the situation as the conditions of possibility or the constraints of producing that object. Those constraints would obviously involve things like land values and the kinds of businesses that want to build in these places. The second way would be to thematize the situation, which is why I mentioned Charles Jencks's writing about the silver standard thematizing the bank itself. The way in which content is thematized in a form often happens in works of art, but it doesn't seem to be the fundamental clue to how they operate. The third kind of mediation, the one I was trying to propose, is that both the work and the situation be seen as different expressions of some common process in terms of the abstraction of the money form — a certain kind of abstraction at one stage of the money form, a very different abstraction at a later stage, which might be ours. The production of new categories and new forms out of a wholly new social situation is potentially a source of utopian, or at least radically different, spaces. I've never quite understood how one could see architectural work as critical in Adorno's sense. As for mimesis, the idea that there has been a constant mimetic principle throughout history has always been the part of Frankfurt School anthropology that I found the least convincing. It seems to me that there are other transhistorical views of the constant repressions of the dialectic in the Enlightenment that are much more satisfying as historical stories.

Sassen I'm finding it useful to think of the transformation of dividing lines, borders, and frontiers — that which separates — in terms of analytic terrains and analytic borderlands. My question about architecture today is, what is the role of architecture, given the production of new types of analytic borderlands? I am interested in another kind of process, and the best approximation is this notion of rethinking the dividing line as an analytic borderland.

Ignasi de Solà-Morales This last question emphasizes methodological analogies as seen in your presentation and in Alejandro's, as well as in Ben's this morning and Nasrine's yesterday. Though in different fields, you both abandon the full interpretation and establish a more profound interest in organization, or ground, as Alejandro said. This means that extremely complex forces have established the basis, the ground, or the organization for the free global market or for the free-flowing, changing architecture. In these meetings a very interesting idea is arising that has to do with architectural attraction, which means no judgment to start. It's a cultural methodology that I remember was also in many conversations when Tafuri said, "Well, our most important commitment is to know as deep as possible how things work." This analogical position is a very interesting methodology between your approach to economic facts today and your approach to architectural basis.

Alejandro Zaera-Polo We discussed the nature of the critical in the last conference. I'm not particularly interested in the critical moment of architectural practice. I am not against it, I am not saying it's irrelevant, but I think processes like the ones that Saskia described open the possibility for something that is more about creating than about criticizing. Production is a moment of emergence that doesn't require a previous ideological position. When we arrive at this $75 trillion, what happens? How do we face this moment in a critical manner when we've never seen anything near it?

Bernard Tschumi Let me try to extend your question. The presence of Fred and Saskia in relationship to the work you've shown is very interesting. Fred talked about ground rent, Marx, and a certain way that property is divided. Saskia talked about analytic borderlands. You talked about ground as a contingent. I'm being terribly literal, but this is the point of architectural functions. Saskia, how would you develop an economic theory that could be compatible with the continuity of Alejandro's ground formations?

Sassen I have been struggling with these issues for 10 or 15 years. I'm not a conventional economist. First, it has to be slightly confined to, for example, the current period. There is a lot of continuity – this is a hot debate outside this community – as well as a lot of discontinuity, and I have very clearly positioned myself as a theorist of the difference. In this confined arena of discontinuities that I'm trying to theorize and empirically reference, I am continuously confronting the need to rethink the border. I don't know whether in architecture the border is the edge, the national border, the border between the formal economy and the informal economy, or the border between the space of the economy that inhabits actual physical space and digital space. I liked Alejandro's shifting ground. It's not clear what the ground is or where the edges are. I don't know where the border fits. With shifting ground, the site of the border is unclear, but that also means that the space of the ground is unclear. Because of this, I can immediately introduce digital space within this shifting ground. When I think of a contemporary office, I think of something that contains both spaces.

Jameson There are several sets of words that cluster around this: land, matter, ground, site, place, space. I don't want to trivialize Alejandro's work by taking it as an example of dematerialization or this theory of making ground porous by separating these forms from those older notions of heaviness, but it could be seen that way. In a tropological sense you have grounds for arguments. To grapple with the business of land speculation there always has to be a little bit of land, right? The money still has to buy something; it has to have some equivalence, no matter how deliriously free-floating it is and no matter how crazy the value of a piece of land. Years ago Kojin showed me a little place in Shinjuku which he said was the most expensive square inch of land in the world. In other words, no matter how extraordinary the price, it still has to be attached to something. We're not talking about complete dematerialization here, but I want to find a difference between the kind of sublimation that takes place in the modern period, which is still very much tied up with notions of mind and body, and what's going on now, which no longer has anything to do with that. In the modern period you have materialisms and idealisms and today we don't have any of those. I certainly don't think we have idealism anymore. Perhaps because we inhabit such a completely dematerialized space idealism is no longer necessary.

Charles Jencks I want to ask Saskia what the $75 trillion refers to and whether it is digitized capital circulating or capital on the ground. I was fascinated by her idea that there are what could be called tranquilizers in the system that calm down the way in which capital circulates. For instance, in 1987 $5 trillion were suddenly lost in interstellar space, causing that famous meltdown on Black Monday. Where did it go? Are you saying that we now have tranquilizers in the system that will stop that from happening again?

While writing on postmodern religion in 1968, philosopher-theologian John Cobb put forth a strong case that money is the religion of today. He said that it's the one thing that everybody takes as given and doesn't really question, and in that sense it is a religion. After hearing you this afternoon, you've proved it is a religion. The way you talk about money is so abstract. Umberto Eco says that of course money is a universal abstract system. You could say it's all been spiritualized. What I saw and heard through your presentations was an incredible universalism. In religion, God is universal, abstract, omniscient, omnipotent, and omnipresent, which is precisely what the global market is. Money produces, as we know, abstract isotropic space in its late-capitalist form. Someone came up with a figure to counter this amount of global world capital and said that the world's resources, all of the living things — the earth, the water, the sky, the air — are worth $120 trillion. At least there is still more real stuff out there than there is real money!

Sassen Let me give you a brief answer that combines the tranquilizers and the universalizing by telling a little story. The People's Republic of China recently launched a very original concept, a 100-year bond that sold very effectively in New York and Hong Kong. This means that there were investors in New York who were buying bonds on Chinese government debt that would mature in 100 years. To do this, China did not have to deal with the United States government, even though it was selling the bonds in New York. It dealt directly with J. P. Morgan, and this was an enormous success. There is today in the global economic system, or in the international system, a specialized intermediary world of strategic agents that can create guarantees on such things as China's 100-year bond. Countries like Romania, Croatia, Brazil, and Mexico have the possibility to create a transaction without engaging another government and somehow — and this is the tranquilizer — to reinvent forms of investment that are enormously risky as gradable investment through the big international services firms — J. P. Morgan, Creditanstalt, Deutsche Morgan Grenfell. In other words, they get graded as worthy investments. Recently they put $3 billion of Brazil's debt on the global market that had previously been Brady bonds. These bonds were invented in the United States, and they are collateralized by U.S. treasuries. Investors are giving up their collateralized instruments, the Brady bonds, for totally unguaranteed, uncollateralized Brazilian debt. This is possible — this is very risky and some people are beginning to say that this is the beginning of the Big Crash — because these service firms have the power to transform (a magician's trick if there ever was one) absolutely unreliable debt into desirable gradable investments. This is an event to which most of us don't relate. This is happening in this impenetrable world of global finance. Those are the tranquilizers. They are enormously powerful. When I speak about the global economy, one question is, who are the strategic agents today in the international system? It used to be nation-states. Today it is these intermediary actors. With universalization, China illustrates one way in which globalization is happening, which is the creation of precisely this universal intermediary world that makes it possible for the specificity of each national system — legal, accounting, cultural — to continue. It is not a homogenizing of national systems; it is a very strategic institutionalized event that encompasses the creation of international standards and allows, in the case of China, for the nation to keep its own accounting system, its financial reporting system, its legal system, which has nothing to do with the new world of international standards. It delegates that to J. P. Morgan. This is often missed in discussions about the global economy, this coexistence of the international, which is a universal, and the continuation of the difference.

Karatani The capitalist economy really is like the world of religion, but it has some limits. There are two things that capital cannot produce: one thing is land, or nature, and the other is human beings, labor power, which is also provided by nature, so to speak. The capitalist economy behaves as if there is no such limit, so it appears to be an idealist world, but there are some material limits. Land and human beings of course form the nation-state that is required by industrial capitalism. The nation and the land or border are also elements that capital cannot produce or get rid of. You can get rid of goods that you don't sell, but you cannot get rid of human beings, of labor, because they will fight back! That's why capitalism, which is almost like a religion, is almost universal, is bound to certain limits, and cannot be but national capitalism.

Time, Information, Numbers

Adriaan Geuze

Manmade Tabula Rasa

Highway near Utrecht, 1989.

CONTROLLING URBAN CHAOS VERSUS ACCEPTING CHAOS

The important issue that has arisen at the Anyhow conference is whether to control urban chaos or to accept it. Since urban development is a matter of extreme numbers, social acceptance of this process is declining. From the Western perspective, the demolition of nature and urban development are now perceived as synonymous.

EUPHORIA IN THE POLDER

After World War II the Dutch started to rebuild their country with great determination and vigor. Cities, roads, bridges, harbors, and railroads were restored, a commercial fleet was built, and trade and industry were renewed. The infrastructure was extended tremendously, and the economy started growing. Large-scale infrastructural works, power stations, and power pylons garnished the polderland, their pinnacles hanging from the clouds.

All of this induced among the Dutch a rare sense of optimism and self-confidence and above all a sense of pride in the prosperity that had been created. Perhaps the most significant symbol of this postwar euphoria was the building of a Dutch whaling fleet, which included the giant factory ship **Willem Barendsz** and 18 hunting boats. The Netherlands, a small country, succeeded in making international treaties on whaling and obtaining a six-percent quota of the worldwide catch, an example of economic enterprise. The whales were not regarded as animals but as giant suppliers: one whale equaled 90,000 packages of margarine.

THE TABOO OF COLONIZATION

This all changed. Along with the panda bear, the whale has now become a symbol of the demolition of nature. This marks a major shift: the public no longer views nature as a primitive force to be overpowered but as something vulnerable that must be protected by regulations. This new concept also marks the end of colonization. Finding, exploring, invading, occupying, and transforming new land, in other words, colonizing, no longer seems valid.

We must realize that in the matter of colonization we are still primitive. Colonization is in fact the ultimate expression of our culture. We identify with the nature we occupy, we transform it into a landscape and make it our home. The cultivation of nature is a necessary and essential act of survival. Like a first step in fresh snow, colonization produces a euphoria that demands and generates creativity. Humankind is not alive without this.

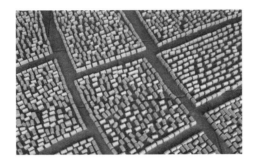

800,000 Houses, 1995,
Installation in the NAI
arcade.

Centuries ago Europeans accidentally discovered and claimed the beautiful virgin ground of Manhattan. This kind of immaculate landscape can no longer be found on Earth; there is no part left to be colonized. In fact, the statistical needs of contemporary mass culture seem to be facing the limits of physical expansion. The Alps are trampled, the coastlines are drowned, and even the nicest parts of Arcadia are absorbed in the sprawl of commercial and suburban development. Colonization has become a taboo. Some people view this as a forecast of the end of culture, I view it as the symbol of the end of urban planning.

EXPERIMENT

In the Netherlands, mass culture expresses itself in the landscape as a mediocre suburban program. After World War II the Dutch landscape was initially reclaimed for agricultural use and infrastructure, but in the past 20 years it has been gorged with monofunctional suburban sprawl. Some 100,000 new dwellings are being built each year, a high rate of production compared with that of other European countries. Dutch planners and architects try to keep a grip on this tremendous housing production with regulations.

An experiment by West 8 illustrates the situation vividly. Thirty architectural students were asked to fill the arcade of the Netherlands Architecture Institute with 800,000 wooden models of houses. They were asked to maintain maximum control over the area appointed to them, each representing a perception of regulation. The experiment visualized very clearly the process of regulation on a national scale, which, as it turned out, is not about regulation at all. In spite of the student-architects' regulatory aspirations, the result was an inarticulate sea of houses. In a very physical and brutal way this exposed the lack of strategies to control mass housing.

Perhaps we should think about planning more in terms of colonization. As it has become physically impossible to colonize new ground, we must develop new worlds, new voids, new tabulae rasae to be colonized. Then regulation, nonregulation, and self-regulation will no longer be an issue.

MANMADE TABULA RASA TO BE TAKEN

On the Dutch coast, between The Hague and the Port of Rotterdam, West 8 envisaged a land-fill in the sea. In collaboration with civil engineers, we developed a strategy to create new land within a period of four years. Two large construction islands are planned for engineering activities; from here other processes will emerge. At the 10-meter depth line a "dune dike" will be made, sheltering a new sand plain that is spread up to a level of five meters below sea level. As the landfill lies along the coastline, the former beach, it creates an inner lake. The southern part of the landfill features an 80-meter-high sand cone visible from the city of Rotterdam. Over five or six years the sand cone will apocalyptically erode into a natural dune area in which wind and rain will cause trenches and creeks. Buckthorn will be sown from airplanes to create an impenetrable vegetation. In this green oasis fire lanes will be laid out.

This new coastal landscape shows all stages of succession, marram on the first dune, buckthorn on the plain behind it, and oakwoods on the old dunes. There are new large-scale landscape textures such as vegetation, swamp areas, manmade beaches, and dunes. The buckthorn grid can be exploited for (sub)urban development, and national highways extending to the shore can connect old and new land, bringing the newborn area into a phase of colonization.

Photo: SPOT image, Toulouse 1991

Buckthorn City, 1995.
Above: Rotterdam harbor.
Below: Scheveningen
Marina. Right: Overview,
looking toward Rotterdam
Europort.

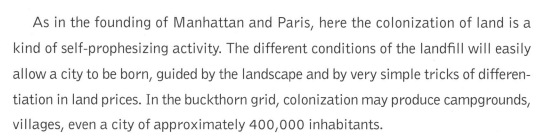

As in the founding of Manhattan and Paris, here the colonization of land is a kind of self-prophesizing activity. The different conditions of the landfill will easily allow a city to be born, guided by the landscape and by very simple tricks of differentiation in land prices. In the buckthorn grid, colonization may produce campgrounds, villages, even a city of approximately 400,000 inhabitants.

Starting off with a tabula rasa of manmade nature and inviting culture to colonize it in a more or less self-guiding process, urban planning loses its relevance. Instead of new cities, we have to make new promised land, new tabulae rasae, new worlds, new landscapes to be taken. The essence of urban development is not the exercising of one's professional knowledge of urban planning, it is the euphoria of the first step of colonization.

ADRIAAN GEUZE IS A DIRECTOR AND THE CHIEF DESIGNER OF WEST 8 LANDSCAPE ARCHITECTS IN ROTTERDAM. HE TEACHES AT DELFT TECHNICAL UNIVERSITY AND AT HARVARD UNIVERSITY'S GRADUATE SCHOOL OF DESIGN. PROJECTS TO DATE INCLUDE LANDSCAPING SCHIPHOL AIRPORT, THE THEATER AND MARKET SQUARES IN ROTTERDAM, AND THE MASTER PLAN FOR A RESIDENTIAL DISTRICT IN AMSTERDAM, NOW UNDER CONSTRUCTION.

Greg Lynn

Geometry in Time

Etienne-Louis Boullée,
Centotaph for Newton:
1784 drawing, section
showing daylight effect
of artificial sun.

I would like to discuss several issues that have been raised in a fairly technical and simplistic way during the conference. One involves a frustration with the term *flow* in regard to architectural design. This frustration stems from the assumption that time, force, and motion are concepts inherently opposed to architectural form. The fiction that architecture is a discipline defined by stasis is as old and conservative as architecture itself. More than perhaps any other discipline, architecture resists the incorporation of an ethics of motion into its thinking. During the 20th century the conceptualization of motion and time has been a common issue for nearly every intellectual discipline. The dilemma for architects has been that they understand their cultural role to be providers of shelter, stasis, and permanence. Unfortunately, most architects separate force from form because they assume that an ethics of motion is contradictory to the central tenet of architecture: that it is timeless, inert, and static.

The first assumption about the combination of force with form is often that architecture must become literally animated and interactive. An ethics of motion, however, does not mandate that architecture must literally move or be movable but that it cease to be conceived of as static.[1] This difference between virtual movement and actual movement is critical, as the two imply very different consequences. Both conceptual and methodological problems arise when these two concepts are casually exchanged. An alternate model of time and motion would resist the separation of form from the forces that animate it. Form could be conceived in a space of virtual movement and force rather than within an ideal equilibrium space of stasis. For example, analyses of Gothic architecture often refer to the space in which the vaults and buttresses are designed as a gravity space in which load-bearing moments and vectors are generated. The shift from an ideal space of inert coordinates to an active space of interactions implies a move from autonomous purity to structural, programmatic, material, and contextual specificity.[2]

If there is a manifesto on the table I would like to contribute the idea that architects must begin by advancing their general knowledge of motion and time in order to design and think in an animate rather than a static space. One principle put forward by Sanford Kwinter at the opening of the conference was a shift from analysis to design research. I would suggest that motion techniques be added to the architect's toolbox. The topological entities that the computer brings to the architect's design space are the first instance of what is later described as timed geometry. Topological surfaces are not merely shapes or figures as most architects, theorists, and historians persist in understanding them, and there is a big difference between framing questions of geometry in terms of shape and performance. Contemporary architectural designers, historians, and theorists tend to have a hypertrophic ability to attribute architectural shapes to one another and an atrophied knowledge of mathematics and geometry. Geometry is not merely a collection of shapes but a rigorous and technical discipline with its own historical development and logic. In architecture today, there is an explosion of new geometries available to designers, yet these are being understood critically as just another set of shapes that look a little like shapes we have seen before.

Topological geometry differs significantly from orthogonally projected geometry in that it is composed of vectors rather than points. It is the responsibility of architects who design with these tools to develop a rudimentary understanding of the difference between points in static X, Y, Z coordinate space and in U, V topological space. This difference between vectors and lines is the topic of this discussion. The questions raised by the relationship of motion, time, and architecture constitute a "space race." We cannot continue to have discussions about motion and time as if we were living in the intellectual climate of Palladio. These concepts mandate an understanding of mathematics and topology as rigorous and detailed as Colin Rowe's understanding of mannerist villas. In short, we need to become

1 For the work of Chuck Hoberman, see Architectural Design, "Folding in Architecture" (London: Academy Editions, 1993).

2 Jeffrey Kipnis has criticized this aspect of the argument but it is integral to any discussion of parameter based design that there be both an unfolding of an internal system and the infolding of contextual information fields. This issue is discussed more extensively in Architectural Design, "Folding in Architecture" (London: Academy Editions, 1993).

From Anthony Vidler, Claude-Nicolas Ledoux (Cambridge, Mass.: MIT Press, 1990), 275.

more advanced in our technical knowledge of time-based forms and to develop at least a working understanding of topological surfaces and their underlying mathematics. Motion and time have been rethought in virtually every discipline to date except architecture. The next advancement of architectural design will emerge from a historical and theoretical engagement with the mathematics and geometry that produced the reductionism of Descartes. This will require architects to distinguish between actual and virtual movement and forces. The most expedient approach has been for architecture to borrow time and motion structures from the disciplines that have used these tools since the turn of the century. In addition to biology and physics, from which many architects are borrowing metaphors, aeronautical design, naval design, and automobile design model form in a medium of movement and force. For example, naval design occurs in a hydrodynamic space of fluid flows. The medium for hull design is wet and animate, yet the hulls remain stable forms; we know that the shapes of boat hulls do not actually change as they move, yet they were designed in an environment of virtual motion.

Architects need to familiarize themselves with the basic developments in mathematics and geometry initiated by Isaac Newton's and G. W. Leibniz's invention of differential calculus. The key development in their mathematics is the replacement of exactitude by either a limit theory of reducible "derivatives" (Newton) or infinitesimal monadlike "integrals" (Leibniz). A similar knowledge of probability studies from the mid-18th century is useful, as the Compte de Buffon's needle experiments are still used as a simplistic basis for spatial probability studies. In all cases, the characteristics of these geometries are such that they are not exact but temporal, probabilistic, and differential.

Two existing and well-known models of time are already used by architects today. The first is seen in the processional model of architecture as a static frame through which motion passes. This motion-picture-based model of time consists of a superimposed sequence of static frames that are later reassembled with motion. In this processional model, architecture does not store time in its form but instead measures or calibrates time with a sequence of temporal sections. Rather than understanding animation techniques within the cinema paradigm, architects can reconceive motion as force rather than as a sequence of frames.[3] An example is the model of formal time, which can include shearing, shifting, and rotating operations based on superimposition. In formal time, architecture stores motion in its form through traces of transformational operations. Kenneth Frampton's description of Charles Gwathmey's early work as "rotational" is one example of formal movement between coincident positions of an object.[4] This second model of formal time conceives matter as the storehouse of motion operations that can be unfolded through perception. This formal time is limited by the motion processes that are marked as instances, or traces, which mandate a detached and static perception, as in the reading of an alignment between coordinates.

In cinema, motion is added at the end, to give form and shape to a simulated vitality. In computer animation, force is an initial condition. In cinema, the multiplication and sequencing of static snapshots simulates a linear indexing of time and motion. Animation is based on nonlinear, dynamic, and kinematic motion techniques. In these systems motion is defined by interacting vectors that unfold in time perpetually and openly. Animation involves the creative unfolding of a dynamic order through the interaction and inflection of vectors in a field that is not neutral, rather than in a regimented linear sequence. With these techniques entities are given vectoral properties and are released in a space of forces, collisions, and boundaries where they move in a continuous dynamic sequence.

Statics is not essential to architectural thinking as much as it is a lazy habit or default that architects choose to either reinforce or contradict for lack of a better model. Throughout its

3 One instance of this cross over is certainly evident in the work of Brian Boigon. See "The Cartoon Regulators," *Assemblage* 19 (Cambridge, Mass.: MIT Press, 1992).

4 Kenneth Frampton, "Frontality vs. Rotation," *Five Architects* (New York: Oxford University Press, 1975), 9–13.

history, architectural design has systematically identified itself with retrograde concepts of motion and time. This understanding holds that gravity is a simple, uniform, unchanging, vertical force acting on a system of independent components. This reductive model of gravity eliminates time and force so that the elements' positions can be calculated discretely. In a complex or relative model, time and force constitute position in space, thus positions must be calculated continuously. The shift from a discrete to a continuous model

as discrete and reducible to what is still held as a central truth — that buildings stand up vertically. In fact, there are multiple interacting structural pressures exerted on buildings from many directions, including lateral wind loads, uplift, shear, live loads, and earthquakes. Any one of these nonvertical "live loads" could easily exceed the relative weight of the building and its vertical "dead loads." A reconceptualization of ground and verticality in light of gravitational orbits and movements might not change the expediency of and need for

Greg Lynn FORM, Michael McInturf Architects, Martin Treberspurg, H2 House, Schwechat, Austria, (design 1997). Deformation of company logo.

of gravity involves the shift from a space of neutral timelessness to a space of procedural temporal change and dynamic interaction.

Structure relates to a concept of force and gravity, and these relationships are by definition multiple and interrelated. Yet architecture remains the last refuge for members of the flat-earth society. Architects treat these issues

level floors, but it would open up possibilities for structure and support that take into account orientations other than the vertical. One must remember that gravity is a concept, not a fact. The history of competing concepts of gravity is extremely nuanced and still unresolved. That gravity is the mutual relative attraction of masses in space has been agreed upon in almost every discipline with the exception of architecture. In a more complex conception of gravity, mutual attraction generates motion, and stability is the ordering of motion into rhythmic phases. The simple static model of gravity, eliminates motion at the beginning. In the complex stable model of gravity, motion is an ordering principle. It is no coincidence that the combinatorial model of gravity without a static equilibrium was put forward by Leibniz in his *Ars Combinatoria*[5] in opposition to Descartes. Leibniz argued that combination

reduction of systems to their constitutive identities in a steady-state equation. Leibniz initiated an alternative epistemology founded on the systematic nature of combinatorial changes in identity that take place with increasing degrees of complexity.

The difference between static and stable models of gravity is defined by the difference between reduction and combination. Discreteness, timelessness, and fixity are characteristic of stasis, and multiplicity, change, and development are characteristic of stability.

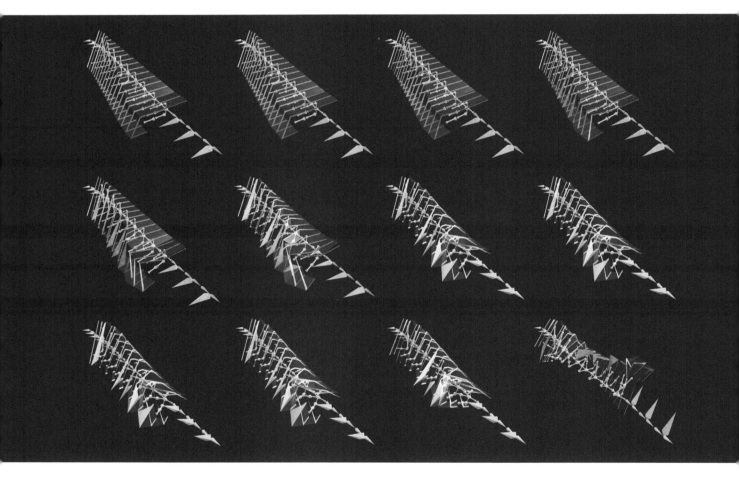

itself would generate a creative movement and development in time that cannot be conceived through ideas of reducible organization. For Leibniz, combination generates motion, and motion becomes the primary mode of organization, construction, composition, and stability. Cartesianism, on the other hand, is associated with the isolation and

These differences are apparent in the two models of gravity debated by Descartes and Leibniz. For Leibniz, any component reduced from its field of influences and combination was provisional and needed to be examined in a larger contextual field and within a developing temporal continuum. The name that he attributed to any provisionally reduced com-

As the site is situated along a major highway, the design of the skeletal system considers the sequence as viewed from the automobile. Later, a series of studies attach deformable surfaces to this skeleton.

ponent or primitive element is "monad." Once gravity is rethought within a Leibnizian monad logic, models for structuring architecture may also become monadological. A monadological architecture would embrace both an ethics of micro- and macrocontextual specificity and a rethinking of developmental time and motion intrinsic to stability.

The geometry and mathematics that Leibniz invented to describe an interactive, combinatorial, and multiplicitous gravity are the foundations for the topology and calculus upon which contemporary animation technology is based. A shift in sensibility from reduction to combination is necessary to compose stability in time-based, topological design mediums. Likewise, this sensibility would shift from mechanisms of stasis and equilibrium, such as the compass and the orrery, to abstract machines of differential stability and unfolding structures of movement and temporal flow.

This brings me to an announcement that Kwinter neglected to mention. Critical linguistic models of architectural thought have been and continue to be virtually bankrupt in their ability to generate architectural design or theory. The disappearance of many architectural theorists who promoted the use of linguistic models for a generation of design and their reappearance as archival historians is an indication of the diminishing faith in linguistic paradigms used as design tools. The shift from linguistic models to proto-linguistic or machinic models of organization has subsumed those earlier, now bankrupt techniques. Where there used to be a confluence between theory and design, there is now a polarization of practices presently comprised of two camps: one of the archive, the other of the diagram.

Any abstract machine, such as an orrery, can be understood as both a technical statement and as a signifier. Neither its representational nor its technical structure can be understood independently. For example, in Etienne-Louis Boullée's Cenotaph for Newton, the orrery operates as both an abstract model and as a sign. The difference between its abstract and representational roles can be located precisely at the moment it crosses the technological threshold from diagram to concrete assemblage. The use of a sign as a representational device assumes a legibility and instrumentality at primarily an aesthetic level; there are many types of organization and structure available to architecture that are not primarily aesthetic. The primary difference between critical and experimental architecture is that in the former concepts are represented and displayed through signs and language, whereas in the latter concepts are developed and expressed initially through more abstract techniques. The use of the term *abstraction* here should not be confused with the purist or modern notion of generic aesthetic abstraction mentioned earlier in the conference. In those instances, abstraction involves an aesthetic reduction to fixed formal essences by a paring away of differences. An alternative concept of abstraction is more generative and evolutionary and involves proliferation, expansion, and unfolding. This marks a shift from a modernist notion of scopophillic abstraction based on form and vision to an abstraction based on process and movement. To understand such a diagrammatic regime, it is helpful to cite Michel Foucault's concepts of "abstract machine" and "diagram." Gilles Deleuze has referred to these ideas as "asignifying concepts" because Foucault preceded questions of representation and linguistic attribution with a more fluid and mobile regime of asignifying concepts, statements, and diagrams. By definition, an asignifying concept is instrumental before it is representational. This model depends on the precise distinction between "linguistic constructions" and "statements." Linguistic constructions, such as propositions or phrases, can always be attributed to particular referents. Statements, on the other hand, are not initially linguistic but are machinic processes. An easily grasped example of a statement is the sequence of letters Q, W, E, R, T, Y as they are organized on a computer keyboard. The distribution of the letters in time and space is abstract and can be deployed in many possible variations to produce linguistic

5 Gottfried Wilhelm Leibniz, "On the combinatorial art," *Philosophical Papers and Letters*, trans. L. E. Loemker (Boston: D. Reidel, 1969).

constructions. The logic of their sequential distribution is based on the control of the speed at which one can potentially type words in the English language. No single sentence or word tests this distribution, rather it is the combination of an indefinite series of words. Because there is an open series the system must be characterized as indefinitely structured. The keyboard is an actual machine, or concrete assemblage, because it is technological, whereas the distribution of letters on keys in space is a virtual diagram, or an abstract machine, because it is proto-technological and is therefore a statement. Statements such as these are machinic techniques, discursive concepts, or schemata that precede the representational and linguistic effects they facilitate. Signifiers are not rejected but delayed toward the moment that they are "found at the intersection of different systems and are cut across by the statement acting in the role of primitive function."[6] Linguistic constructions are merely postponed, not abolished, and a regime of abstract, schematic statements are seen to preempt and sponsor them. From the particular discursive formation of multiple, diagonally intersecting statements emerges some form of expression. Through the interaction of a multiplicity of abstract statements, signifiers emerge in a more dynamic manner than do mere representational effects. The shift from linguistic models to the proliferation of asignifying statements marks what Deleuze terms a move from the "archive" to the "diagram." Deleuze defines this shift: "Foucault gives it its most precise name: it is a 'diagram,' that is to say a 'functioning, abstracted from any obstacle . . . or friction [and which] must be detached from any specific use.' The diagram is no longer an auditory visual archive but a map, a cartography that is coextensive with the whole social field. It is an abstract machine."[7] The move from linguistic constructions to statements or, more properly, from meaning to machine, is a necessary shift in sensibility if one is to tap the potential of abstract machines such as computational motion geometry and time-based, dynamic force simulations.

This difference between the virtual regimes of "abstract machines" and the actualization of those diagrams as "concrete assemblages"[8] is a difference that architects can easily comprehend because architecture is one of the few disciplines in which the virtual not only precedes the actual, but is the end product of the design process. Robin Evans has debunked the popular myth that architects build, arguing that the practice of architecture involves the production of drawings of buildings rather than the buildings themselves. These drawings and specifications both describe and organize construction processes. Architecture involves the production of diagrams that are conceptual techniques of the virtual organization of material technologies of concrete assemblage. Perhaps more than in any other discipline, the negotiation between concrete constructions and abstract concepts has been the responsibility of architects.

Because architectural design involves the virtual description of buildings through geometry and measurement, it is defined by the limits of technical description. Throughout the history of architecture, descriptive techniques have impacted the way in which architectural design and construction have been practiced. The advent of perspective, stereometric projection, and other geometric techniques have extended the descriptive repertoire of architectural designers. Action geometries are presently introducing a constellation of new diagrams based on the computer. Where previously Cartesian geometry limited the description of materials and spaces to a system of fixed-point coordinates in X, Y, Z coordinate space, action geometries define form in terms of directional vectors and splines. These entities are themselves directional and multiplicitous and therefore cannot be easily reduced to static points. These geometries allow for the description of time and force in geometry through curvature and inflection. In Cartesian space, force and time have been reduced from the measurement of form due to the fixity of the three-coordinate system of points, lines, and volumes. The diagrammatic characteristics of contemporary animation technology are first, topology-

6 Gilles Deleuze, Foucault, trans. and ed. Sean Hand (Minneapolis: University of Minnesota Press, 1988), 8.

7 Ibid., 34.

8 For a discussion of abstract machines and concrete assemblages see Gilles Deleuze, A Thousand Plateaus, trans. Brian Massumi (Minneapolis: University of Minnesota Press, 1987), 502–14.

9 Donna Haraway, Simians, Cyborgs, and Women (New York: Routledge, 1991), 149–82.

based, second, parameter-based, and third, time- and motion-based. Force, motion, and time, which have continually eluded architectural description due to their vague essence, can be experimented with once the tools of exactitude and stasis are supplemented by tools of gradients, flexible envelopes, and temporal flows and forces.

Architects have been taught to eliminate questions of flow and motion from the rigorous description of space; thus these qualities have been relegated to personal taste and

ask the technology what it would like to do to architecture. It is more interesting to begin with an inventory of what machines can do to us rather than pose the question of what we desire from the machines.[9] The computer, like more conventional methods of drafting and measurement, presents a limited medium for experimentation and conceptualization with space and form. The limits and tendencies of this tool as a medium must be understood conceptually before they can be grasped by a *systematic* intuition. Three fundamental proper-

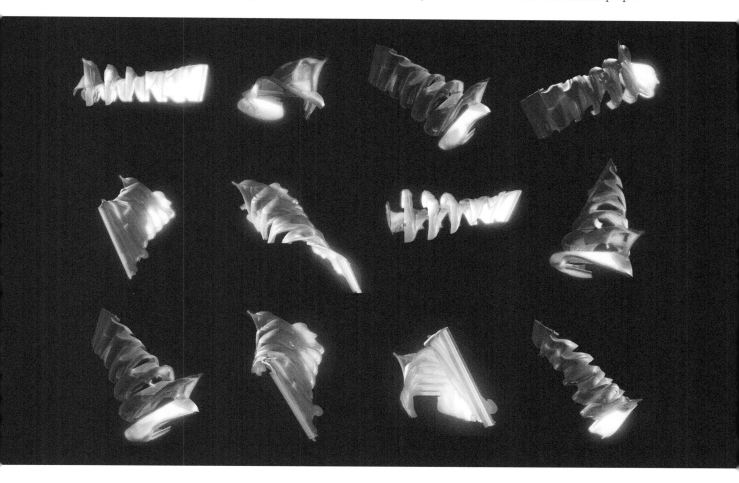

Surface sweeps as phase portraits.

casual definition. Architecture's present lack of experience and precedent with motion and force make it necessary to raise these issues from within the technological regimes of the tools rather than from within the history of architecture. Since it is not clear what architects would want to do with action geometries, it might be better to reverse the question and

ties of organization in a computer — time, topology, and parameters — are very different from the characteristics of inert mediums such as paper and pencil.

First, time is built into animation software as the possibility to keyframe changes in shape as well as to allow objects to interact dynamically with one another. Both the possibility for formal transformation or "morphing" and the nonlinear interaction of objects add a temporal dimension to the modeling of form. Second, topology describes forms in terms of flexible surfaces made of curvilinear splines rather than Cartesian volumes made of lines and points. Splines can be understood as vectors hanging from weights. As entities in and of themselves, they are seen as motile. As they exist in a time-based environment, even if they do not move within that space they are always already defined as directional vectors. Along a spline,

is reducible neither to a single entity nor to a collection of multiple entities. A multiplicity is neither one nor many but a continuous assemblage of heterogeneous singularities such that it exhibits both collective qualities of continuity and local qualities of heterogeneity. This implies a very different concept of experiential time as there are no points of definition or contemplation; instead, splines must be understood as a serial flow of coordinates. Finally, parameters are used to define these complex entities and their interaction in time with one

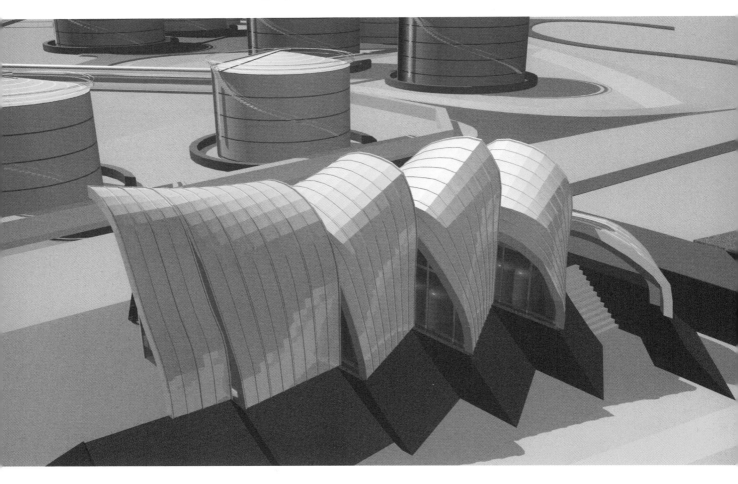

instead of points, there are moments that cannot be defined with coordinates but must be defined as a flow through a sequence of particular points in a continuous rather than discrete series. Because splines are vector flows through sequences of points they are by definition multiplicities rather than discrete entities. A multiplicity is a collection of components that

another. These parameters can also be keyframed and changed as well as linked through "expressions" to one another, generating nonequilibrium and nonlinear organizations. In addition to mere changes in shape, these parameters control gradient characteristics of fields such as directional forces, gravity, warps, and particles. These entities, which have no envelope or

Perspective view from northeast.

boundary, are used to transform objects placed within their influence. Parameters of decay, wave behavior, attraction, and density effect shape without mechanical transformations of form. These parameters are used for modeling in a more numerical and less formal manner. The linkages between these characteristics of time, topology, and parameters combine to establish the virtual possibilities for designing in animate rather than static space. Each of these characteristics can be used to rethink the familiar Cartesian space of neutral equilibrium as a more active space of motion and flow.

Splines are entities defined by flow, direction, and motion and are therefore capable of modeling time. Action geometries are inherently temporal due to their sequential definition. Likewise, because they are defined by weight, gravity, and force they are structured by curvature. Curvature is the graphical and mathematical model for the imbrication of multiple forces in time. The shift from linearity to curvilinearity is a feature of contemporary mathematics and geometry that has been discussed elsewhere. Curvature in a temporal environment is the method by which the interaction of multiple forces can be both analyzed and expressed. Beginning with D'Arcy Thompson, the term *deformation* signified not the loss of structure in a system but rather the curvilinear structure of a dynamic system of differential performance. His analyses of variations in the morphology of animals using deformable grids yielded curvilinear lines due to changes in form. These deformations correspond to different performance and contextual criteria such as speed, temperature, and weight, among other factors. The curvature of deformations in formal configurations was compared with the curvature of statistical data. Deformation, inflection, and curvature all involve the registration of force and performance on form. Rather than thinking of deformation as a subset of the pure, deformation can be understood as a system of regulation and order through variable curvilinear structures.

This is to say that everything is a curve, even what seems to be a straight line. For example, a curve drawn between two points

looks like a line. Similarly, a curve drawn between multiple sequential points in the X axis with the same Y and Z values will also appear to be a straight line. Finally, a curve between multiple points defined with one degree of inflection will look like a polyline because it is segmented. What appears to be a line, in terms of calculus, is merely a curve with a minimal inflection of differential values. To oppose the curved and the straight is to misunderstand the mathematical and geometrical principles by which curves are constructed. Curvature can be a mode of integrating complex interacting entities into a continuous form. Curvilinearity is a more sophisticated and complex form of organization than linearity in two regards: it integrates multiple rather than single entities, and it is capable of expressing vector attributes and, therefore, time and motion. Curvature such as this was described by Jules-Henri Poincaré in his three-body problem, in which he showed that these calculations must involve time as a continuous sequence; that is, to calculate the moment of intersection of three vectors. The fact that any system of three or more linked differentials must be thought in series implies a new relationship to those kinds of diagrams and geometry.

Curvature as a mathematical and intuitive system can be explained with the classic example of throwing a Frisbee to a running dog. Plotted in space, the dog is given a vector of direction and speed and the Frisbee is given a vector for direction and speed at its release; if a wind is blowing, the environment is given a velocity and direction as well. In order to intersect with the Frisbee at a future moment in time the dog does not follow the Frisbee but performs a differential equation to calculate both its and the Frisbee's position in time as vectors moving toward an intersection in both space and time. The paths of the dog and the Frisbee are described by curved lines. From the inflections of these curved lines the velocities, directions, and timing of each of the imbricated vectors in space and time becomes apparent. The bad news for the old dogs in the audience here is that the mathematics of this new trick is a differential equation.

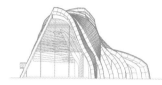

East (top) and west elevations.

GREG LYNN TEACHES AT THE SCHOOL OF ARCHITECTURE, PLANNING, AND PRESERVATION AT COLUMBIA UNIVERSITY IN NEW YORK AND AT THE UNIVERSITY OF CALIFORNIA, LOS ANGELES AND IS PRINCIPAL OF THE STUDIO FORM. HIS BOOK, ANIMATE FORM, WILL BE PUBLISHED IN DECEMBER 1998 BY PRINCETON ARCHITECTURAL PRESS.

Hubert Damisch

How We Deal with History

Ours is a time that seems to have no way of dealing with history other than as strictly retro-spective, in the past tense. A time that doesn't want to know of any form of ideology other than the laissez-faire, the mere and mechanical submission to the rules of the "market." A time that leaves no room for utopias other than the degenerate, as in Disneyland. A time that precludes any projection into the future, unless evolutionary, in terms of profit, fic-tional (the so-called "science fiction"), or fantasmatic, in the guise of identity or of virtuality, which in some way amounts to the same (there is no identity but virtual, no virtuality but "identitarian," **identitaire**, both in trompe-l'oeil). My thesis will be that no matter the con-ditions, architecture indicates the new paths, or non-paths, the new ways, or non-ways, that are or could be – I dare not say "or should be" – the ones of history (or non-history) today. Architecture also indicates the margin of "play," in the sense of play in a machine or gear, that is left, beyond irony, for any form of creative, critical, or subversive activity.

1. Is there any way for a building, public or private, large or modest, to be declared "his-toric" or a "landmark" without reference to the past or to "style?" Is there any way for architecture to deal with "history" in its very process or activity, as well as in its appearance, in terms of structure or form? One of the most common criticisms of modernist archi-tecture is that it had no concern for history. Indeed, the ideology of modernity implied a rupture with the past, under the labels of newness or rationality or both. As Walter Gropius once said, "Modern architecture is not a new branch added to an old tree, but a new growth, that sprouts directly from the roots."[1] The architecture of the "moderns" involved

1 Walter Gropius, "Architect – Servant or Leader?" in *Scope of Total Architecture* (London: G. Allen & Unwin, 1956), 94.

a projection into the future, the very notion of "project" being related to the forthcoming dimension of time, to the opening of things to come, things to conceive and construct, things to "plan" and to "project," eventually to the detriment of the remnants of the past. Project and utopia hand in hand, as Manfredo Tafuri recognized.[2] For the constructivists, history

2 Manfredo Tafuri, *Architecture and Utopia*, trans. Barbara Luigi La Penta (Cambridge, Mass.: MIT Press, 1976).

had to do with expectations rather than with memories; with looking forward rather than with looking back; with construction rather than with conservation.

Architecture is not only a product of history, a product to be studied, analyzed, criticized in relation to its context, conditions of appearance, or possibility. Architecture is an essen-tial thread in the fabric of history, most especially in the fabric of "context." It is an agent, or tool, in the making of history, in the development of new forms not only of dwelling but of production and sociability, of power and exploitation – new modes of historicity. This may sound like mere commonplace, but it needs constantly to be reassessed. The very activity of building, of projecting, is, by definition, future-oriented. Even the great monuments that celebrate the past are a way of getting rid of it. Adolf Loos claimed that the tomb is the epitome of architecture: it is, first, a way for the living to come to terms with the dead, a way for people to come to terms with death itself. This is part of history and part of archi-tecture, but only one part of it.

No one has better formulated this issue in contemporary architecture than Fredric Jameson. The same Fredric Jameson who, in a daring move, shifted gears from "postmodern" to "postcontemporary," as if even contemporaneity, such as we have to live it, think it, be part of it, is already and irremediably lost as such. As if we could live it, think it, be part of it only in retrospect. As if history, be it contemporary history, history in the present tense, had from the start to be narrated in the past tense while failing to attain any form of coherence.

Peter Eisenman's project for the University Art Museum in Long Beach, California is perfectly in tune with such a scheme, taking its form from – I quote Eisenman – "the overlapping registration of several maps" corresponding to various time zones, the coordinates of which are incompatible: "Beginning with the settlement of California in 1849, the creation of the campus in 1949, and the projected 'rediscovery' of the museum in the year 2049. The idea was to imagine the site in the year 2049, 100 years after the founding of the university and 200 years after the period of the gold rush."[3] Projecting into the future equates with reducing the future to its own archaeology, with making up for the lack of deeper layers of time, the lack of "history" in the past tense that is supposed to be characteristic of America.

3 Peter Eisenman, *Recent Projects*, 25, as quoted in Fredric Jameson, *The Seeds of Time* (New York: Columbia University Press, 1994), 170–71.

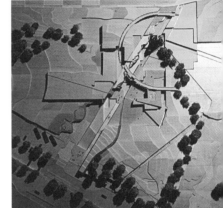

Eisenman Architects, University Art Museum, Long Beach, California, competition entry, 1986, model with and without roof.

I quote, somewhat freely, from Jameson's **The Seeds of Time:**

Now the new individual building does not even have a fabric in which to "fit," like some well-chosen word . . . rather (consistent with the freedom of the market itself) it must **replicate** the chaos and the turbulences all around it. . . . Replication means the depoliticization of the former modern, the consent to corporate power and its grants and contracts, the reduction of social conscience to manageable, practical, pragmatic limits; the Utopian becomes unmentionable, along with socialism and unbalanced budgets. Clearly also, on any materialist view, the way the building form falls out is of enormous significance; in particular the proportion of individual houses to office buildings, the possibility or not of urban ensembles, the rate of commissions for public buildings such as opera houses or museums (often recontained within those reservation spaces of private or public universities, which are among the most signal sources of high class contemporary patronage), and not least the chance to design apartment buildings or public housing.[4]

4 Jameson, *The Seeds of Time*, 143–44.

From the small private house rebuilt by Frank Gehry to what Jameson calls "the grandiose new totalities" of Rem Koolhaas, the contemporary (or shall we say, the post-contemporary?) praxis of architecture demonstrates the narrow range of possible interventions left to architects in a world in which any form of planning has been subverted by building regulations and zoning laws that are applied in a strictly defensive and negative way; and at the public level, the process of decision is reduced, at its best, to a choice between different moves that mechanically follow the weakest lines of resistance. The paths of "history" are such that today there seems to be only one way of dealing with this in a creative way: to accept the constraints and to try to take advantage of them in order to develop new ideas. (As Koolhaas likes to say, in a Goethean way, with respect to New York City zoning law: "The more you stick to the rules, the more freedoms you have." The **more freedoms**, in the plural.)

2. Among the types of public buildings that are publicly or privately commissioned today, Jameson mentions opera houses and museums, that is, buildings explicitly related to the

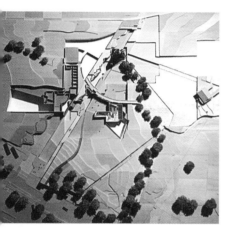

issue of history or "heritage." Strangely enough, he omits airport terminals, yet these are among the most important public commissions today, and they may eventually be turned in the future into museums, as train stations already have been (think of the Musée d'Orsay in Paris; in Washington, D.C., a former department store is being turned into an opera house). For the moment the museum is desperately attempting to resemble a terminal, with its halls, counters, escalators, zones of gathering, security booths, shops, parking lots, and herds of tourists that make us believe that museums are enjoying a vogue that equals one of the great pilgrimages of the past, even though the number of visitors they attract is in fact constantly declining.

The museum as a terminal, inside or outside the city. Not very far from here, set in the park of Upper Veluwe, is the Kröller-Müller Museum, a good example of the museum as part, in Jameson's terms, of a reservation space. Here in Rotterdam, when the city council agreed, in 1928, that a new museum was needed, it seemed logical that the plan for the building retain the parklike character of the same site on which the museum of architecture, the Netherlands Architecture Institute, stands today: "A tranquil stretch of land in the midst of the city's hustle and bustle."[5] Similarly, the Museum of Modern Art in New York has for a long time been

5 Séance du 30 décembre 1926, as quoted in Frederike Huygen, *Het museum Boijmans van Hannema: gebouw, geschiedenis, architectuur* (Rotterdam: Museum Boijmans Van Beuningen, 1992), 78.

conceived as a public oasis, an island of culture in the center of the metropolis. In fact, the architects who recently participated in the competition to remodel the museum were asked to treat it as a "campus," that is, as a reservation space under high-class patronage.

The great collections that historically have been developed into museums were by no means restricted to a retrospective view of artistic production and to the celebration of antiquity or the great schools and periods of the past. When Velázquez was commissioned in 1629 to go to

Italy to buy works of art for King Philip IV of Spain he mostly acquired paintings by his contemporaries or immediate predecessors. The first museums were not conceived as monuments of the past, and still less as tombs or funerary sites but rather as repositories of models for living artists. Things changed when, in the 18th century, the erudite sense of history and archaeology overrode the concern for the present and when, partly due to the success of the salons, the art of the past and the art of the present were sharply divided while at the same time the institution as such pleaded for continuity, often to the detriment of living art.

A symptom of the way in which we now deal with history is evident in the same split between the art of the past and the art of the present that gave way to the creation of museums of modern art, a split now reverberating inside those relatively new institutions as a split between modern and contemporary (and post-contemporary) art. The best way to avoid the apparent contradiction between the diverse approaches to history seems to be to dodge it by carefully isolating each layer of time in its own container, thereby avoiding or preventing any form of communication, exchange, or contamination between them. The museum has become some sort of air terminal. But in opposition to the imaginary one, or to what I would call the "paper museum" – in the sense in which we speak of "paper architecture" – it doesn't offer flights to all destinations.

Hubert Damisch, curator, "Moves: Playing Chess and Cards with the Museum," interior views of exhibition (Summer 1997).

In 1979, referring to Cesar Pelli's model for the new museum tower, Bill Rubin, then director of the Museum of Modern Art, declared: "This new building solves the problems of the past but not the future – you can't predict what art's going to do." We are aware of the problem that curators at the Centre Georges Pompidou face with each new installation because programmers in the 1970s thought they could predict where art was heading and what it would need: a museum without walls. But we also know what an extraordinary challenge the spiral of the Guggenheim Museum still offers to artists 40 years after its completion. This is exactly what makes it "historic" in the sense I am trying to suggest.

Not only do we not know what art is going to do, it also looks as if one of the main concerns of art was to deceive any prediction, to evade any enlistment. This doesn't mean that plans for new museums, or for the remodeling of existing ones, should only solve problems of the past, as Rubin put it. The "historic" quality of a project depends on its capacity to generate a margin of play, as well as a set of situations to which both the visitors and the artists must react. As far as the museum is concerned, this means breaking with the strictly linear development of a master narrative. Frank Lloyd Wright's scheme for the Guggenheim Museum represented a drastic move beyond Le Corbusier's Mundaneum, a museum that developed concentrically as a snail shell, providing no room for any confrontation or short circuits, not to mention the impossibility of introducing a new piece in the game without having to reorganize the entire itinerary. In the Guggenheim Museum the visitor is allowed, at any moment along the spiral, to take a transversal view, either upward or downward, backward or forward. In a recent show there, Ellsworth Kelly played systematically, and dramatically, on the constraints that the spiral form imposes, as well as on the possibilities it opens.

A museum is at once a narrative and a system that assumes an architectural form: a narrative that "precipitates" – in the chemical sense – according to constant accretions and redistributions; a system that corresponds to the mapping of diachrony into synchrony, of succession into simultaneity, and through which one has to open a path in some transversal way. When the new Boijmans Museum opened in 1935, it was much criticized for its traditionalism by the adepts of the modern movement. However, due more to its intricate plan than

to its technically advanced system of lighting, the building retains an extraordinary quality. Distributed on several levels, with a circular hallway at the crossroads of various possible itineraries, it functions according to an unprecedented principle, mirroring in its very structure the evolution of art – itself ramified, arboreal, bushlike – and the multiple pathways of its history.

We still need to learn from Karl Marx that history is not only a matter of narration. We still need to learn from Lucien Febvre and Marc Bloch, creators of the French school of **Les Annales**, that history has to be constantly rewritten according to the needs and anticipations of new generations. In the museum such rewriting takes the form of new additions and the remodeling of former parts. For the curators at the Boijmans it meant dealing simultaneously with ancient, modern, and contemporary art. My own move in the exhibition that I curated there is consistent with this. "Playing Chess and Cards with the Museum" amounts to an experiment in having art from the past working, with no intermediaries, with art from the present and vice versa. An experiment in the ways in which history can be dealt with not only according to sequential lines but through simultaneity and the constant confrontations, overlappings, and short circuits of which the history of art is constituted.

3. A more delicate, even painful question concerns the uses and abuses of history, as well as the uses and abuses of architecture in a "museum" like the Holocaust Museum in Washington, D.C., a structure, according to its supporters, that is specifically about the nature of memory.[6] This issue seems to defy any attempts to deal with it in a seemingly detached and objective way, hence I will only pinpoint in the most discrete way two problems of special relevance to my argument here.

6 Adrian Dannatt, *United States Holocaust Memorial Museum: James Ingo Freed* (London: Phaidon Press, 1995), 5.

First the problem of linearity. Notwithstanding the architects' efforts to provide visitors with a succession of choices between different itineraries and to induce (here again, I borrow freely from different sources) "a sense of imbalance, distortion and rupture," the story of the Holocaust unfolds linearly on three levels surrounding "a large hollow interior that resembles another hall of arrival" (itself described as both "a non-place and a central space"), that is, strictly speaking, another kind of terminal. How are we to deal in a narrative way with an event so beyond measure that it not only evades the grasp but blasts the very notion of it? I do not want to sound polemical, but the way in which the story starts in 1918 and implacably continues to 1945 with General Dwight D. Eisenhower discovering the atrocities of the death camps; the way in which the tale is told to play on the sense of guilt that Western democracies should develop for having refused to welcome the great numbers of refugees who would have otherwise supposedly been allowed to leave Germany; the claim that one would have had to wait until 1942 and the Wansee Conference for the Nazis to engage in the "final solution"; and, last but not least, the tale abruptly ending on the two interrelated historical destinies left to the Jews after the Holocaust, the State of Israel and the American Jewish community; all the supposed subtleties of the setting lead to the same conclusion: there is no way to deal in critical terms with such an endeavor other than strictly architecturally. At stake is no less than the capacity of architecture to ensure a visible grasp on an unspeakable past: for the enormity of the event, the way in which, as Jean-François Lyotard once put it, it destroys all instruments of measurement, is measured by the way in which it implies the negation of any form of bigness other than the merely quantitative, as well as the total, or totalitarian, elimination of any architectural trace, or any archaeological remnant of the boundless atrocities that took place on the premises.

There is no other way to discuss such a "monument" in the etymological sense of the word than the strictly architectural. A more general question concerns the different ways in which architecture can relate to history today, the different ways in which architecture can deal with the challenge of history.

This leads to the second problem, that of style: for the way in which the architects of the Holocaust Museum played on style reveals the degenerate Nietzschean way in which we now indulge in dealing with history in stylistic terms. Starting with the "architectural language" of the Hall of Witnesses, conceived as "an ironic criticism of early modernism's lofty ideals of reason and order that were perverted to build the factories of death"[7] and ending, regrettably,

7 Quoted from the leaflet "The Architecture and Art of the United States Holocaust Memorial Museum," published by the Holocaust Museum, Washington, D.C., 9.

with an unbearable touch of so-called "concentrationary atmosphere." A sequence of events one is forced to watch in strict chronology down to a horse-stable barrack treated as the canonical representation of German camps. In a way the Holocaust Museum, in its limitations and given the issues it raises, amounts to an urgent call for the museum to come to terms with history in ways other than the merely retrospective and narrative, in the past tense. An urgent call for architecture to be "historic" in ways other than the stylistic, mimetic, or allegorical. An urgent call for architecture in the future tense, the future of metaphor.

HUBERT DAMISCH IS DIRECTOR OF STUDIES AT THE ÉCOLE DE HAUTES ÉTUDES EN SCIENCES SOCIALES IN PARIS.

Rem Koolhaas

I want to talk about numbers and, indirectly, about the effect of numbers on architecture. I will present a research project – Pearl River Delta – that is the first installment of the so-called Harvard Project on the City, in which eight thesis students participated. The China project is a field report on the production of urban matter and some of its consequences both for the city and for architecture. In September 1995 we made a circular journey to six cities in the Pearl River Delta: Hong Kong, Shenzhen, Dongguan, Guangzhou, Zhuhai, and Macao. Some of the demographics are well-known, especially the rate of China's urbanization, which accelerates continuously and, given the numbers of China, now implies the generation of, in Western terms, unbelievable quantities of new urban substance. We then extracted from the situation a glossary of about 50 newly minted and copyrighted concepts that we offer as an extension to the inadequate vocabulary that now dominates urban discourse. The numbers are incredible, exacerbated by the present status of communism as it moves from red to **INFRARED**©, a kind of underground control of the situation where there is an attempt at making two previously incompatible systems – the market economy and the system of state control – compatible. The mediating agent between those two dogmas or ideologies we have called **CORRUPTION**©, the only agent that can bridge the contradictions. The general theme of this gold rush is the statement Deng launched in 1978, "To get rich is glorious," the subtext for this entire hyperdevelopment.

At this point, Pearl River Delta is inhabited by about 15 million people; by the year 2020 that will be 34 million, so that what is now still a collection of disparate parts will become an "entity" – we will talk about that later – and will simply through its incred-

Pearl River Delta

ible quantities – 34 million – become an "important" city, prototype of a new kind of importance that lies in wait for us in the next century – importance given by quantities or by economic activity, not by our previous qualities such as culture or history.

For the economy of this presentation I will talk here about the two most "mutant" cities, Shenzhen and Zhuhai. Shenzhen is a "Special Economic Zone," a cynical parasitic construction conceived by the Chinese to drain off some of the excess energy of Hong Kong. Zhuhai is also a Special Economic Zone, territories **SACRIFICED**© – to be urbanized, raped, or colonized, transformed. If you look at the statistics, Hong Kong is, compared to Shenzhen, actually a relatively stable condition, in spite of its seeming dynamism . Its population has increased only marginally in the past decade. Shenzhen, projected to the north of Hong Kong as an urban parasite, has truly exploded. In 1980 it was a fishing village, and in '91 it was already a metropolis of a million and a half people – permanent and temporary residents – and since then has grown into a city of three million. The entire urban system of the Pearl River Delta – the future metropolis of 34 million – generates 500 square kilometers of new urban substance per year, a speed at which no city has ever been produced before. Between 1982 and 1993, 500 skyscrapers were built.

Obviously architecture can be read in many ways, and I think this is where a comparison with Greg Lynn's incredibly exhilarating presentation becomes interesting: in Shenzhen architecture is mostly read in terms of figures, in terms of money. The newspapers are obsessed with the value of buildings. Everyday, each major building in the city is listed and its increase or decrease in value recorded, like the stock market, allowing each citizen

to invest or sell at the right moment. Architectural fluctuations are economic fluctuations; predominantly, the speed of production has a drastic effect on the architecture. Through sheer programmatic pressure and sheer demand, parking garages are appropriated for human occupancy. Each occupant is made manifest through a unique fragment of curtain wall. Here a building is converted before it is finished, partly destroyed and then partly rebuilt because the program changed before the building saw the light of day. We are interested in the implications of this kind of architecture, of this kind of production, this speed, and these numbers for architecture. Is it a unique, and therefore irrelevant example or is it a premonition of a condition where even we will not have time for "Architecture?" We wanted to find out under what conditions architecture was being produced and the implications of this kind of architecture for the city. Perhaps the most "architectural" building in Shenzhen is triangular; it has decoration; it manipulates different kinds of curtain wall and, uniquely, it also has exposed concrete. The architects are two men in their twenties. They produced the design in four days on a Macintosh computer at home. Four days is actually a fairly long time for a building in Shenzhen. We then investigated under what conditions the Chinese architect works.

If you look at all these factors, the Chinese architect is a thousand times more efficient than his nearest colleague. There are 15 times as many architects per 1,000 people in England as in China. Chinese architects earn one seventh of their American colleagues; they produce 30 times the architectural substance of their Spanish counterparts. Yet a typical view of Shenzhen is not very different from our contemporary cities. With so much more

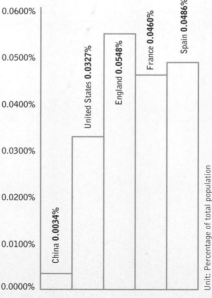

1994 Architects Index

tradition, money, education, and insight, is there so little difference between the average architecture in Europe and the average contemporary architecture in China?

Practically nothing in Shenzhen is older than eight years. I don't know anyone in this room who will argue that Shenzhen is a defensible urban condition. We inhabit a profession forced by its own traditions to interpret the most exciting events that occur on its territory as worthless and as aberrations. Yet Shenzhen is a city of unbelievable richness and unbelievable contrasts with a fantastic proximity between the town center – or at least the major intersection – and rice fields. The intersection is dominated by two important things: a billboard of Deng with the major terminal Communist slogan, "Hundred years of no change," and a fish pond. The final repertoire of architecture is completely polarized: only two typologies remain, high and low. Every condition in between is disappearing under the pressure of constant acceleration. Together these conditions of course imply an incredible relish for destruction: the former fishing village is not only destroyed but actually pulverized.

While whole parts of the world and entire continents are extremely reticent about the use of the **TABULA RASA**©, there are other continents for which it is seen as a *sine qua non* for urban production. Ultimately the question is whether this separation and this compartmentalization are tenable in globalization or if sooner or later we will also undergo the influence of this kind of condition. In China even **TABULA RASA**© itself can be inhabited. Where with our humanist sentimentalities we constantly censure what is possible and what is impossible, in Shenzhen a field of burnt-out grass between a highway viaduct and a

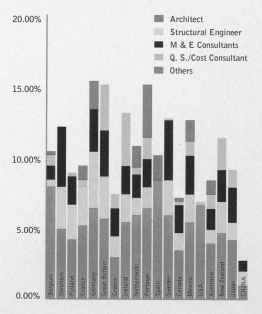

1994 Design Fee Schedules

Legend:
- Architect
- Structural Engineer
- M & E Consultants
- Q. S./Cost Consultant
- Others

Categories: Belgium, Denmark, Finland, France, Germany, Great Britain, Greece, Ireland, Netherlands, Portugal, Spain, Sweden, Canada, Mexico, USA, Australia, New Zealand, Japan, CHINA

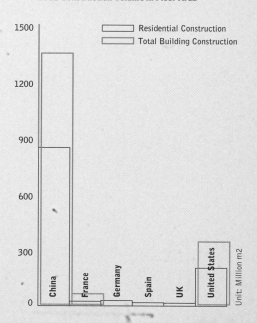

1992 Construction Volume in Floor Area

Legend:
- Residential Construction
- Total Building Construction

Categories: China, France, Germany, Spain, UK, United States

Unit: Million m2

railway becomes a perfectly inhabitable urban plain. Now I ask you to go back in your mind to Manhattan and imagine the contrast between Central Park and the cliffs of buildings around it, a contrast between vegetation and architecture that probably took at least 150 years to reach its full fruition. In Shenzhen, the same contrast is established in a decade. But where the park in Manhattan is a void in the center, in Shenzhen the void is the center. Downtown Shenzhen is a golf course amalgamated into theme parks and other *terrain vagues*. In retrospect, perhaps the La Villette competition in 1981 was an early intuition of such a mutation that architecture can contain only certain predictable programs, no matter how ingenious it becomes, and that increasingly the raw territory itself becomes the field, the "event space" where program now takes place without inhibition. The golf course in downtown Shenzhen is open 24 hours a day; a lot of deal-making is going on at two o'clock in the morning or even later. The golf course is becoming a major urban topology in Asia where it is merging with housing estates and other highly charged places to generate a seamless condition. All previously separate categories are now merged or morphed – whatever language you want to use – into not urban substance – I think that the old urban substance is becoming of secondary importance – but morphed into a new urban condition that has largely superseded architecture. Therefore here we have the typical view of Shenzhen, an empty plain with a reference point that attempts to be the Eiffel Tower. This is the new urban condition, and the question is whether *we* will soon work with the same frivolity, whether our present anxiety, agony, or even seriousness about the city could be entirely misplaced. Frivolity offers enormous potentials for everybody.

Short-circuiting the journey, I now switch to the west bank of the Pearl River, to the city of Zhuhai. It is also a Special Economic Zone, but one that in spite of its claims of vigor is a phantom city that is preparing itself very seriously for the role that it eventually will have to play when the 34 million inhabitants are there, a city that has now only grown to a very modest 700,000. What in Shenzhen is still a contrast between vegetation and skyscrapers, between the solid and the void, here seems as if the city itself is **THINNING©**. **THINNING©** is an important word in the series of copyrighted words that we offer for the discussion of new urban conditions. In Zhuhai the architecture is cardboard and the program indeterminate. More and more accommodation is designated as hotels, motels, or vacation camps in the search for at least a provisional or occasional occupancy. In spite of this liteness, in Zhuhai they are not frivolous but are serious about urbanism: they are creating a system of **POTEMKIN CORRIDORS©** that announces a city without the presence, yet, of a city. The eventuality is crisscrossed by future boulevards and even the beach is equipped for its future metropolitan status in this way. The most daring **POTEMKIN CORRIDOR©** prepared by Zhuhai's planners is a bridge that connects Zhuhai to Hong Kong. Eighty kilometers long, it has a fixed beginning and an uncertain end. It will start in Zhuhai and then leap in a few steps across the Pearl River. If Hong Kong remains the essential city on the east bank, the bridge will end in Hong Kong. If Shenzhen will eventually dominate, it will end there. We are here confronted with an entirely new interpretation of both the city and infrastructure. Why connect Hong Kong, the metropolis par excellence, to Zhuhai, a flowerbed? Asking the question is answering it:

of course each flowerbed needs a metropolis and vice versa. It suggests a new notion of **A-SYMMETRY©**. The bridge's profile could be unequal: privilege flows from Hong Kong to Zhuhai – make it a Metropolis – hinder traffic in the opposite direction.

In the Pearl River Delta we are confronted with a new urban system. It will never become a city in the recognizable sense of the word: each part is both competitive with and has a relationship to each other part. Now these parts are being stitched together by infrastructures, so that every part is connected, but not into a whole. We call this new model the **CITY OF EXACERBATED DIFFERENCE (COED)©** – a city that does not imply the stability of a definitive configuration because each part is unfixed, unstable, and in a state of perpetual, mutual adjustment, defining themselves in relation to all other parts. At first sight the model of the **CITY OF EXACERBATED DIFFERENCE©** appears brutal, to depend on the robustness and primitiveness of its parts. The paradox is that it is in effect delicate and sensitive. The slightest modification of a detail in any one point requires the readjustment of the whole to reassert an equilibrium of complementary extremes. I think there is an analogy to some of the models that are current in avant-garde architecture. The city has become a **BUBBLE DIAGRAM©**. That contemptuous term that has haunted the avant-garde with its implications of the diagrammatic is now at the end of the 20th century coming back with a new luster of the primitive and clarity. In this model, infrastructures which were originally reinforcing and totalizing are becoming more and more competitive and local. They no longer pretend to create functioning wholes, but now spin off functional entities. Instead of network and organism, the new infrastructure creates

This thesis project was conducted at the Graduate School of Design at Harvard University as part of the author's Harvard Project on the City. Rem Koolhaas and the China Group: Bernard Chang, Mihai Craciun, Nancy Lin, Yuyang Liu, Katherine Orff, Stephanie Smith, with Marcela Cortina and Jun Takahashi.

REM KOOLHAAS IS PRINCIPAL OF THE OFFICE FOR METROPOLITAN ARCHITECTURE (OMA) IN ROTTERDAM AND PROFESSOR AT HARVARD UNIVERSITY'S GRADUATE SCHOOL OF DESIGN.

enclave, separation, and impasse – no longer the *Grand Recit* but the parasitic swerve. This new definition of **INFRASTRUCTURE**© is closely related to the new use of **A-SYMMETRY**©: all phenomena that restore, maintain, or intensify the inequalities that define the **CITY OF EXACERBATED DIFFERENCE**©.

I want to conclude this presentation with this image, in which you see a city that is undeniably a city but also unrecognizable in our terms: an endless, formless amalgamation of the urban condition merged with/turned into a landscape. At a smaller scale each fragment/visual frame of this condition always contains a mountain, a rice field, and a skyscraper. We propose **–SCAPE**© as a name for this condition to suggest that the focus of need, the focus of usefulness is shifting away from architecture, not entirely to landscape but to an intermediate condition. **–SCAPE**© is neither city nor landscape. It is a new urban condition. It will be the arena of a terminal confrontation between architecture and landscape. It can be understood as an apotheosis of the **PICTURESQUE**©, in itself a hybrid of the English and Chinese traditions. Only the **DICTATORSHIP OF THE EYE**© can establish the relationships between these objects savagely arranged on the **TABULA RASA**© for our inspection. Any one of us is able to talk with a certain authority about events in Asia, how urbanism is rampant there, etc., even if it goes without saying that we have no Chinese architects in the audience today. For me, the critical question is whether every construction in China doesn't irrevocably change the notion of architecture everywhere else, even here. Does this "new" city change the notion of city everywhere else?

Beatriz Colomina

Reflections
on the
Eames House

The theme of this conference, "Anyhow," has presented me with a dilemma. How architects practice is the stated issue. But since, like many theorists of my generation, I am an architect who writes rather than builds, should I talk about my own practice of research and writing or about the practices of the architects about whom I write?

It is, of course, a non-question because we cannot separate our work from that of the people about whom we write. Some kind of complex interaction takes place. In writing about architects you reconstruct their practice and at the same time their practice reconstructs yours. That's why every time is different. I am not the same when I write about Adolf Loos or Le Corbusier or Mies van der Rohe or Eileen Gray or Frederick Kiesler or Charles and Ray Eames . . . because in each situation I become infected with a different bug.

So I'll talk about the architects on whom I happen to be working at the moment: Charles and Ray Eames. They had a unique mode of practice, which raises some questions for both designers and writers. The Eameses were experts on "time, information, and numbers," the theme of this session. In fact, they made famous films on all three subjects. But what interests me here is that they had a very sophisticated theoretical position, even though they didn't theorize their work in a traditional way. Nor did they have somebody doing it for them. There is no Sigfried Giedion or Nikolaus Pevsner of the Eameses. Nevertheless, they were able to communicate their philosophy with considerable precision.

The oldest published photograph of their most famous project, the Eames House, shows a truck on the site, occupying the place of the house, taking its place, anticipating it. The windshield happens to lie exactly where a glass facade will terminate the building. The

steel frame of the house is being assembled from a crane on the back of the truck as it steadily moves down the narrow site carved out between a steep hillside and a row of eucalyptus trees. It is said that this process took only a day and a half.[1]

The Eameses immediately celebrated. A sequence of photographs shows the ecstatic couple holding hands under the frame, then stepping off the retaining wall onto a thin beam suspended like a tightrope across the space, and finally posing in the middle of the beam, still holding hands. Ray has a white bird in her raised hand.[2]

The Eameses liked to celebrate things. Anything. Everything. This was not just whimsy, a distraction from the work. It was part of the work itself. Walking along the beam of the house under construction was the beginning of the occupation of the house. They were literally moving in, even if the crafting of the basic fabric of the building was to take almost a year. The house became an endless process of celebration over the course of their lives.[3] When they walked across the steel tightrope before the tent had been pulled up over the frame, they were launching an intense program of construction through festive play. Every stage of the play was recorded, photographed, and disseminated to an international audience.

Circus, it turns out, was one of the Eameses' fascinations. So much so that in the mid-1940s, out of work and money, they were about to audition as a clown act when a financial deal related to the production of their plywood furniture came through.[4] When in 1970 Charles gave the prestigious Charles Eliot Norton Lectures at Harvard University, he concluded the first of his six talks by presenting a three-screen slide show of circus photographs that he had been shooting since the 1940s. The 180

Previous page: Charles and Ray Eames on the steel frame of the Eames House under construction, 1949, from John Neuhart, Marilyn Neuhart, and Ray Eames, Eames Design: The Work of the Office of Charles and Ray Eames (New York: Harry N. Abrams, 1989), 108.

images were accompanied by a sound track featuring music and other sounds recorded at the circus. Eames turned to the circus because what "seems to be a freewheeling exchange in self-expression, is instead a tightly knit and masterfully disciplined organic accumulation of people, energies and details."[5] In a lecture given before the American Academy of Arts and Sciences in 1974, he elaborated:

The circus is a nomadic society which is very rich and colorful but which shows apparent license on the surface. . . . Everything in the circus is pushing the possible beyond the limit. . . . Yet, within this apparent freewheeling license, we find a discipline which is almost unbelievable. There is a strict hierarchy of events and an elimination of choice under stress, so that one event can automatically follow another. The layout of the circus under canvas is more like the plan of the Acropolis than anything else.[6]

In many ways, this is what Eames thought architecture was, the ongoing theatrical spectacle of everyday life, understood as an exercise in restrictions rather than self-expression. The endless photographs of the

ridiculously happy Eameses displaying their latest inventions are part of an extraordinarily precise and professional design practice. We see them on top of the frame of their house, "pinned" by metal chair frames, holding Christmas decorations, waving to us from inside a Christmas ball, wearing Easter hats or masks, photographing their own reflections in the house, and so on. In almost all of the

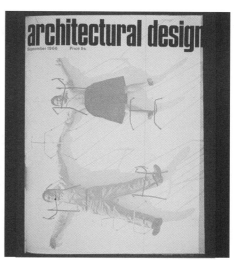

early photographs they wear matching outfits as if to emphasize the performative aspect of their work. The Eameses were very precise about their clothes, commissioning them from Dorothy Jenkins, the Oscar-winning costume designer for such films as *South Pacific*, *The Ten Commandments*, *Night of the Iguana*, and *The Sound of Music* (Ray Eames's distinctive pinafore dresses are even reminiscent of Julie Andrews's dresses in this film). The effect of the Eames costume was that of the professional couple as a matching set, carefully positioned like any other object in the layout. The uniform clothes transformed the couple into a designer object that can be moved around the frame or from picture to picture. The layout, not the objects, was always the statement. And the layout was constantly reworked, rearranged.

If design was not the designer's self-expression, it was the occupant's daily life that left its mark on the house. All the ephemera of daily living would take over and define the space. In the Eames House, the real architecture was to be found in their endless rearrangement of collectibles within it, the

real space in the details of their daily life.

For the Eameses, everything was architecture, from the setting of a table for breakfast to a circus performance. Everybody was a designer. Employees arriving at the Eames office were routinely assigned tasks for which they had no previous experience.[7] It was thought that anybody who applied his or her attention totally, obsessively, to a problem would come up with a good solution, especially if there were many restrictions, such as limited time, materials, or money. Charles spoke nostalgically of his days at the MGM studios, where he often had only one night to make a whole new set out of a limited range of props.

This idea of design as the rearrangement of a limited kit of parts was a constant in

their work. Everything they produced can be rearranged, no layout is ever fixed. Even the formal lectures were sometimes rearranged in midstream. Kits of parts, movable partitions, "The Toy," plywood cabinets, the House of Cards, the Revell Toy House, and the Kwikset House are all infinitely rearrangeable.

The Eames House is a good example. Not only was it produced out of the same structural components as the utterly different Entenza House (designed by Charles Eames with Eero Saarinen), the Eames House was itself a rearrangement of an earlier version. After the steel had been delivered to the site, Eames decided to redesign the house. He put the same set of steel parts together in a completely new way.[8]

Not just the frame got rearranged. Rather than produce a complete, fixed environment for the postwar consumer, the Eameses offered a variety of components which individuals could construct and rearrange themselves. Their own house was the paradigm: panels shift, furniture moves in and out. The house became a kind of testing ground for all their work. Everything moves in the end. Only the basic frame stays still, and this frame is meant to be almost invisible. A necessary prop – no more than that. As Esther McCoy wrote in a caption for an image of trees reflected on the glass walls of the Eames House: "After thirteen years of living in a house with exposed steel frame, Ray Eames said, 'The structure long ago ceased to exist. I am not aware of it.' They lived in nature and its reflections – and

Left to right: Revell Toy House, Eames Design, 235; Charles and Ray Eames, Kwikset House, Ibid.; Models of Case Study Houses 8 and 9, from Arts and Architecture (March 1948).

reflections of reflections."[9] The house dissolves in a play of reflections, restless images that immediately caught the eye of the world. The Eames House was published everywhere, exposed, scrutinized.[10] The images multiplied and became the objects of reflection. Their appeal was part of the general fascination with postwar America that extended from pop-up toasters to buildings.

of what they saw as new in the Eameses: the attention to seemingly marginal objects (which the Smithsons perceptively understood as "remnants of identity"), the love of ephemera, of colored wrapping paper, and so on.

For the Eameses, gifts were all important. They maintained that the reason they began to design and make toys (the House of Cards, The Toy, the masks) was to give

Perhaps nobody was so captivated by the Eameses, and more lucid about their work, than their buddies the British architects Alison and Peter Smithson. In a 1966 *AD* issue devoted exclusively to the Eameses and prepared by the Smithsons, they wrote:

> There has been much reflection in England on the Eames House. For the Eames House was a cultural gift parcel received here at a particularly useful time. The bright wrapper has made most people – especially Americans – throw the content away as not sustaining. But we have been brooding on it – working on it – feeding from it.[11]

The house as an object, a gift all wrapped up in colored paper. This comment reflects so much of the Smithsons' obsessions, so much

them to their grandchildren and the children of staff members and friends. But the concept of gift extends far beyond the toys. Not only were the Eameses extremely generous with their friends (they once paid for airline tickets so the Smithsons could visit them in California), they understood all of their work as a gift. In an interview Charles said:

> The motivation behind most of the things we've done was either that we wanted them ourselves, or we wanted to give them to someone else. And the way to make that practical is to have the gifts manufactured. . . . The lounge chair, for example, was really done as a present to a friend, Billy Wilder, and has since been reproduced.

Wilder wanted "something he could take a nap on in his office, but that wouldn't be mistaken for a casting couch."[12] In addition to the "nap" chaise, the Eameses designed a "TV chair" for Wilder. An article in a 1950 issue of *Life* magazine shows a multiple-exposure photograph of Wilder moving back and forth on the plywood lounge chair of 1946, claiming that it was designed so that the "restless

work: from house to cabinets, to children's furniture, to toys, to miniatures. Even the architectural models are treated like toys, played with by excited architects and clients acting like curious children. Eames once said that in the "world of toys he saw an ideal attitude for approaching the problems of design, because the world of the child lacks self-consciousness and embarrassment."[13] In Eames

Wilder can easily jump around while watching television."

From the toys, to the furniture, to the houses (which were either designed for their closest friends, John Entenza and Billy Wilder, or as toys like the Revell House and the Birthday House designed for Hallmark Cards in 1959), to the major productions (such as the film *Glimpses of the U.S.A.*, which they understood as a token of friendship to the Russians), to their most complex exhibitions, the Eameses always concentrated on what they were giving and how it should be presented. Everything was thought of as a gift. Design was gift-giving.

The sense of the Eames House as a gift also points to the constant shift in scale in their

architecture everything is a toy, everybody is a child. Perhaps this explains the constant presence of children in the photographs of their work. Since when have we seen so many children in architecture?

Charles and Ray saw everything through the camera. This accounts for the astonishing continuity between work in so many different scales. If the eye is the eye of a camera, size is not fixed but continuously shifting. They used to shoot at everything. This was surely not just an obsession with recording. There is that, no doubt, but they also made design decisions on the basis of what they saw through the lens, as is evident in Ray's description of the process of decision-making in the Eames House:

Left to right: "What is a House?" Charles's illustrations of the activities that new houses should be designed to accommodate, from **Arts and Architecture** (1944); Reflections of trees through glass walls of Eames House, from Esther McCoy, **Case Study Houses**, 55. See also Pat Kirkham, **Charles and Ray Eames: Designers of the Twentieth Century** (Cambridge, Mass.: MIT Press, 1995), 113.

Photo: Charles Eames

We used to use photographs. We would cut out pieces from photographs and put them onto a photograph of the house to see how different things would look. For instance – there was a space in the studio we wanted filled. It was between the depth of the floor where it opens for the stairs. We wondered what to do. We had some pier pylons from Venice pier (we had wanted to keep something of it to remember it

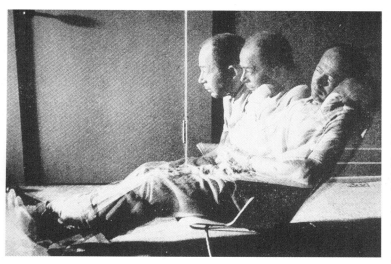

Billy Wilder in Eames chair, from Life (1950).

by). Well, we had pictures of it, glued them onto a photo and decided it worked so we went ahead and did it.[14]

To remember the Venice pier they take a piece of it with them. This is characteristic of the Eameses, who over the years accumulated an astonishing quantity of objects. The pylons can be seen standing outside the house. But to see if they could keep a memory of the object inside the house they used photographs and collage. Indeed, a photograph of the Venice pier ends up filling the space in the house they had tested using collage.

The photocollage method had already been important to architects of the early European avant-garde. Mies van der Rohe photocollaged a drawing of his office building of 1919 onto a photograph of the Friedrichstrasse, glued photographs of landscape, materials, and a painting by Paul Klee to the Resor House drawings of 1938, and glued together photographs of landscape, sculpture, and paintings in the project of the Museum for a Small City of 1942. The structure of the building gives way to a juxtaposition of photographic images. But the Eameses transformed the strategies of the avant-garde. The Eames House "triggered," in Peter Smithson's words, "a wholly different kind of conversation."

The Smithsons wrote: "In the 1950s the Eames moved design away from the machine aesthetic and bicycle technology, on which it had lived since the 1920s, into the world of the cinema-eye and the technology of the production aircraft; from the world of the painters into the world of the lay-out men."[15] This shift from the machine aesthetic to color film, from the world of painting to that of the layout men, from Europe to California, can be traced in the shift between the first and second versions of the Eames House. The first version, the so-called Bridge House, published in *Arts & Architecture* in 1945, seems to be based on Mies's 1934 sketch of a glass house on a hillside. The scheme was rejected in 1947, after Charles went to the Museum of Modern Art to photograph the Mies exhibition, in which the sketch was first made public. Charles must have already known. In fact, he said that he didn't see anything new in the projects that were exhibited, but he was impressed by Mies's design of the exhibition itself. Shortly afterward, the Eameses came up with a new scheme for their house.

The first version, which Charles designed with Eero Saarinen, faithfully followed the Miesian paradigm in every detail. The house is elevated off the ground as a kind of viewing platform. The sheer glass walls are aimed at the landscape, lined up with the horizon. In the original drawings, published in *Arts & Architecture* in December 1945, we see the occupant of the house standing behind the glass, an isolated figure looking out at the world that is now framed by the horizontal structure. The interior is almost empty. In the model of the house published in March 1948, the only

thing occupying the house is the reflections of the surrounding trees, which the Eameses went to considerable trouble to photograph by placing the model on the actual site and carefully superimposing an image of the trees in the foreground. The effect is classic Mies. As in the Farnsworth House, there is a stark elevated interior with at most a few isolated pieces of furniture floating near the glass in a fixed pattern prescribed by the architect.

In the second version the house drops to the ground and swings around to hug the hillside. It no longer faces the ocean. The view is now oblique and filtered by the row of eucalyptus trees in front of the long east facade. A low wall wraps around the patio on the south facade, partially blocking the ocean from the

view of someone sitting in the space and focusing attention on the patio as an extension of the house, as an interior. The dominant focus is now in rather than out. The house abandons the Miesian sandwich, where floating slabs of floor and ceiling define a strictly horizontal view. The floor is treated like a wall with a series of frames defined by rugs, tiles, trays, and low tables on which objects are carefully arranged. In fact, floor, wall, and ceiling are treated in a similar way. Not only are they now given the same dimension (the sandwich being replaced by a box); they start to share roles. Hans Hofmann paintings used to hang horizontally from the ceiling. Ray said that it was necessary to protect them from the strong light and that they "would be able to see them well from that position."[16] Many photographs of the house are taken from a very low angle, and we often see the Eameses sitting on the floor surrounded by their objects. The west wall is clothed in birch because they needed something on which to hang objects. On the east wall, much of the glass has become translucent or is wired ("to make people realize it is there")[17] or replaced with opaque colored panels. The sheer surface is broken up with louvers. The occupants can only see fragments of the outside, fragments that have the same status as the objects that now take over the interior. The view is there but restricted to a few of the many frames. Everything overlaps, moves, and changes. The singular unmediated view is replaced by a kaleidoscopic excess of objects.

The eye that organized the architecture of the historical avant-garde has been displaced by a multiplicity of zooming eyes. Not by chance, the Eameses 1955 film *House: After Five Years of Living* is entirely made up of thousands

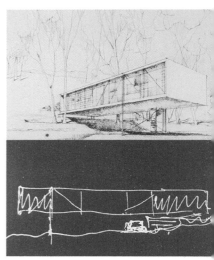

Left to right: Philippa and Miranda Dunne, daughters of screenwriter Philip Dunne, in the Eames lounge chair of 1956, from **Eames Design**, 207; (above) Charles Eames, Bridge House, 1945, from **Arts and Architecture** (December 1945); (below) Sketch for a glass house on a hillside by Mies van der Rohe, 1934, from Philip Johnson, **Mies van der Rohe** (New York: MoMA, 1947, 1978), 109.

of slides. Every aspect of the house is scrutinized by these all-too-intimate eyes. The camera moves up close to every surface, every detail. But these are not the details of the building as such, they are the details of the everyday life that the building makes possible.

The film as a succession of slides is consistent with the house itself. It is impossible to focus in the Eames House in the same way that

Left to right: Mies van der Rohe exhibition at MoMA, 1947; Charles and Ray Eames, Glimpses of the U.S.A. projected on seven screens suspended within Buckminster Fuller geodesic dome, Moscow, 1959.

we do in a house of the 1920s. Here the eye is that of a TV watcher. Not the 1950s TV watcher but closer to that of today – multiple screens, some with captions, all viewed simultaneously. It helps to follow more than one story at once.

To some extent the Eameses pioneered this mode of viewing. They were experts in communication. In 1959 they brought Glimpses of the U.S.A. to Moscow, projecting it on the seven screens suspended within Buckminster Fuller's geodesic dome. Twenty-two hundred still and moving images presented the theme of "A Day in the Life of the United States." Fuller said that nobody had done it before and that advertisers and filmmakers would soon follow.[18]

The Eames House is also a multiscreen performance. But Mies is not simply abandoned.

Indeed, the house takes an aspect of Mies's work to its extreme. When Eames gave up on the first scheme after seeing the Mies exhibition at MoMA, he did so because he saw something else there. In fact, it was the exhibition technique that inspired him. When he published his photographs of the exhibition in *Arts & Architecture*, he wrote: "The significant thing seems to be the way in which he has taken documents of his architecture and furniture and used them as elements in creating a space that says, 'this is what it is all about.'"[19]

Eames was very impressed by the exhibition's zooming and overlapping scales: a huge photomural of a small pencil sketch alongside a chair towering over a model next to a twice-life-size photograph, and so on. He also noted the interaction between the perspective of the room and that of life-size photographs. The visitor experienced Mies's architecture, rather than a representation of it, by walking through the display and watching others move. It was a sensual encounter: "The exhibition itself provides the smell and feel of what makes it, and Mies van der Rohe great."[20] What Eames learns from Mies, then, is less about buildings, more about the arrangement of objects in space. Exhibition design, layout, and architecture are indistinguishable, as Mies had demonstrated in his layout for the magazine G, his numerous exhibitions with Lilly Reich, the Velvet and Silk Café, the Barcelona Pavilion, and so on. Eames picked up on the idea that architecture is exhibition and developed it.

Once again, the Eames House takes something from history and transforms it. The house is an exhibition, a showroom, but it is a different kind of showroom from those of the modern movement. The multiple eye belongs to a completely different consumer. It is the eye of the postwar acquisitive society. While Mies is famous for his comment "Less is more," the Eameses said that their "objective is the simple thing of getting the most of the best to the greatest number of people for the least."[21] The glass box gives way to such a density of objects that even the limits of the box blur. The role of the glass changes. With Mies, reflections consolidate the plane of the wall. The complex lines of trees become like the veins in marble. With the Eames house, the plane is broken. The reflections of the eucalyptus tree endlessly multiply and relocate. The Eameses even replaced a panel on the south facade with a photograph of a reflection of the trees, confirming that every panel is understood as a photographic frame.

The showroom quality of the Eames House was confirmed by its repeated use as a site for fashion photographs. Magazines such as *Life* and *Vogue* inserted their models into the building, lining them up with the architecture, even merging them into the interior elements. In this, the house participates in another long tradition of the historical avant-garde. Ever since the turn of the century, modern architecture has been used as a setting for fashion publicity. In fact, the history of modern architecture is the history of the showroom, the history of a blending of architecture and exhibition. But the Eames House is no longer just a uniform backdrop for fashion designs as discrete innovations. The garments blend into the fabric of the house, mingling with the objects. The accompanying text bounces backward and forward between the "California bold look" of the architecture and the fashion. What is on display in the showroom is the equal status of all kinds of objects. The announcement of Case Study houses 8 and 9 in the December 1945

issue of *Arts & Architecture* shows the silhouettes of the Eameses and Entenza surrounded by the galaxy of objects that defines their respective lifestyles. The role of the architect was simply that of happily accommodating these objects.

Nowhere are the differences between Mies and the Eameses more clear than in the photographs of their houses under construction. A photograph of the Farnsworth House shows the lonely figure of Mies with his back to the camera somberly appraising the empty frame. His enormous figure cuts a black silhouette into the frigid landscape. With his coat on, he stands like a Caspar David Friedrich figure confronting the sublime. At about the same time, but a world away, the Eameses put on their new outfits, climb into their frame, and smile at the camera.

Left to right: Fashion in the Eames House, from Life (June 1954): 90–91; Fashion in the Eames House, from Vogue (April 15, 1954); Mies van der Rohe on the building site of the Farnsworth House, 1945–51, from Mies van der Rohe: The Villas and Country Houses, pl. 21.9 (original photo in Mies van der Rohe archive at MoMA).

BEATRIZ COLOMINA IS ASSOCIATE PROFESSOR IN THE SCHOOL OF ARCHITECTURE AT PRINCETON UNIVERSITY. SHE IS THE AUTHOR OF PRIVACY AND PUBLICITY: MODERN ARCHITECTURE AS MASS MEDIA AND EDITOR OF SEXUALITY AND SPACE AND ARCHITECTUREPRODUCTION. SHE IS CURRENTLY WORKING ON A BOOK ON THE RELATIONSHIPS BETWEEN WAR AND MODERN ARCHITECTURE.

1 The Eameses said that the structural shell of the Eames House was raised by five men in 16 hours. "Life in a Chinese Kit: Standard industrial products assembled in a spacious wonderland," *Architectural Forum* (September 1950): 94.

2 The first one was published in *Blueprints for Modern Living*

(Cambridge, Mass.: MIT Press, 1989), 182, and credited to the Eames office. The second, in "Steel in the Meadow," *Interiors* (November 1959): 109, is attributed to Jay Connor. The third, reproduced here, was printed in John Neuhart, Marilyn Neuhart, and Ray Eames, *Eames Design: The Work of the Office of Charles and Ray Eames* (New York: Harry N. Abrams, 1989), 108. It is attributed to John Entenza.

3 Not by chance they moved into their house on Christmas Eve 1949.

4 Pat Kirkham, *Charles and Ray Eames: Designers of the Twentieth Century* (Cambridge, Mass.: MIT Press, 1995), 150. See also Saul Pett, "Charles Eames: Imagination Unlimited," *St. Louis Post-Dispatch* (July 27, 1971): 3.

5 "1970, Charles Eliot Norton Lectures: Lecture 1," *Eames Design*, 356.

6 *Bulletin of the American Academy of Arts and Sciences* (October 1974): 13–25, as quoted in *Eames Design*, 91.

7 Kirkham, *Charles and Ray Eames*, 89.

8 While many sources insist, following the Eameses, that the new version used only those parts already delivered to the site, with the exception of one additional beam, Marilyn and John Neuhart question this: "A count of the seventeen-foot vertical girders needed for both house and studio yields a total of twenty-two for the first and sixteen for the latter, considerably more than would have been needed for the first

version of each. In addition, there do not appear to have been any seventeen-foot girders in the original house. Additional trusses would also have been required to accommodate the reworked plan." *Eames House* (Berlin: Ernst & Sohn, 1994), 38.

9 Esther McCoy, *Case Study Houses 1945–1962* (Los Angeles: Hennessey & Ingalls, 1977), 54. First published in 1962 under the title *Modern California Houses*.

10 In addition to *Arts and Architecture*, the Eames House was published in *Architectural Forum* (September 1950), *Architectural Review* (October 1951), *Arquitectura* (Mexico, June 1952), *L'Architecture d'aujourd'hui* (December 1953), *Interiors* (November 1959), *Domus* (May 1963), *Architectural Design* (September 1966), etc.

11 Alison and Peter Smithson, "Eames Celebration," *Architectural Design* 36 (September 1966): 432.

12 "Q&A: Charles Eames by Digby Diehl," *Los Angeles Times WEST Magazine* (October 8, 1972): 14.

13 "Eames, Charles," entry in *Current Biography* (New York: Wilson, 1965), 142.

14 Ray Eames in an interview with Pat Kirkham (July 1983), Box 61, The Work of Charles and Ray Eames (WCRE), Manuscript Division, Library of Congress.

15 Peter Smithson, "Just a Few Chairs and a House: An Essay on the Eames-Aesthetic," *Architectural Design* (September 1966): 443.

16 "We hung them off the ceiling for two reasons — one was because they needed to be kept away from strong light and the second was because we thought we would be able to see them well from that position." Ray Eames, interview with Pat Kirkham (July 1983), Box 61, WCRE, Library of Congress.

17 Charles Eames as quoted in "Life in a Chinese Kit," 94.

18 Letter from Buckminster Fuller to Ms. Camp (November 7, 1973), Box 30, WCRE, Library of Congress.

19 Charles Eames, "Mies van der Rohe" (photographs by Charles Eames taken at the exhibition), *Arts & Architecture* (December 1947): 27.

20 Ibid.

21 Charles Eames quoted in "A Designer's Home of His Own," *Life* (September 11, 1950): 152.

Discussion 4

Charles Jencks Greg Lynn said that his supplier told him that it didn't matter how many changes he wanted to make in his bananas, because they just weighed the bananas to determine the cost. I asked the people who are building Frank Gehry's Guggenheim Museum in Bilbao how much more it cost to make each of the 26 petal shapes slightly different. They said that it cost maybe 10–15 percent more, which is not a greatly appreciable difference. I then asked them why the exterior skin is made up of titanium shingles that are all the same. Why, on these big forms that are self-similar, do you get a self-sameness as if Mies van der Rohe had detailed Gehry's building? The answer: it would have been incredibly costly if they had to change all of the panels. Each titanium panel was prebent at the factory — prefabricated for a particular curved context. The building had been designed all the way through with one kind of thinking, but when it came to the skin, the old thinking prevailed for cost-effectiveness.

Greg Lynn One issue that connects this question with Rem Koolhaas's and Adriaan Geuze's presentations is that of scale. In another project that we are working on, the Korean Presbyterian Church of New York [see **Anybody** (MIT Press, 1997), 162–73], we could use every element as standardized, mass-produced. Because of the scale of the repetition, by subtly realigning each one we didn't have to redetail it to achieve a continuous undulation and curvature. In the Austrian project, which is much smaller, we had to engineer the curvature into every component. There are two approaches: one uses stock, standardized systems and varies them slightly — slight variations within a series that add up to a large-scale curvature; and the other details every curve in the building. There are certain scales of construction at which things are either cheap or exponentially expensive. We assumed that you wouldn't want to touch structure because it's more expensive than cladding, which is just simple sheets. But we found that structural systems, especially wood, aren't as low-tech as you might think. Most of the fabricators are already computerized, in some cases more computerized than the architects. Basically, the constraints are site- and context-specific.

Rem Koolhaas Your presentation was really exhilarating, but very close to the end there seemed to be a break that you didn't talk about. Your other project — like my other car is a Porsche, your other car is a Korean church — intensifies it. When it came to the sections there was a point of acute disappointment because, in spite of your bold declaration that linguistic issues were utterly misguided, it looked like a church of a very well-known typology. Giovanni Michelucci, an Italian architect, did a series of autostrada churches, and your project reminded me of it. That's a neutral comment. Then you claimed that you never change your mind — and I don't understand why anyone would be proud of that — but obviously that gives great importance to the initial triggering decisions. It seems that the most critical triggering decisions were an alignment with the sun and an alignment with the motorway, so in the beginning there is crushing banality and at the end there is churchlike architecture; in between there is spectacular and exciting intelligence. Will it ever be different, or do we have to find a moment that the initial parameters are more intelligent or have more to do with culture? Will there be at the end a way in which you can control the religious dimension?

Lynn I'm aware of the Michelucci similarity, although it's more a relationship to speed, more an autostrada church than just a church. I was shocked and concerned when I saw the Swiss highway pavilions yesterday, but that was another resonance. Ours has to do with a certain speed at which you experience the exterior of the building and a certain relationship to the autobahn that gives it its particular scale and shape.

Koolhaas Yet we're used to the high percentage of cubic objects next to autobahns.

Lynn Those cubic objects aren't designed to take advantage of the sequence, they are more like billboards for moments. The scale, repetition, and alignment of the components in Michelucci's work might be similar to this because you are about 10 meters away when you drive by.

Koolhaas The intelligence in a project like this is of a highly abstract nature. It's only able to absorb program with incredible limitations, like the receptacle of a projection. It's empty, and you use the walls. Now I'm beginning to understand the Jeff Kipnis strategy. Maybe his absence here is even part of that. There was going to be a series of connected statements that you probably worked out with a great amount of coordination that somehow would explode like a small landmine and in the end completely change the landscape.

Lynn The approach is highly improvisational at the level of equipment and machinery. The most important triggering decision in all of the projects is the software. We know the limitations and techniques in the software; we know what it can show, what gradients it can produce. We start by making the decision about what software we're modeling on and then progressively build information into the system. We start very generically with combinations of off-the-shelf software and improvisationally try to build our design strategy. The initial decision isn't a judgment so much as it is an envelope of potential. Now, the strategy for the conference with this group was highly loose. I don't know who these supposed five are, or even if there are five, but the idea was to come and improvise and see if we could make connections.

Koolhaas There's still the issue of the religious overtones. Greg, do you think you can ever cure, or are you a mystic? I am trying to write a better conclusion for you.

Lynn I always feel a little out of control of the symbolism and the reception of this work. I've got a good handle on the techniques and the machinery, but the expression it produces is something we can't anticipate at the beginning. Part of working machinically is that you don't know what it's going to look like and you don't know what it's going to symbolize. You just know how it's going to work.

Beatriz Colomina This reminds me of our previous conversation about Frederick Kiesler in Buenos Aires, and some claims that were made about the way new technology produces forms that didn't exist before. Arata Isozaki pointed out the similarities between Ben van Berkel's project for the Yokohama International Port Terminal and Kiesler's Endless House. Michelucci didn't have your software. Would it be disingenuous to say that his mechanistic somethingness comes from your history, from your archive of images from architecture? I think that's an important issue in light of the discussions that we're having today on the question of the relationship between theory and architecture and history and architecture. You are quite adamant that we have no use for history. You don't think that it's relevant to the practice of architecture today.

Lynn The representational effects of the projects aren't usually used as representational effects. Like the project in Austria, we decided ironically to use this triangular logo as a structure for the building knowing that in the end it wasn't going to be a triangle. We also tried to use it opportunistically because we knew the corporation would be excited about having a logo building.

Koolhaas Ironically? Isn't that a horribly charged word?

Hubert Damisch It's not only the triangle, which is a two-dimensional figure. You also called it a tent, an idea that is very loaded with symbolism. You cannot speak in terms of representational effect when you start with representation. Tent is representation.

Lynn It's also a structure.

Damisch I agree, but it's a structure that is a metaphor from the very beginning.

Koolhaas Do you see any similarity between yourself and the Chinese architects I discussed?

Lynn They don't seem to be very technically advanced. It seems that given the scale, the volume, and the time in which they have to produce, the projects could be facilitated by the kinds of technology we're using. Things such as repetition and differentiation, for example. With a computer program like the one I use, you could spit out urban plans in an afternoon that would probably give you a number of different qualities.

Koolhaas The Chinese issue is not that they don't have plans but that there is no planning, no kind of activity that needs planning.

Lynn It would allow certain kinds of improvisation you couldn't have otherwise.

Ignasi de Solà-Morales Rem, what are you saying? Do you think that the patch-work system in Chinese cities works more like an auto battery than as a sophisticated geometric system? It's important to understand the logic behind this very fast production of large built-up areas. More than Greg's overdetermined geometrical process, it has to do with the decoration of Chinese restaurants or what I like to call a patchwork system or auto-battery system. Both Ben and Greg made many general statements, and I do not understand why Sanford's presentation, which was supposed to be the theoretical umbrella, didn't work in the same way. We have seen a strong range of work where the theoretical bases are more individually elaborated than something that should be considered as a group. The idea of a manifesto suggests that there is a group of people working in the same way. This is very exciting, and the process and the tools are quite evident. The use of schemes as starting points, as in Alejandro Zaera-Polo's work, project ideological statements and are connected to scientific research related to differences in geometry. They have more to do with chaos theory, with the uncontrolled process in which form/shape happens.

Sanford Kwinter I fear I'm going to disappoint you greatly. We were interested in a set of problems that have merged to become a forefront in thought and knowledge today. To embrace and to engage those things some people felt was a kind of imperative for design. All we want to share in common is an approach to, and a willingness to approach, a certain set of problems. The aborted aspect of the manifesto is very important because it means you don't know where you're going. It means that in a sense you are laying down a path as you walk. The insistence on research was really to say we are not afraid of mistakes, we are not afraid of dead ends, and we're also not afraid to make provisional gestures without having an entire overview of what is to come. We would like to feel that our freedom to invent is embodied in the concept of a chaotic system or an ergodic system. We don't know where it is going, and we would like to reserve the right to incorporate all ideas and technologies that even provisionally seem appropriate at a given time. It's a wavering response, but we're interested finally in establishing the foundations and the conditions of possibility of a program.

Phyllis Lambert I want to discuss changes in technology. Charles Eames, for example, was extremely interested in technology. He felt that mass production allowed you in principle to produce many different shapes, and he was distressed by the failure to do that. Jørn Utzon's Sydney Opera House, similar to Greg's project but designed before the advent of the computer, was very complicated to draw and build. Frank Gehry is very conscious of the fact that you can only take so many elements that are skewed out of a regular pattern to build economically, which leads me to China. How do these people build so fast? How do they design so fast? Are they using a computer system that allows them to speed up the process? Gehry incorporates the building process within the computer, and if a specification isn't right, he changes it and they import it right into the machine and fabricate the pattern from within the computer itself. Is this happening in China? How else could they build so fast?

Koolhaas China relies on an incredibly limited repertoire of moves. The issue of fixity or stability in the building is addressed in a very new way. First you finish a building, and then you start to convert it, it's like a two-phase operation. First you make it unfit, and then you retrofit it. This is also happening in planning. For instance, we asked if they work according to **fengshui**, and everyone said that they don't recognize it as a very interesting issue. In other words, first they do it in a Western way, and then when things don't work, they have a retroactive **fengshui** that corrects any number of mistakes. It's an idea about the provisionality of everything, and that's why China represents a challenge.

What maybe should be revealed to the conference is that underlying this whole discussion is the notion that maybe five years ago the point had come in architectural history to write a manifesto for a new architecture. I remember discussions with Kipnis and being excited about the new but remaining totally unexcited about the architecture and about the notion that there even was architecture. For me, the Chinese condition fundamentally erodes the status of architecture because ultimately you replace one incredibly intricate architecture and one very intellectual architecture with another very intellectual architecture. Therefore, even though your revolution/manifesto is partly bold, it is also extremely sedate in the sense that it is another version of the same thing. I recognize the originality and the potential, because it obviously has enormous potential, but there is still something that fundamentally assumes that architecture is important, that it will remain important, that form is important, that this sacredness which you cannot control so far is finally an important part of a whole continuous thing.

Saskia Sassen This is a question about capacities and resistance at the most abstract level, and it comes out of Greg's and Rem's presentations. Greg seems to be dealing with a technology that allows him to play with endless permutations. The temporality issue matters here – having the computer allows you to run through sequences in a duration that makes it viable. You have a resistance, which is why these rounded shapes come out as religious. Your resistance is that you have to gain some sort of container or closure, because you could run those same permutations on very different kinds of axes. I'm wondering how you negotiate the illusion of indefinite permutations. I say "illusion" because on some level they could be endless, but it is an **illusion** of endless permutations. To what extent can the resistance that you negotiate alter the outcome? There is a certain tendency to go in a certain direction once your resistance is a container rather than a totally open space. In the case of Rem's Asian urbanscape – enormous capacities, no plans, no constraints, this rolling building machinery – what are the constraints? What are the resistances that are also at work besides the geography? Is there something more complex that's at work that counteracts the sense of an undifferentiated operation that you often get from reading about cities and urbanism in Asia? I'm sure there are resistances.

Lynn I need to respond to both Phyllis and Saskia. I think the industrial model of mass-produced standardization was a certain impasse, but the more we ask the right kinds of questions, the more we find out that shape has nothing to do with mass production anymore. Instead of asking how we are going to achieve these kinds of variations, the question really becomes, how do you do a box? What's the logic to do a box when the construction industry is set up to give you variations that don't need those kinds of standard components? It becomes an aesthetic question about the kind of repetition you want, and we try to temper the aesthetics with constraints. The computer programs give us an open system for development, and then we ask, what are the structural constraints, what are the programmatic constraints? We build those things in and let different kinds of contingencies set up the rules that regulate our design process.

Peter Eisenman I was struck by the similarity among the three architects who presented – Greg, Rem, and Beatriz. First of all, Rem speaks of Greg's work as intellectual, but all we have to do is walk down the street a few hundred meters, and we find a very intellectual project by Rem. We are looking at three architects presenting three very intellectual aspects of their work. What I'm struck by is that when I look at the pictures of the towns in China that Rem showed, the question becomes, what to do? When I look around Rotterdam and see these three little white houses over here, I think, aren't they fantastic in the context of this place? Isn't it fantastic that we have Rem's building in the context of this place? Architecture is always about an intervention, it doesn't matter what the scale is, but it's always about the quality of the work. Great cities are not made by great architects, they are made by pieces that intervene in the urban fabric. I would love to see pieces by Greg, Rem, and Beatriz in the fabric of that Chinese town, but they're never going to change the whole thing. Ninety percent of the working architects can't make buildings of quality no matter how much they learn. It's not a question of scale or time, it's a question of being able to do qualitative work. I for one would like to applaud Greg, Rem, and Beatriz and the others for their presentations because I still believe that quality will always overcome quantity.

Hans van Dijk How does this work relate to the traditional concept of the body of architecture, the library of knowledge? Rem said that Greg had a very banal start and ended up with a church and that in between there was a lot of intelligence and process. It's not very interesting to discuss Michelucci or origami as we did last year with reference to Eisenman's Church for the Year 2000. The process in between is very interesting and new, but is there a beginning to these kinds of design processes that can be related to the library of architecture or the body of architectural knowledge? Greg, is it important whether you start with a logo or a triangle or a tent with a symbolic meaning? Does that relate your work to the body of architecture? In a few years can we expect a lecture from Beatriz that shows as many complexities in your work as she showed in the work of the Eameses?

Colomina One of the issues today is the question of the relationship between writing and design in architects' work. It's a long tradition; architects have always written, always theorized their work. But what is the relationship between writing and design? In architecture we are in a very peculiar situation in relation to other disciplines, other artistic forms. For example, artists may say something about their work, but they never pretend that this theory will explicate their work. This takes place on the side, as another thing that is said in a different medium. I question this necessity to make this kind of pronouncement that presents the work. I agree with Rem that what happens in the middle is more interesting, though I would prefer that the walls stay where they are and the drawings and the designs where they are rather than attempt to explicate the work or to justify it in some possible dimension.

The other question is, does the architect need a lawyer? Do we need a Sigfried Giedion for every significant architect of our generation? We don't need that any longer; in fact I'm more interested in what the architects have written than in the explanations given by history and art historians and theorists of their time.

Lynn What ties this whole panel together in my mind is that the emphasis was put on methods or techniques, which seems right for an Anyhow conference. This allows me not to be too phased when I get hit with Utzon, Michelucci, or Gehry, all things that stick to the work but don't stick to the process or the broader sensibility. You don't need a Giedion for process, and you don't need a Giedion to explicate the work, but you do need a Giedion for a sensibility. What is missing is a kind of design sensibility about an approach to process and constraints. How is a shared sensibility about what's important set up? Is it about the end product and what it looks like and what its affinities are with history or about the affinities of the process? I liked the Eames talk because there's a certain sensibility in the Eameses' work about process and improvisation and continually reworking a design that I think would be a shared affinity.

Colomina The Eameses are interesting because they didn't have that lawyer; they were on their own and they were profoundly nonverbal people. We don't need critics for their sensibility, perhaps for something else, like publicity.

Koolhaas I want to combine Saskia's question about the limits of resistance and Hans's question about the moment. Would it be possible for Greg to connect this work to the cultural trigger rather than to a purely mechanical trigger? This kind of conference is an enclave where both architects and critics can believe in their own importance, but actually the situation is very different because the fact that Greg's initial point of departure was a logo is the cultural statement. What are the limits of resistance, or where is the resistance? What is happening is that architecture for the first time is in a situation without real supporters because there is the market. We all float up and down with it. That phenomenon, which is actually pretty new and characterizes the last 10 years, is overwhelmingly at odds with the pretension of architecture to be important and to be able to make important statements. We, as Sanford is saying, are at a forefront of new thoughts, at a forefront of new techniques, but we are not at a forefront of new needs. On the contrary, we are spinning in an increasing banalization of need, and Greg's exhibition stand for an oil company is one of them. This may be one of the rare moments that you can actually lose something. The denial that we collectively share is this banalization of need and our dependence on it.

Lambert I want to take up this issue of sensibilities. Beatriz said that she likes to read what the architects say, that we don't need a Giedion, although she becomes the Giedion for the Eameses. We might consider, similar to what Damisch was saying, that the NAI and the Canadian Centre for Architecture (CCA) are about creating sensibilities in a much broader public and about creating sensibilities for the architects who cannot get their information in other ways. You cannot leave the public out of it. You cannot leave out the fact that architects work in an environment in which people have to **want** to build these things. In China it's a bit different.

Damisch My point was about the capacity of architecture to deal with history. When you deal with the issue of the museum of architecture, it is a place to deal with history — what you're doing at the CCA is typical and emblematic in a modern way. We have to deal with history in the making, not with the history of the past — collecting beautiful objects, models, projects. You are working in the same way as they did in the 18th and early 19th centuries, providing models, in the epistemological sense, for living architects, for architecture as it can be. What does that mean that architecture still has to do? It has to demonstrate its capacity to deal with history. I like the idea of a Holocaust Museum because it's very important to deal with in terms of a museum and how such an institution can deal with something that represents such a blast in history that it destroys the very idea of history. This is not the past because it represents the State of Israel and the American Jewish community. The only way of approaching the issue of the Holocaust Museum is in strictly architectural terms, not in ideological or political terms, which means that we have to understand how architecture has the capacity to deal with that history. What's going on in China is very revealing. Do they have a project or not? We all heard about the organization, about the global market being very structured and organized, but what about the project behind it? Is it only a project in terms of growth and profit, or is it a historical project?

Project, Program, Future

John Rajchman

I would like to suggest a kind of pragmatism. One might say a "new pragmatism," as it takes up lines started by the classical pragmatist philosophers, but under new conditions. I will call it a pragmatism of diagram and diagnosis. Its role in this session of the conference is odd, for it supposes a relation to a future that we can neither program nor project. It is about forces that we can't predict, with which we can only experiment – about what William James once called "things in the making." My larger question is how to engage in pragmatism at a time when we are told with an air of self-evidence that we have entered the brave new world of "global information societies." I think we need to break a bit with this self-evidence. What I have in mind is not a pragmatics of communication or information typical in such societies, but rather a manner of questioning, of seeing unforeseen singularities that those societies serve to unleash.

Of course there are more familiar senses of "pragmatism" that fit better with the erosion of the powers of the state in which globalization discourse delights. For example, in opposition to Mao Zedong, Deng Xioping is called a pragmatist. He declared practice to be the sole criterion of truth, though the pronouncement derives authority from the Party – an odd destiny for what the first pragmatist Charles Sanders Peirce said was incompatible with any party, any church, since it works through dissent and divergence. Today a pragmatist is often thought to be someone proud to have nothing to do with ideological program, theory, position, or larger vision, content to devise efficient ways of solving specific local problems. My "diagrammatic pragmatist," while concerned with a future that one can neither program nor project, while working outside anything like a party bureaucracy, is quite different from this. Let's take an example. We might talk of "diagramming and diagnosing" the new geographies that emerge with the crisis in the great invention that is Imperial Europe, the national-social-state, as it was overdetermined by colonialism and then the Cold War.[1] For globalization is more than a "transnational" homogenization of conditions; it is, at the same time, a loosening, a vacillation of borders shown in mixtures or "hybridities" and the questions they pose. We might thus talk of "diagramming" spaces in Europe in contrast to inserting them in the old geopolitical map of the "great nations" of the last century or even in that supranation called "Europe" with its unelected Brussels administrators. We might thus diagnose new forces of a European racism: focused on immigrants, assuming different guises according to the different "imagined communities" or nationalisms of the states in which it figures. But what then does such "diagrammatization" mean – what does it do? I'll start with some conceptual distinctions.

In some philosophical circles, words like "functional," "instrumental," "operational," and "utilitarian" have gotten a bad name – what Max Weber called *Zweckrationalität*.[2] Immanuel Kant elaborated a strong view in relation to the "disinterest" that he thought was required by moral imperative, political reason, or aesthetic judgment. One consequence is the place that falls to architecture in Kant's hierarchical classification of the beaux arts. He thought architecture the

[1] For all of these issues see Etienne Balibar, *La crainte des masses* (Paris: Galilée, 1997), especially the essays on what a border is, what the borders of Europe are, and what European racism means.

[2] By this Weber meant the kind of rationality set by goals or ends in contrast to the kind concerned with deciding which ends, or goals one ought to pursue.

most "interested" of the free liberal arts – the most tied to money, market, government, and instrumentality, hence the lowest, the least free, the least beau of all. Of course, there would be many avatars of this idea of disinterest that Kant took to be freedom. It is found in the heroic image of a reductive or self-critical formalism railing against an increasing functional society, in the "critique of instrumental reason" proposed by Max Horkheimer and Theodor Adorno, and again when Martin Heidegger, reacting to Friedrich Nietzsche's diagnosis of the "ascetic ideal" in Kant's doctrine of aesthetic disinterest, proposed to "retranslate" it as mystical *Gelassenheit* ("letting be").

It is therefore interesting that the term *pragmatisch* (pragmatic), which Kant introduced into philosophy, had another purpose or "point of view" that expresses another kind of question. That in any case was the thesis of Michel Foucault's *thèse*, which consisted of a translation of Kant's *Anthropology from a Pragmatic Point of View* lectures. Foucault stressed that *pragmatisch* is neither instrumental nor practical and may even problematize the exclusive division between the two. It is rather "experimental" in the sense of that word found in writings of pragmatists and in Nietzsche when Zarathustra declares, "Society is an experiment, o my brothers – and not a contract!" Foucault associated the "pragmatic" in Kant with a problem that even Jürgen Habermas would later agree besets much post-Kantian critical philosophy: that of the empirical and the transcendental. Looking back we can now see that the various "transcendental conditions," subjective or objective, which the post-Kantian philosophers would propose, were in fact all patterned on some element from empirical domains that they were supposed to condition or ground. The "pragmatist" way out of this dilemma was then to rethink the very sense of "critical." The critical question becomes how to see and to conceive new forces that exceed and problematize assumptions that normally function as "transcendental." It becomes a question of how, in the absence of a priori or transcendental conditions, prior to what "determines" us as subjects, objects, members of communities, we may yet "invent ourselves" and our worlds. Peirce derived his word "pragmatism" from Kant; and in all of the philosophers whom we today call pragmatists we find formulations of this basic question – in Peirce's attempt, against Laplacian determinism, to introduce chance into the question of how, in Dewey's attempt to introduce "contingency" into social history, and again in what James called "the problem of novelty" – the problem of how to deal with "things in the making," how to see and respond to the emergence of things for which we have no preset manner of seeing or responding.

Foucault himself went on to develop this pragmatist question in a new way when, following the events of 1968 in Paris and Prague, his work took a more explicitly political turn. He then tried to elaborate a "strategic" (not to be confused with "instrumental") conception of the workings of power and the role of critical philosophy in them – power as strategy, philosophy as conceptual toolbox. I'd like to look at one aspect of this process that focuses on the word *diagram*, as when Foucault said of Bentham's *Panopticon* that it is a "diagram of power reduced to its ideal form." When Deleuze called Foucault a new cartographer, a new archivist in the city, we might then say he was a man with a diagram rather than a plan, a program, or a project.[3] He was someone who had worked out a diagram of a partially unseen kind of power or power strategy at work in many different institutions and situations — an ingenious "abstract machine" functioning in many ways, not to be found on the official map of policies and prescriptions, planned as such by no one. The basic problem to which the machine was addressed was a problem of population — in Foucault's words, what to do about "the accumulation of men."[4] In effect it was a machine to "individualize a population" by dividing up the space and time of its activities, which would gradually prove useful for a wide range of things and in a great variety of settings. We see it, for example, in new differentiations of domestic space, in the emergence of worker cities, and in colonial modernizations.

4 Michel Foucault, "The Eye of Power," in Power/Knowledge, trans. Colin Gordon (New York: Pantheon Books, 1980), 151.

Of course, to sketch a diagram of a "disciplinary society" was not to say everything was completely, hopelessly "disciplined." It was only to say that this partially unseen "abstract machine" was still at work in it. But what then was the point of drawing this diagram? One answer comes from Foucault's conception of the archive. What is the point, for example, of establishing the archive, which lets us see why "prisons resemble factories, schools, barracks, and hospitals which all resemble prisons?" Foucault said he wanted such an archive to function as a sort of "diagnostic" — he wanted it to suggest an untimely future that we can't program or project, but with which we can only experiment. Thus he declares that the archive is not concerned to "sketch in advance what we will look like" but, on the contrary, with breaking with such continuities, to confront us with the fact that we are in the process of becoming something other, we know not yet what.[5] With the archive would go a "pragmatic" sense that we are made up of "differences," or processes of complexification and differentiation of futures unknown. Deleuze proposed this precept for the Foucauldian archive: "not to predict but to be attentive to the unknown that is knocking at the door." In this sense, it is through the archive that Foucault tried to introduce a "time of the diagrammatic" into history; in Deleuze's words, he wanted to turn history into the "negative condition for an experimentation." Such was the pragmatism of his diagram, his diagnosis.

Put another way, we may say that Foucault's diagram and diagnosis came at a time when the great abstract machine of the disciplines was in fact not working so well, when it was entering into a crisis in relation to new forces that it was no longer able to contain. Having advanced it, Foucault himself entered into a crisis. He came to a fresh conjecture concerning the "failure of political theories nowadays." He thought we could analyze the various strands of "liberalism," whether they appeal to markets or to civil society, as attempts on the part of the modern state deliberately to limit itself so as to better perform its characteristic functions with respect to populations and their relations with territories and resources; one outcome of such a "reason of state" was the geopolitical confrontations of the great nations of Europe that began in the 19th century. In other words, in the mid-1970s Foucault "diagnosed" that we were living through a crisis in the "welfare-warfare-state" as a basic matrix of our "political rationality" and were in the process of becoming something

3 See Gilles Deleuze, Foucault, trans. Brian Massumi (Minneapolis: University of Minnesota Press, 1988). In Politics/Poetics documenta X – The Book, Daniel Defert describes in some detail how architects close to Tafuri helped make the theme of "heterotopia" seem basic to Foucault's analysis of space, as such it would later be introduced into geography by Edward Soja and others. Perhaps Deleuze's focus on "diagram" (around the same time) might today indicate another direction.

5 See Gilles Deleuze, "What is a dispositif?," in Michel Foucault, Philosopher, ed. and trans T J Armstrong (New York: Routledge, 1992), 164ff Deleuze draws attention to the relevant passages concerning "diagnosis" from the Archaeology of Knowledge, saying that they fit with all of his work. For example, the "diagnosis" consists in asking what new "subjectivization" we might yet invent given that there is a sense in which, in relation to sex, we are no longer Greek, no longer Christian, no longer even Freudian. "Diagnosis" is one sense of the word kritis, from which we get our term critical. It belongs to the link between "critical" and "clinical" that Nietzsche helped introduce into philosophy.

else, we could not yet quite say what; and I think that our worries and divisions 20 years later over how much of the welfare apparatus to retain while insuring that we are "competitive in global markets" would have seemed for Foucault only to confirm and extend this diagnosis.

In any case, we might distinguish two aspects of the "diagram of discipline" that Foucault had worked out archivally in the 1970s, both emphasized by Deleuze. The first is that it came at a "diagnostic" or critical moment, a pragmatic interval between the disciplinary formation and something as yet undefined such that we must experiment, and experiment with ourselves, in order to see it. The second is that among the "new forces" of this "critical moment" were those of biotechnology and digital devices and the new arrangements or assemblages that they help create in and among us – forces now taken for granted as part and parcel of "globalization." These forces or arrangements called for new diagrams, new diagnoses, new experiments. Of course, the diagram of the disciplines had been, among other things, one of architectural and urban spaces, and the question thus arises whether we might find something like this "pragmatic cartography" of new assemblages or arrangements in what is called "the new urbanism." I think several features of this urbanism might usefully be seen in this light.

First, the crisis of the decline in the centrality of Taylorism and factory discipline might also be seen urbanistically in the relics of declining industrial sectors photographed, for example, by Bernd and Hilla Becher. The new forces that displace the diagram might then be found in formations that tend in one way or another to depart from the "reason of state" with which the disciplines came to be tied up, leading to a new kind of problem. The problem is not so much of environments or spaces that are excessively organized, controlled, or "rationalized" in the Weberian sense but rather of ones that are increasingly random, diffuse, disparate, thin, often even surreal, ones that therefore *work* through other forms of the accumulation and interconnection of men and women – through other "diagrams." To see what is at work in them, we need to readjust our mapping techniques. In particular, in the ultrarapid, large-scale developments that we see in Asia and may yet see in Africa, we need to draw new diagrams, which, in the absence of fixed models or maps, suggest discrete possibilities of intervention.

Second, this cartographic readjustment requires new ways of thinking about space and time or about *espacement* (spacing). For the disciplinary diagram basically worked through segmentations of space-time in interlocking closed environments, and against it arose the protest of another time, another memory, and "duration" prior and irreducible to it, as for example in the waves of Virginia Woolf, where a life is imagined to be composed of multiple irregular bits combined in ways that can never be turned into a perfect narrative continuity – what Foucault at one point called a revolt of time against space. Now, however, we have formations that look rather different from the segmented assemblages of the mechanical city as depicted, for example, by Fernand Léger in his 1919 painting *Men in the City* or in Fritz Lang's 1927 film *Metropolis*. We have other "smoother" sorts of accumulation and interaction, and the question of how to diagram and creatively or experimentally deal with them arises, as earlier with the critical question of a duration irreducible to segmentation.

Third, to "diagram" these new kinds of *espacement* is in effect to deal with them through something akin to the pragmatism I am trying to sketch; one might say that a "gay science of the city" works through diagram and diagnosis rather than through a plan, program, or project. It is a style of analysis, thinking, perhaps even of design, in which a city-diagram-experimentation relation replaces the older state-program-ideology relation typified by Marxism, in which the old mystico-literary theme of allegory and utopia is replaced by the pragmatic one of diagram and diagnosis of new urban conditions.

Understood in this way, the "diagrammatic" in the gay science of the city brings us back to the old questions of form and meaning. They are formulated in one way in Deleuze's attempt, in contrast to the assumptions of classical perspective, to envisage looser and more dynamic sorts of "spacing"; at the close of his study of the "images" in postwar cinema, he drew a contrast between the mechanical city and a new "brain-city" that displaces it. Different diagrams, different "automatisms" go with each city, and they serve in turn to bring out the differences between the mechanical and energetic or the mechanical and digital or smart kinds of machines and machinic arrangements. In particular we see relations between brain and city, nervous systems and environments unlike those we previously imagined through the classical paradigms defined by relations of eye to nature or figure to landscape. Problems of "diagramming information" take over from the problems, tied up with earlier techniques of drawing and painting, of inserting distinct objects or figures into compositional wholes, as if seen through a classical Italian window or located within an existing frame or fixed set of coordinates. The question then becomes: What kinds of images, signs, meanings are thus made possible?

Pragmatism is not opposed to the question of how things, including buildings, make sense. Perhaps one could say it is a matter of introducing a certain indefiniteness, multiplicity, vagueness (or, as it is now said, a certain "complexity") into it. Thus Peirce, inventor of pragmatism, experimenter, and philosopher of chance, also helped start semiology; with his transformation of the idea of truth went an altered "logic of sense." Today Peirce is admired for a semiology that is directly visual and not subordinate to language as in Ferdinand de Saussure's work; Peirce's concept of the "index" is still alive in art-historical debate. But if we then think of signs or images as specific to "mediums" and their possibilities, their conditions of invention and reinvention, what about architecture – what about "diagrammatic" signs or images in it?

The diagram was of course part of Deleuze's own semiology. He worked out a contrast between diagram and code in the pictorial arts as well as in music. It was part of his general attempt to envisage an interstitial "spacing" prior to Albertian procedures to depict distinct figures in perspective and recount illustrative stories about their interrelations. Thus in contrast to Vasily Kandinsky's dream of a pure pictorial code of shapes and colors, there would be the diagrams of "other movement" in Paul Klee, the contourless abstract lines in Jackson Pollock, and the "a-signifying marks" in Francis Bacon, which suggest other possibilities within a given "pictorial fact." But can we then conceive of such an uncoded "diagrammatic" dimension in architecture or the specific ways that it acquires its meanings? Today's talk of "dynamic topologies" and "vectoral images" seems to suggest one idea.

We might recast the diagram-code distinction in architecture in this way. We might call "diagrammatic" those images or spaces that introduce other "possible movements" not predetermined by an overall program; they are those that, in contrast to classical composition of fixed elements in well-formed or organic wholes, work through connections in multiple disparate spaces, allowing for relations of mixture, hybridity, contamination, simultaneity; they thus let unforeseen things happen rather than trying to insert everything into an over-arching plan, system, or story. The diagrammatic dimension thus helps free an older idea of "function" from absorption or negation by a purist aestheticism while undoing its identification with preprogrammed stories or sets of interrelations. One might thus talk of a "new functionalism" concerned with the complex insertion of architecture into an environment, characterized by a new problem: that of "re-singularizing" a milieu or environment by releasing something unforeseen, as yet "pre-subjective" or "a-signifying" into it. The "sense" of a building would then no longer be given through an "embodiment" of something that predates it, not even a "world" in the phenomenological sense of the word; it would "make sense" in ways that depart from monumentalizing or commemorative impulses traditional to architecture. For where a monument conserves and makes public something one is supposed to remember, a diagram sets into motion unforeseen connections and the new possibilities that they release or introduce. It is thus concerned with accumulations and connections of people in another way and through a different kind of "spacing," which Deleuze suggests when he talks of an architecture of *trajets et parcours* – not "the pharaoh's tomb in a central chamber at the bottom of the pyramid," he writes, but rather "more dynamic models: from the drift of continents to the migration of peoples."[6]

What then does the "new pragmatism" – the pragmatism of diagram and diagnosis that I have been trying to imagine – involve? What does it do? In the first place, the diagrammatic supposes a pragmatic relation to a future that is not futuristic, not imagistic. It is concerned in the present with those multiple unknown futures of which we have no image just because we are in the process of becoming or inventing them. It follows that the diagrammatic requires and excites different kinds of solidarity or "movement" among us than those of the traditional avant-garde group, the organization of a political party, or even a nice progressive social-democratic public sphere, inasmuch as those forms rest on the presumption of a future we are able to know and master. The diagrammatic "mobilizes and connects" us in other, indirect ways that work more through linkages, complicities, and alliances that grow up around new questions or in response to new conditions or forces than through adherences to the prior supervenient generalities of a theory, a project, or a program. Perhaps in this way the pragmatism of diagram and diagnosis might help transform the sense of what is "critical" in our thought and our work. It might help move beyond the impasses of older images of negative theology, transgression, or abstract purity and introduce a new problem: that of resingularizing environments, of living an indefinite "complexity," prior to set determinations, which questions the simplicities and generalities of our modes of being and suggests other possibilities. Such a pragmatism would differ from the "communicational" or "informational" pragmatics promoted by globalization discourse – it ties creation and resistance to the present.

6 Gilles Deleuze, "Ce que disent les enfants," in *Critique et clinique* (Paris: Minuit, 1993), 81ff. What children say (that they try to explore the milieu through dynamic maps, and draw out the map or diagram) is shown in particular by Fernand Deligny's diagrams of odd movements of autistic children. They might well be read in tandem with Klee or Bacon. The terms *trajet* and *parcours* often occur together in Deleuze's late writings in *Essays clinical and critical*, notably in the introduction, where they are used to say what a work or "oeuvre" is. For example, the expression "architecture of *parcours* and *trajets*" is used to describe Nietzsche's labyrinthine motion of Earth in the essay "Ariadne's Mystery" first published in English in *ANY*, no. 5 (March/April 1994). "Trajet" means passage, crossing, journey, way; as a verb, "parcourir" means to travel through or traverse, and so see or look-over, and a "parcours" is then such a course, line, way. The conceptual use Deleuze makes of the pair of terms seems to be connected with two problems: (i) the "trajectories" or "goings-through" suggested by the terms may be said to make or draw a space, or to involve a time, that is not pregiven or predetermined as by a prior plan. (ii) the "jet" in "trajets" comes from the sense of "throwing," that Latin puts into such words as "subject" and "object", and one might say thus that "trajets" here refer to a kind of "throwing through" space and time prior to one given by the traditional sense of objects represented for subjects.

JOHN RAJCHMAN IS PROFESSOR AT THE COLLEGE INTERNATIONAL DE PHILOSOPHIE. HE IS THE AUTHOR OF TRUTH AND EROS: FOUCAULT, LACAN AND THE QUESTION OF ETHICS AND MICHEL FOUCAULT: THE FREEDOM OF PHILOSOPHY. HIS ESSAYS ON ARCHITECTURE ARE COLLECTED IN CONSTRUCTIONS, PUBLISHED IN ANYONE CORPORATION'S WRITING ARCHITECTURE SERIES WITH MIT PRESS (1997).

Joost Meuwissen

The Virtuous Horse or Empiricism In Urbanism

My second home, Austria, has the highest suicide rate in Europe. Because of this, one of the primary functions of architecture, vis-à-vis certain building codes, is to prevent people from killing themselves. One of the main criteria for designing a window, for example, is to prevent a person from throwing him or herself out of it. This is the case for much of Middle Europe.

While we're talking about this, I find it a little astonishing and a bit embarrassing that 30 years after Gilles Deleuze wrote *Difference and Repetition*, architects are still discussing difference rather than repetition. Deleuze argues that all differences, all ideas, are false conceptions, except for what he called free difference, which can only be thought of in terms of repetition – dumb or, as Deleuze puts it, "naked" or "complicated" repetition.

Instead of reality, architects discuss ideas. This might be due to the fact that the American translation of *Différence et répétition* was too long in coming to have an impact on the architectural debate that, at the time of its publication, was dealing with "the fold." The folds and computer curves that have subsequently been generated, however, are even more repetitive than the accompanying theories suggest.

Architecture, as the art of repetition that could eventually produce free difference, offers a preferable alternative. Such an architecture or urbanism would not be about representation, diagram, language, ideas, the construct, or space but about empirical reality, big or small.

It is just such an architectural empiricism that needs to be formulated.

Repetition is the basis of such empiricism because unlike difference, which is generally thought of as difference within a symmetrical world, repetition involves what Deleuze calls an "asymmetrical synthesis of the sensible world." While architects like to establish the vertical asymmetry that unfortunately they consider a matter of gravitation and not of architecture, they show no real awareness that left and right or front and back are fundamentally asymmetrical relationships.

Following a very modest and very simple 19th-century Kantian approach, Deleuze argues that space is ultimately an intensity, not an extensity. However, the possibility of extensity can be said to emerge from the external, from a point or amount, for example. Not a category or idea on its own, a categorical definition of extensive space relies on the Nietzschean question: "What is it to extend space?" or even "Who is extending the space?" The extensity of space thus always refers to some reality. According to Deleuze, these other lines of thought suggest that a specific extension of space is always limited (real *extensio*, or confined extension), that such a real, confined extension is specified by a certain quality or filling in of that real extension, and that its being there must not remain undiscovered – it must be recognized. The latter concept, which Deleuze calls *quale*, is the specific

designation of an extension; space might be a point or a thing or a chimney or even a nonspace but it is *not* a phenomenon![1] This is not only a rejection of phenomenology; it is also and above all about *empirical reality*. As space is part of empirical reality, it is not *merely* extensive.

It is thus amazing that architects still consider space a natural or conceptual extensity in which the folds and curvatures of architectural volumes have to take place. Besides Rem Koolhaas, the only exception to this general naturalist view seems to be Saskia Sassen's nonextensive digital money space. Yet we know from experience that such a progressive conception will be adopted by architecture as yet another dull metaphor within naturalist space.

THE VEGETARIAN DOG

By its nature, or rather by the fact that most architectural theories from the past were about

The architects Matthijs Bouw and Joost Meuwissen overlooking the site at the Maxglan–Stiegl/ASK area, Salzburg, Austria (July 11, 1996), where 600 residential units will be built.

1 Gilles Deleuze, *Différence et répétition* (Paris: Presses universitaires de France, 1972), 298.

Photo: Thomas Pucher

idea, the construct, tectonics, extensive space, and representation and not about architecture as part of reality, there is no general theory of empiricism within architecture. These design methods, however, can be traced to architectural thought from the past, through Karl Friedrich Schinkel, Josef Plečnik, and Ludwig Mies van der Rohe, for example.

There is still no richer source of architectural thinking than Schinkel's *Das architektonische lehrbuch* written in the first half of the 19th century. The book unfortunately remained unpublished until 1979, one year after Koolhaas's *Delirious New York*. (How's that for architecture!) Architecture is awkwardly out of touch with its own history.

Since architectural *thinking*, contrary to the field's various solipsistic and idiosyncratic *theories*, has not been a well-defined category or tradition in the past, even in philosophy, one might argue that a *philosophical* empiricism might be the right approach to the many unanswered questions, unsolved problems, and failures that architecture as a tradition contains. In *Lehrbuch*, Schinkel presents an architectural history of mistakes, the failures of Palladio and Bramante, all of them boiling down to the same reproach: they made shapes that were incomprehensible within their own systems of understanding.[2] A philosophical empiricism would guarantee to

architectural thinking the complete freedom that it has always had, including the freedom to make mistakes, while at the same time stating that such thinking could logically only have been affected by experiences. In *Enquiries Concerning Human Understanding*, David Hume writes, "all this creative power of the mind amounts to no more than the faculty of compounding, transposing, augmenting, or diminishing the materials afforded us by the senses and experience."[3] The two beautiful examples that Hume gives to explain this line of thought – one external, the other internal – are, from the moment one thinks of them as architecture, funny: the golden mountain and the virtuous horse, both of which are not merely collages but simple, buildable architectures.

For many, Hume might be the hero – or villain, for that matter – of representation or of confining thinking through the conviction that thoughts and ideas must reflect reality rather than being real themselves. But for us, as well as for Deleuze, who wrote his first book on Hume, he is a philosopher of empiricism. With Deleuze, we are more Humean than Hume. That is why, in our office, we replaced the virtuous horse with the virtuous dog; the virtues we associate with a dog are more specific than those of a horse. A horse might be thought of (and in our and

Hume's culture is indeed thought of) as virtuous by nature. It is easy to imagine the virtues extending over the whole horse or, rather, any specific virtue extending over the whole horse in the same (and therefore unspecified) way. With a dog, especially the dog that bites you, it is more difficult to find a virtue that permeates the whole dog. We call it "the vegetarian dog," which is highly empirical and not derived from nature: in the history of mankind, or dogkind for that matter, we know for sure only of one vegetarian dog: Adolf Hitler's. And that very special dog is difficult to realize in architecture today. You would have to change the whole idea of our urban iconography. Realizing Hitler's dog would be one of the key projects of empirical architecture today, one which takes its empiricism really seriously.[4]

THE GOLDEN MOUNTAIN

Hume writes, "When we think of a golden mountain we only join two consistent ideas, *gold* and *mountain*, with which we were formerly acquainted."[5] To join these does not presuppose the existence of a third element, say space, in which gold and mountain could be joined. With Hume, they are joined in the mind, not in space, time, language, or diagram.

One might argue that a golden mountain would still

2 Karl Friedrich Schinkel, Goerd Peschken, *Das architektonische lehrbuch*, ed. Margarethe Kühn (Munich: Deutscher Kunstverlag, 1979), 97–100.

3 David Hume, *Enquiries Concerning Human Understanding and Concerning the Principles of Morals*, reprinted from the posthumous edition of 1777 and with introduction, comparative table of contents, and analytical index by L. A. Selby-Bigge; third edition with text revised and notes by P. H. Nidditch (Oxford: Clarendon Press, 1975), 19.

4 This project was published but not very well understood in Monika Zimmermann, ed., *Der berliner schloßplatz* (Berlin: Argon, 1997), 112.

5 Hume, *Enquiries*, 19.

6 Gilles Deleuze, *Empirisme et subjectivité: Essai sur la nature humaine selon Hume* (Paris: Presses universitaires de France, 1972), 138.

7 Rem Koolhaas, *Delirious New York: A Retroactive Manifesto for Manhattan* (London: Thames and Hudson, 1978), 200–4.

Behind: Kendler Street in Salzburg, Austria. The residents complain about the amount of traffic.

Right: Jean-François Millet, **The Angelus**, 1857–59, 55.5 x 66 cm, Bequest of Alfred Chauchard, 1909, RF 1877, Musée d'Orsay.

consist of two natural, extensive elements, gold and mountain, which share their natural extensions within space and time and can only be brought together in that sense. This, however, would not take into account that within natural space and time a golden mountain does not exist and that the extendability of these natural elements as we know them is always limited. Their shared extensions, their possible overlap within nature, would result in golden mountains in nature, something that has eluded even the most persistent prospectors. So the combination must have had another cause or a different origin. The golden mountain is not solely about artifice either; people searched for it because at any moment it might have been found.

Gold and mountain are thought of as two intensities that can extend themselves into each other while never forming a fixed system. Gold might just as well extend itself into something else, like rain. A relationship between gold and mountain does not represent anything, or rather what it might stand for is not a direct result of their relation. It is the opportunity, not the motive, that the mind designs.[6]

Golden mountains are exactly the kind of questions that architects confront when, for instance, people ask for a blissful, quiet, low-density, landscaped, villagelike suburbia combined with all of the facilities that are thought to be only possible in high-density developments: art galleries, museums, Ethiopian restaurants, delis, airports, subways. As John Rajchman has written, the pragmatist's answer to these wishes would be problematic, diagrammatic, and unwillingly critical. It would sound something like: "Sorry, folks, you just cannot have everything. I don't want to promise you golden mountains. You have to make up your mind. It's either city or village. I cannot make both of them at the same time. There's no urbanistic recipe for that. You have to choose. This is a democracy, you have the right to choose."

The empiricist's answer would be: "Ye want a golden mountain? Ye bet ye get it." As the pragmatist deals with what is possible within the framework of existing design techniques, the empiricist looks for the impossible within an existing situation and develops new design techniques to realize the unexpected. The empiricist breaks the frame of existing design techniques, just as people's wishes always break the frame of the reality in which they live. This technique might be called *hyperempiricism*. It results in a reality that is more intensive, more unnatural, and, above all, more public.

That is exactly what Koolhaas was up to when he described Manhattan as a self-transcending project in his 1978 *Delirious New York*, by means of the paranoid-critical method, adding what he calls a "false fact" to reality. The "false fact" destroys the existing reality to reach a new, unnatural reality without the rules and orders by which the previous reality determined the false fact to be false.[7]

The image that Koolhaas uses to illustrate and explain this method is Jean-François Millet's *L'Angélus*, a 19th-century genre painting showing a man and a woman standing in a field near a church, whose bells must have rung to announce that it is time for the Angelus prayer. The couple is frozen in prayer. Koolhaas describes how the Catalan painter Salvador Dali assumed that if the man is frozen, he must be completely frozen not because the prayer would not be complete if some of his parts were not frozen but because this young French peasant finds his parts very easily frozen. He hides his erection by holding his hat in front of his trousers before his erection space.

As a hypothesis, the presence of the erection cannot be easily proven. This was already a general problem within psychoanalysis, which was held unscientific by empiricists like Karl Popper because within this reality we cannot actually *see* the erection behind the hat. What does it look like? How big is it? As an architect, I would be interested in what it looks like, how the thing has been built up, its *tectonics* or lack of tectonics.[8]

THE NORMAL ERECTION

Koolhaas and Dali answer these questions by means of overdetermination, a method at the heart of psychoanalysis. By accident or not, the woman's head and red cap look like the head of her lover's penis. The wife mimics her husband's penis! This commonality is thought to be in turn overdetermined by the two *identical* bags behind them.

This mode of analysis through overdetermination starts with the identity of a symmetrical relationship because otherwise the two things compared, by one overdetermining the other, would not compete at all. Presumably, Koolhaas and Dali did not take the sexual intercourse, the next stop in the image's narrative, seriously. It was not considered to be important or *specifiable* enough to be adopted as a visual or even tactile "fact" *within* the analytic framework of the picture itself. Amazingly, with respect to this paranoid-

critical interpretation, the two things hidden from the picture, the erection and the subsequent sexual intercourse, are not linked at all.

During sexual intercourse the erection again disappears, leaving much to the imagination. An analysis of the picture suggests that Millet was far from naive. In pornographic films, in order to prevent this type of disappearance, which becomes boringly suggestive during actual intercourse, many completely unnatural positions were invented, including praying Angeluses. In the painting, the man and woman have intercourse. He does not cover his erection for moral reasons but because if it were exposed, the intercourse would stop. It is a highly specific posture through which the actual intercourse has been divided into two figures or, as Deleuze would call them, series linked by the fact that they both have hats. The specificity of the scene is drawn from the prayer that gives the painting its title because only at prayer or in church would a man take off his hat and a woman put on hers. Her penis-like hat is not so much a reminder that his erection is rightfully hers but that sex has been painted as something that, as a general idea or program, cannot be simply remembered. The painting shows sex as a complicated repetition.[9]

In the Koolhaas and Dali interpretation, however, the

picture's hidden agenda, its script or program, its "retroactive manifesto" is about sense, not about repetition. (This was the 1970s approach.)

What is politically not correct in this painting or in its interpretation is that within the image the human figures have to be made identical because one serves the other. Within this interpretation, the man is primary and the woman secondary. She is only wearing her pressing cap because the man hides his erection. If the man had shown his erection, the woman would have been able to wear whatever hat she wanted, the beautiful Balenciaga hat she always desired, or the Dior, or even the baglike Paul Poiret dress that would have freed her body from the constraints of traditional clothing and not confined it in some painful, overdetermined, erect tectonic shape.

In his analysis Koolhaas spoke about a "fact" and not about ideas. *Delirious New York* is one of the few books on architecture that talks fact, not idea. As opposed to an idea, a fact is never new. It is not an event either. It is hidden. It was hidden in the past. As in Sigmund Freud's "subconscious," it is defined as a repetition, a neurosis, or an irresistible urge to mistakenly repeat something from the past. In the Millet painting, such a fact, Koolhaas says, looks quite normal, and the more normal it looks, the

8 A short survey of Dutch architects – Rem not being the only one – who in the 1970s adopted psychoanalysis instead of the then more generally accepted semiotics, as a method of reading architecture, and their tremendous influence on Dutch urbanism is provided by Crimson, *Re-Urb: Nieuwe plannen voor oude steden*, intro. Michelle Provoost and Wouter Vanstiphout (Rotterdam: Uitgeverij 010, 1997), 48–59.

9 Deleuze, *Différence et répétition*, 136.

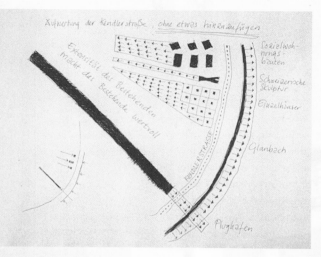

Behind: Master plan for the Maxglan–Stiegl/ASK area, Salzburg, Austria, 1996–97, model.

Above: Master plan for the Maxglan–Stiegl/ASK area, Salzburg, Austria, 1996–97, diagram showing the principle of repetition. The whole of the scheme consists of only repeating what is already there: social housing, electricity plant, single family houses, airport landing strip, and river.

better it succeeds in destroying the reality that held it to be false. Accordingly, from the programmatic point of view, if there existed such a thing as a normal erection, this erection would look normal.

As such, a fact in no way represents the reality to which it contributes, nor does it represent the reality resulting from adding the fact. It has nothing to do with small, differentiated ideas that thematize whole projects and buildings as cozy individualities. The question is how to find this "fact" that hides itself, that looks pretty normal, and that definitely does *not* contain the new. One answer might be that if we would consider any fact to be a false fact, this problem of recognizing the falseness of a fact would be solved easily and smoothly. From that might result an empiricism without the criticality and without the paranoia of the paranoid-critical method, as Koolhaas calls it, an empiricism not obsessed with the

falseness of repetition. Such empiricism would not work through overdetermination, as in the case of the two human figures overdetermining each other in the Millet painting, but through underdetermination, liberating each figure, element, or thing from the constraints exerted by the configuration in which it happens to find itself.

If we remove the paranoid and the critical from Koolhaas's 1978 position, acknowledging that the two were the result of having had one too many picnics with Michel Foucault while discussing discipline and punishment as a general disposition of institutions producing false facts, then empiricism suggests an architectural pragmatism that transcends and breaks the frame of existing design techniques, thus breaking the frame of what seems possible now, and developing new ones. As such, empiricism can substantiate a positive pragmatism, without which it would have no direction and no possibility to generate the new.

THE COMING-OUT GARDEN

If repetition is the basis of difference, we do not know beforehand, when repeating things, what kind of difference will emerge. Dumb repetition, because it always repeats something, involves a careful and highly empirical research about what is actually repeated.

But then the repetition starts to differ slightly from what is repeated, or rather the repetition always becomes more complicated. From this complicated repetition comes a difference yet unknown.

In developing our housing scheme for Salzburg in 1996, we worked along these lines. People in the area were very happy with the loose configuration of meadows, single-family house settlements, social housing, and commercial buildings. They did not want anything new. They loved living in their "European suburbia," without the walls that U.S. suburbs use to lock themselves out of the cities. We agreed with them. They knew best. We didn't build anything new. We decided not to impose a rigorous new scheme on the area but to intensify carefully all that was existing and all that was beautiful.

So we started to repeat. Starting from the main road, we repeated the social housing by proposing social housing. We repeated the single-family housing with single-family housing. We repeated the power station proposed by the Zurich-based architects Bétrix & Consolascio, which they describe as "a sculpture in the landscape," by proposing a series of "sculptures in the landscape." We repeated meadows, dead-end streets, and, most importantly, the looseness of the area. We took this looseness very seriously: it meant the collapse of all things systematic and all overdetermination.

Subsequently we could differentiate the existing in order to incorporate all programmatic and other requirements in our master plan.

At the southern side of the planning area we insisted on keeping the meadow open to maintain the continuity of landscape. To do so, we increased the density of the projected dwelling areas. For the elderly housing, however, financed by a Berlin firm and to be sold to affluent retirees, we wanted to keep the housing low and accessible. The existing houses

were repeated and subsequently differentiated according to the programmatic needs of the future residents.

If we don't think of a garden as a plot of land, in a "territorial" way, we can argue that having a party and barbecuing, growing flowers and vegetables, and looking at it all have different territorial requirements. The first is pretty fixed, the second depends on the

individual, and the latter is not territorial at all.

In order to keep the meadow open we had to give it a fixed status. We divided it to accommodate every house in the elderly complex. Each received a garden measuring one meter wide by up to 350 meters long. In this public-private partnership, the 200 retired lawyers who rent the plots make future development of the meadow impossible.

These strip gardens, in function and appearance, move from suburban garden out into the landscape. Near the homes they will be used and cultivated but farther out into the meadow, many gardens will stop being cultivated and become meadow themselves.

Together, they also form a plowed field. This is illustrated by a drawing derived from Koolhaas's reference to Millet's L'Angélus in Delirious New York. In realizing L'Angélus, 20 years after having read Delirious New York, we had become so delirious that we made the simple mistake of thinking that the painting was in the book because architecture, according to Koolhaas, should look that way. We mistakenly thought of the painting as an example of good architecture or urbanism. We sought to realize a Koolhaas proposal that he himself had completely forgotten to realize. In this, we added to the tradition of mistakes that is architecture, a new and highly unexpected mistake.

To underline the public character of the gardens, we established a public function in the collective garden of the nursery home, replacing Millet's 19th-century church with a 20th-century Duchampian beer pavilion. The beer pavilion, which we are now designing with artist Berend Strik, designates the area's public character and acts as a pivotal point within the landscape.

Territorially, the scheme made it feasible to think aspects as different as land ownership, leases, maintenance, infrastructures, and parking in a very unsystematic way. Instead of the usual coincidence of zones and resulting overdetermination of boundaries that impede the continuity of the existing landscape, each of these could be negotiated independently. Land belonging to owner A could be leased by developer B, maintained by corporation C, feature a road primarily used by D, but appear completely public.

To find the tools or techniques to deal with the swift economy of public/private and private/private partnerships within the planning process, we have to give up the overall systematic of the spatial and territorial a priori of planning. Space and territory, or language and diagram, no longer mediate content. Instead, they become a product of hyperspecific questions, demands, and desires.

Behind: Josef Plečnik, Reconstruction of the Castle of Prague, Czech Republic, 1920–32. The obelisk from 1928 ties two irregular squares together. Situated near the corner of the building that divides the irregular squares, it makes the corner disappear by means of repeating it. This solution, of course, was derived from the bell tower in St. Mark's Square in Venice, Italy.

Left: Master plan for the Maxglan–Stiegl/ASK area, Salzburg, Austria, 1996–97, model of beer pavilion designed with Berend Strik.

Right: Master plan for the Maxglan–Stiegl/ASK area, Salzburg, Austria, 1996–97, drawing of the one-meter wide strip gardens at the houses for elderly people, referencing Millet's **Angelus**.

Photo: Michel Boesveld

JOOST MEUWISSEN IS A PARTNER OF ONE ARCHITECTURE, AMSTERDAM, TOGETHER WITH MATTHIJS BOUW. HE IS A PROFESSOR OF URBAN PLANNING AND DESIGN AND ACADEMIC DEAN OF THE FACULTY OF ARCHITECTURE AT THE UNIVERSITY OF TECHNOLOGY IN GRAZ, AUSTRIA. HE IS ALSO PRESIDENT OF THE WIEDERHALL FOUNDATION, WHICH PUBLISHES THE **WIEDERHALL** ARCHITECTURAL JOURNAL. HIS MOST RECENT BOOK IS **ZUR ARCHITEKTUR DES WOHNENS**.

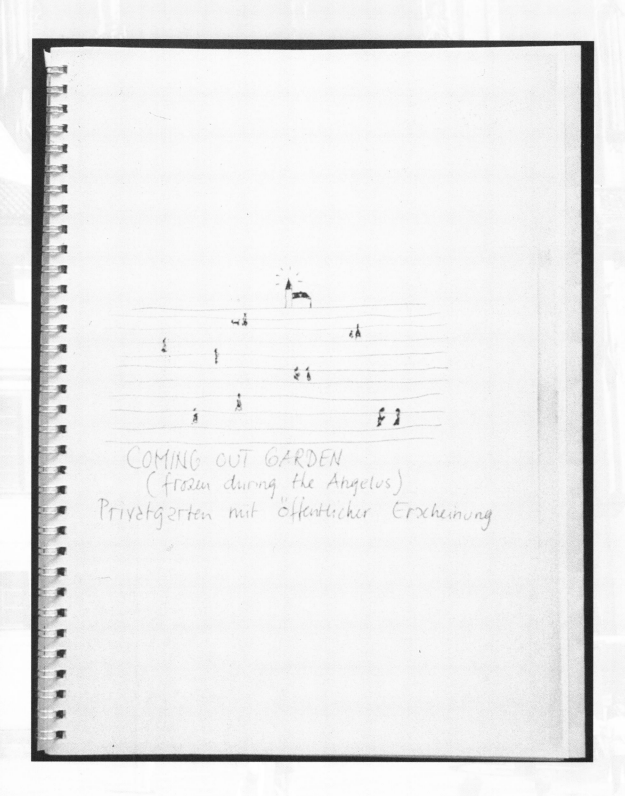

COMING OUT GARDEN
(frozen during the Angelus)
Privatgarten mit öffentlicher Erscheinung

Rosi Braidotti

on Enflesh Memo Power of

In order to practice critical theory today, you
need a new kind of political sensibility. You need
a flair for complexity that does not give in to relativism. I want to defend a political style that is
fluent in the language of complexity and multiplicity yet remains rigorous. Fluidity does not mean
ever-receding boundlessness or amorphousness.
I call this the philosophical style of "as if." This
refers to a practice of strategic repetition aimed
at engendering difference as a conceptual form of
creativity or a qualitative leap out of the **aporias**
of postmodern discourse. I will enact here a few of
these strategic repetitions in the mode of a conceptual opera. They are variations on the theme of
bodies and memories in the geopolitical space of
the European Union.

PROLOGUE

There is a shared conviction among many
"post-" intellectuals (modern/industrial/
colonial, etc.) that the critical task of accounting for the social reality of a fast-changing
world that is disaggregating under the acceleration of the digitally clad global economy
is both more necessary and more complex
than ever before. Along these lines I would
argue that the notion of diagrams of the present – in Michel Foucault's sense of the
term – needs to be revised in light of Gilles
Deleuze's nomadic philosophy.

In an attempt to provide a critical redefinition of power relations that moves beyond the
humanist residues of modernism, Foucault
introduced the notion of philosophy as a diagrammatic reading of the present. At the heart
of Foucault's critique of Marxist notions such
as ideology, repression, and hegemony is the
idea of "mapping the present" in terms of intersecting networks of power effects that simultaneously enable and constrain the subjects.

The notion of the diagram undergoes a radical conceptual revision in Deleuze's work, notably – and perversely – in his book on Foucault. Here, the diagrams are not only cartographical devices that enable the tracking of power effects but also concepts, embedded and embodied abstractions that aim at re-designing a framework for the subject that comes *after* – after all the "posts" mentioned above and especially after Foucault.

In an attempt to set the variables that frame our discussion of how to enforce difference through repetition, I will start, following Deleuze's notion of nomadic subjectivity, with the assumption that we can only really know where we are coming from, that is to say, what we no longer are. Retrospective, external, and relational accounts of subjectivity are all that we have. We can only know what we have already ceased to be. I want to stress this because I am aware that, in architectural discourse, the notion of the "diagram" has very different meanings and functions. This clarification may contribute to a clearer discussion between the philosophers and the architects engaged in the Anyhow conference.

Even more important for me is the element of *affectivity* or *desire* invested in and shaped by the diagram of the present. Here too the subject is off-center or external in relation to the flow of affects: desire is what remains unthought at the heart of thinking because it triggers and sustains the power of thinking. This is why – upon closer scrutiny – Foucauldian cartographies must be amplified and made more useful by taking up the challenge of the abstract conceptual devices that Deleuze proposes.

ACT I: RECASTING

As if radically materialist forms of reembodiment and reembeddedness were not only desirable but actually possible.

ADAGIO

A Deleuzian "body" is an assemblage of forces or passions that solidify (in space) and consolidate (in time) within the singular configuration commonly known as "individ-ual." This intensive and dynamic entity is not, however, the emanation of an inner essence along the lines of the classical axiom "Man as a thinking, speaking, mortal animal." Nor is it merely the effect of biologically or genetically inscribed codes. The intensive Deleuzian body is rather a concentration of forces that is stable enough – spatiotemporally speaking – to sustain them and undergo con-stant, though necessarily contained, fluxes of transformation. It is a field of transforma-tive affects whose availability for changes of intensity depends on its ability to sustain and to encounter outside forces or intensities.

In this field of transformative forces, *sustainability* is crucial. It is a socio-symbolic idea of ecological stability in which changes in intensity are directly proportional to the ability to sustain the shifts without cracking. The borders of the framing, or containing, exercise are crucial to the success of the out-come, an affirmative and not dissipating process of becoming.

This is extremely important to prevent nihilism and self-destruction. That the subject for Deleuze be a transformative, affective apparatus is not meant to suggest infinity or limitlessness: that would be the expression of a delirium of megalomania that would flip the subject into a pit of regressive passions. It is a sustainable system that encounters clear limits and, in that encounter, frames a territory or an affective space tolerable for him/her.

ANDANTE

The subject lies at the crossroads with external forces. "Becomings are a matter for geography: it is a question of orientations, of points of exit and entry."[1] The question for Deleuze's subject is not "what" but rather "where" it is.

Neither a sacralized inner sanctum nor a purely social construction shaped by external "forms of production," the subject is rather an in-between: a folding in of external influences and a simultaneous unfolding outward of affects. A mobile entity, an enfleshed sort of duration, the subject lasts in and through a set of discontinuous transformations and remains extraordinarily faithful to itself.

This faithfulness is not to be understood in the mode of sentimental attachment to an "identity" that often is little more than a social security number. Nor is it authentic voice expressing a belief in the importance of one's starving ego, one's petty likes and dislikes. Rather, it is all the more rigorous because it is a more pragmatic expression of a sustainable self-in-process, of faithfulness of endurance. It is the expression of one's continuing adherence to certain dynamic spatiotemporal coordinates. Deleuze's view of subjectivity owes a great deal to Friedrich Nietzsche's anti-humanism. For these philosophers, subjectivity needs to be disengaged from the liberal view of the thinking subject. Rather, subjects can be analyzed in terms of latitudinal and longitudinal forces that structure subjectivity. It is a deeply materialistic view that argues that subjects come in different mileages, temperatures, and beats. Of course, one can change gears and move across these coordinates, but one cannot claim all of them, all of the time. The contemporary fascination of our culture for multiple mutations has come so far that it has engendered (a very genderized) flirtation with disembodiment via a multiplication of virtual embodiments, such as the cyberpunk flight from the body and the fashion industry's obsession with the anorexic body.

Deleuze warns us that a little *less* abstraction would be welcome in contemporary debates about subjectivity. In reflecting upon the subject as a site of multiple becomings, due attention must be given to sustainable limits. That means that the rhythm of the sequences, the selection of the constitutive elements, and other geopolitical variables framing the process of becoming have to be taken into account. This careful selection of the forces involved in the process of becoming prevents a slippage into the fantasy of megalomaniacal expansion. For Deleuze, the reenfleshments of the "intensive" subject take the form of radical immanence: the actualization of a field of forces apt to frame the *singularity* of a subject.

ALLEGRO MA NON TROPPO

Becoming is intransitive, it's becoming nothing in particular, nothing more than what one is capable of sustaining. It is life on the edge, but not over it; it is excessive, but not in a sacrificial sense (exit Bataille). It is not devoid of violence, but is deeply compassionate insofar as it begins with the recognition of one's limitations as the necessary counterpart to one's forces or intensities. It is ethical, following Spinoza's notion of the adequacy of one's passions to the modes and times of their enactment. It is collective-minded and social because it is interrelational insofar as it requires impact with and upon others. It can only be embodied and embedded and is thus a radical form of immanence.

Deleuze's central figuration is a general becoming-minority, or becoming-nomad, or becoming-molecular/woman/animal, etc. The minority is the dynamic or intensive principle of change in Deleuze's theory, whereas the heart of the (phallogocentric) majority is dead. The space of becoming is posited as a space of affinity and symbiosis between adjacent forces; it is a space of dynamic marginality and of affinity between entities at the point where they intersect (Deleuze's "plan of immanence"). Proximity is both a topological and a quantitative notion, both geography and meteorology, which marks the space of common becoming of subjects as sensible or intelligent matter.

1 Gilles Deleuze and Claire Parnet, *Dialogues* (Paris: Flammarion, 1977), 8.

The process of becoming requires the decolonization of the thinking subject in the grip of dualism. This also implies the dissolution of all sexed identities based on gendered opposition. Thus, the becoming-woman is the necessary starting point for the deconstruction of phallogocentric identities precisely because sexual dualism and its corollary, the positioning of woman as figure of otherness, are constitutive of Western thought.

Insofar as Man represents the majority, there is no "becoming-man": he is stuck with the burden of Being. By implication, the various minorities (women, children, blacks, animals, vegetables, molecules) are the privileged starting points for the process of becoming. This is to say that the multiple variables of difference or of devalued otherness are positive sites for the redefinition of subjectivity.

Deleuze suggests an asymmetrical starting position between minority and majority. This means that the process of deterritorialization is dual and minorities can undergo the process of becoming only by disengaging themselves entirely from the unity imposed upon them by opposition to the majority. Common asymmetrical becomings turn the former dialectical opponents (men and women, old and young, white and black, etc.) into traveling companions in the process of undoing the common grounds for their formerly unitarian – albeit dualistically opposed – identity.

Thus, "as if" in the sense of recasting subjectivity is the patient repetition of steps aimed at approximating, through a series of adaptations, the raw simplicity of the forces that shape one's embodied intensity or existential temperature. It is the unfolding of a subject that appears in its bare skeletal structure as speed of remembrance, capacity for perception, empathy, and impact over others. De-essentialized vitalism.

ACT II: REMEMBERING

As if memory could be disengaged from its attachment to and indexation on a fixed identity.

I become, therefore I will have been.

Crucial to this process of becoming is the question of memory. Fixed identity is predicated on a molar or majority subject: white, heterosexual, property-owning, male, and fluent in a standard Western language. A huge data bank of centralized knowledge is relayed through every aspect of his activities. The "majority subject" holds the keys to the central memory of the system and has reduced to the rank of insignificant, or rather asignifying practices, the alternative or subjugated memories of the many minorities. Homogeneous and centralized, the majority subject functions by organizing differences and relaying them to the periphery. Saskia Sassen gives a perfect example of this model: the most digitalized information centers in the world are also the largest urban agglomerates.

In reaction to this vision of memory as data bank, Deleuze activates a minority memory, a power of remembrance without a priori propositional contents, or memories. This intentive power does not retain and retrieve information in linear order. It functions instead as a deterritorializing agency that dislodges the subject from his/her sense of a unified and consistent identity. "I" is not the owner of the portion of space/time that I occupy; "I" is only a rubber stamp, and I am actually only passing through.

What do you do when you remember? According to Deleuze you reinvent yourself on the basis of the very fragments that remain from whatever you are capable of retaining from the past. Like trying to remember a face and sequence of events after a particularly bad hangover, one needs to try and string the pieces together. Remembering in this nomadic mode is active reinvention of a self that is joyfully discontinuous, as opposed to mournfully consistent. It's like picking up a family photo that has nothing to do with your family and finding ample family resemblances. As Deleuze suggests, paraphrasing Virginia Woolf's style of remembrance: it will have been *a* childhood, though not necessarily my own. We must shift from the reassuring platitude of the past ("I remember when I was young") to the openings offered by the future perfect (*le futur antérieur*). This is the tense of virtual reality in that it builds a bridge between past and present. It also conveys the force of the imperative: "We will have been free" amounts to "We have to manage to become so!"

Memories (in this molecular mode) are virtual, that is, perfectly real insofar as they already act as a propelling force within the subject. They are not potential; rather, they exist as embodied modalities in him/her/it and simply await the possibility for actualization: they propel toward and compel to action. It is like walking the tightrope between the possible, the plausible, the half-thought, and the only remotely likely. Actualization requires careful orchestration, i.e., the arrangement of empowering conditions – or spatiotemporal coordinates – that would enable the unfolding of these propelling forces.

In this regard, Deleuze's theory of subjectivity is like a choreography of passions that require an adequate script in order to become (actualized). Whether or not the script is adequate is determined by the correspondence between the structuring elements of the forces at the point of their intersection (plan of immanence). These elements are speed, intensity and capacity to create connections, and the immediate surroundings. The *adequatio* in question is therefore a question of cohesion and empathy between the constitutive elements,

not the correspondence of the individual becoming to some general model or paradigm.

When you remember in this mode, you reinvent yourself as the expression of a longing for the self-in-becoming or the self-as-process-of-transformation, that is, for the self-as-other. It is not about being what I was like before (before what?) but rather about differing from myself as much and as often as possible: a personal overthrowing of the internalized simulacra of the self. Remembering is less about forgetting to forget than about retaking, as in refilming a sequence. It is about differing from oneself: "I will have been free."

In terms of the propelling and compelling power of enfleshed memory, Deleuze's theory of becoming is also a theory of desire: a fundamental attraction to change, to wanting to construct oneself as different. Black feminist theorist bell hooks calls it "yearning." Contrary to those who fear that the proliferation of micro-discourses and molecular practices of becoming will result in a relativistic drift into nihilism, I see this as a productive and affirmative process.

The diversification of the process of memory in Deleuze's philosophy both rests upon and requires a more complex understanding of time. We can distinguish Aion from Chronos as the time of the event, the indefinite, the speed of constant comings and goings; this is the time of becoming. Chronos is the fixed time of being, of stasis and measure. Deleuze's project consists of disengaging memory from the latter and attaching it to the former.

More attention should be paid to the gendered structure of time in Deleuze's thought. Aion, as the feminine mode of becoming, stands for the cyclical and the repetitive, and Chronos, as the masculine mode of Being, for the linear and teleological. One is the longer time of in-depth transformation and the other is the linear time of historical change. As I will argue later, feminism acts on both levels.

All minority subjects, including women, need to act on both times, though the subversive potential is on the side of positive affirmation or becoming. The dual structure of memory also needs to be made more complex. It is absolutely the case that, for the majority, the line of becoming requires an antimemory that would vehicle a nomadic or deterritorializing force. It is equally true, however, that for minorities, it would be of the utmost significance first to have their own data bank of accumulated experience recognized as an official "memory." I must stress this dyssymetry in the respective positions of the majority and the minority vis-à-vis the question of memory.

All this notwithstanding, I would suggest that to enact a Deleuzian becoming, we need new conceptual coordinates. These are not elaborated by voluntaristic self-naming but rather through careful revisitations and retakes. I would describe it as a process of peeling off, stratum after stratum, the layers of signification that have been tattooed on the surface of the body and – more importantly – in its psychic recesses and in the internalized folds of one's sacrosanct "experience." Like a snake shedding an old skin, one must ultimately remember to forget it.

I would like to propose therefore that the classical axiom "Man is a thinking, speaking, mortal animal" should be processed in the same way that Gertrude Stein (who, among other texts, also wrote a great opera) composes her texts. It would then become "Man is a is thinking is speaking is mortal is animal is. . . ." The sequence is open.

As in Stein's operatic prose, what matters ultimately is the recurrence of that process whereby Being – the only verb that, according to Deleuze, has no workable infinitive – gets an irresistible beat and actually starts whirling, opening new spaces of becoming.

ACT III: THE RETURN OF FIGURATIONS

The politics of "as if," or the strategic practice of mimesis.

Feminist thought is a laboratory for picking up the challenge of learning how to think differently. Feminist theory has emphasized both the notion of embodied subjectivity and the need for conceptual creativity. The latter has been expressed as the need for new "figurations," following Donna Haraway, or "fabulations," to quote Marleen Barr. They are needed to express the alternative forms of female subjectivity developed within feminism, as well as the ongoing struggle with language to produce affirmative representations of women. The array of terms available to describe this new female feminist subjectivity is telling: womanist, cyborg, postcolonial, lesbian, queer, post-Woman women, etc.

A figuration is no mere metaphor but rather a diagram, a politically informed map of the present that renders one's embodied and embedded location. I read figurations in terms of the feminist politics of locations that, from Adrienne Rich to Haraway's "situated knowledges," provided the foundations for both feminists' knowledge claims and political accountability. Second, I read figurations with Deleuze's notion of the diagram as an attempt to move beyond the "image of the thought" embedded and inscribed in logocentric philosophy.

The starting point for feminist refigurations of subjectivity is a new materialism that emphasizes the embodied and therefore sexually differentiated structure of the speaking subject. The body, or the embodiment of the subject, is understood as neither a biological nor a sociological category but rather as a point of overlap between the physical, the symbolic, and the sociological. In other words, feminist emphasis on embodiment goes hand in hand with a radical rejection of essentialism. In feminist theory one *speaks as* a woman, although the subject "woman" is not a monolithic essence defined once and for all but rather the site of multiple, complex, and potentially contradictory sets of experience defined by overlapping variables such as class, race, age, lifestyle, sexual preference, and others. One speaks as a woman in order to empower women, to activate socio-symbolic changes in their condition. Accountability is a form of "embodied genealogy."

A figuration expresses one's sense of spatiotemporal location; it marks a point of origin in space and in the sense of historical memory. A location is where one takes one's departure. Highlighted is the political practice of self-reflexivity about one's own location (in both the spatial and temporal sense of the term) and of accountability for it.

Accountability can best be explained in terms of making visible one's implication in the very power formations against which one is fighting. It is a form of self-criticism in terms of one's relationship to power and/as knowledge that Foucault and Deleuze inaugurated in philosophy, even though feminism invented it as a practice. Accountability is a form of "embodied genealogy" that makes one responsible for understanding the conditions of one's existence, a radical critique of one's own embedded and embodied foundations. In its antifoundationalist stance, feminist postmodernism has redefined the political in terms of radical accountability.

One of the crucial points of intersection between contemporary social and political theory and feminist thought is the desire to leave behind linear intellectual thinking, the teleologically ordained style of argumentation that most of us have been trained to respect and emulate. The point for me is not loyalty to existing philosophies but accountability for one's gender: a nomadic feminist is necessarily an undutiful daughter.

In this regard the feminist project intervenes at the level of historical agency in the linear time of patriarchal progression (Chronos) and that of individual identity and the politics of becoming (Aion). It thus engages both conscious and unconscious levels of subjectivity. Identity becomes a site of "as if" formations. Let me give you an example: feminist women go on functioning in society as female subjects in these post-metaphysical days of the decline of gender dichotomies, as if "Woman" were still a significant location. In so doing, however, feminists treat femininity as an optional extra, as the site of available poses and costumes, rich in history and social relations but no longer fixed and compulsory. Woman is simultaneously asserted and deconstructed in a strategy of mimetic repetition.

Strategic mimesis is the process of revisiting and consuming the old, both within and without. What counts as "the old" here is the established definition of the feminine as "the Other of the Same." Mimesis is a constant renegotiation of the forms and the contents of female identity, an inner erosion of the feminine by women who are aware of their own implication in that which they attempt to deconstruct. The purpose of this mimetic exercise is not deconstruction for its own sake but the political project of breaking down old social and mental habits and forms of identification.

To practice "the politics of as if" one must have a flair for these complexities; a political culture of difference must support what would otherwise be only an intimate project of transformation. To illustrate this politics, I would like to take the (hopefully) classical feminist axiom "Woman is a subject inscribed in power via class, age, race, ethnicity, and sexual orientation" and activate it as a set of inner differences that go on multiplying themselves. Once again, Stein's operatic prose. The logocentric gravitational pulls of the sentences would implode under the strain of the repetition: "Woman is a subject is inscribed is in is power is via is of is class is age is race is ethnicity is sexual is orientation is" and so on indefinitely.

What matters ultimately to this feminist politics is repetition. Being gets dislodged from its fundamentalist pedestal and loses the dogmatic authority of its essentialist predicates, exposing at last the multiple "differences within." Being thus becomes activated as a force whose function is to stitch together the different moments that it enacts but does not encompass. The metaphysical weight of Being is reduced to a mere shifter: it drops the pretense of essential continuity on which it erected its imperialist power of signification in order to return each subject to the specific multiplicity of one's singularity. "We," the female feminist subjects of an-other discourse, will have been free.

ACT IV: REFRAMING EUROPE

What if Europe could rethink itself as periphery not as center?

In European philosophy, the project of the politics of "as if" coincides historically with the decline of classical humanism, thus opening up that proliferation of discourses about "otherness" that Arjun Appadurai takes as one of the traits of our era.

This is a topical question because in these days of the renegotiation of the treaty of Maastricht/Amsterdam and the 50th anniversary of the Marshall Plan, no notion is more contested in social theory than that of European citizenship.

Historically, Europeans have perfected the trick of turning themselves into the center of the universe while the rest of the world becomes one huge periphery. The postmodern predicament is — among other things — about the shift of geopolitical power away from the North Atlantic in favor of the Pacific Rim and especially Southeast Asia.

This shift in geopolitical power becomes both confirmed and theorized in terms of the decline of the Eurocentered logocentric system. Philosophers such as Deleuze, Jacques Derrida, and Massimo Cacciari have pointed out one perverse aspect of this shift: what makes Western philosophical culture so perniciously effective and so seductive is that it has been announcing its own death for over one hundred years. Since the apocalyptic trinity of modernity — Marx, Nietzsche, and Freud (and Darwin) — the West has been thinking through the historical inevitability and the logical possibility of its own decline; so the state of "crisis" has become a hegemonic theme. Nobody, let alone critical thinkers, should take the "crisis" of Western humanism naively or at face value; this state of prolonged and self-agonizing crisis may be the "soft" form that Western postmodernity has chosen in order to perpetuate itself.

The convergence of the discourse of "crisis" within poststructuralism and the postcolonial deconstruction of imperial whiteness is not a *sufficient* condition for a political alliance between them, though I would argue it is a *necessary* one. Anthony Appiah[2] reminded us of the need *not* to confuse the "post" of postcolonialism with the "post" of postmodernism but to respect instead the specific historical locations of each.

I do think, however, that facing up to these contradictory demands is our historical responsibility because Europeans, as early-21st-century North Atlantic people, are historically condemned to our history, insofar as we come after the historical decline of the promises of the Enlightenment. Whether you choose to call our predicament "postmodern," "post-humanist," or "neo-humanist" makes little difference. What does matter is our shared awareness that we must make ourselves *accountable* for the history of our culture without burying our heads in the sand and without giving in to relativism. Relativism is not an option because it erodes the possibility of both political coalitions and intellectual discussions.

Postcolonial thinkers like Stuart Hall, Avtra Brah, and Paul Gilroy have stressed the extent to which the political focus has shifted from the 20th-century question about essences: from "What is European Civilization?" to the 21st-century question about genealogy, entitlement, agency, and participation: "Who is entitled to call him/herself a European?"

As a white European and a first-generation migrant, I would like to emphasize, out of the many conflicting answers that are circulating on this point, the ones that offer a potential reframing of Europe. This positive approach goes hand in hand with reactivating a minority memory of European consciousness that aims at undoing the power of the centralized memory or data bank that jealously maintains European identity. One needs to forget the heroic definitions of Europe and remember against the grain, focusing on the other side of that heroic tale.

The starting point for this project is the acknowledgment that a state of crisis has been constitutive of Europe at least since modernity, arguably earlier if you follow Derrida and Cacciari. The *decline* of Europe is the condition of possibility for its redefinition or framing — historically, Europe has done this over and over again. Note that this discourse of the crisis of European hegemony — as Cornell West puts it — is radically set apart from the nostalgic discourse about the decadence of European culture, society, and the economy, itself a very popular discourse on the right. Reminiscent of the panic-stricken accounts of Otto Weininger[3] and Oswald Spengler[4] at the end of the last century, this proto-fascist view of Europe, like most discourses about decadence, merely paves the way for reactionary solutions.

Not so in the radical frame I would like to defend. Suppose that we start from the assumption that one of the defining features of Europe is its capacity to think through its own decline. What if Europe were the site where the infernal dance of sameness and difference ended by releasing difference from that fatal embrace?

What if, under the impact of the global economy, Europe could become the site of multiple internal differences, flowing and needing to be framed in a new geopolitical philosophy? This radically embedded vision of this geopolitical zone allows for unprecedented forms of *accountability*. What if we thought of the European Union, in its most progressive and even radical potential, as a possible frame for this new accountability?

To start with, this project assumes the decline of the nation-states as principles not only of economic but also of political organization. Being deeply antinationalistic, I find this rather a relief and I fancy the idea of nation-states becoming little more than museums of national folklore or guardians of the symbolic capital of countries.

2 Anthony Appiah, "Is the post- in postmodernism the post- in postcolonial?" in *Critical Inquiry* 17 (Winter 1991): 336–57.

3 Otto Weininger, *Sex and Character* (Vienna: Braumuller, 1904).

4 Oswald Spengler, *The Decline of the West* (Munich: Beck, 1920–22).

5 See also: Philomena Essed, *Understanding Everyday Racism: An Interdisciplinary Theory* (London: Sage, 1991); *Confronting the Fortress. Black and Migrant Women in the European Union*, a report to the European Women's Lobby by the European Forum of Left Feminists and Others (September 1993); Beverly Guy-Sheftall, *Women's Studies: A Retrospective* (New York: Ford Foundation, 1995); Helma Lutz, *Obstacles to Equal Opportunities in Society by Immigrant Women, with Particular Reference to the Netherlands, the United Kingdom, Germany and the Nordic Countries*, paper presented at the meeting of the Joint Specialist Group on Migration, Cultural Diversity and Equality of Women and Men (October 1994); Kum-Kum Bhavnani, *Towards a Multi-Cultural Europe?*, met Nederlandse vertaling (Bernardijn ten Zeldam Stichting, 1992).

6 Rosi Braidotti and Judith Butler, "Feminism by any other name," in *Differences: More Gender Trouble: Feminism Meets Queer Theory* (Summer–Fall 1994): 27–61.

7 Arjun Appadurai, "Disjuncture and Difference in the Global Cultural Economy," in Patrick Williams and Laura Chrisman, eds., *Colonial Discourse and Post-Colonial Theory: A Reader* (New York: Columbia University Press, 1994), 324–39.

ROSI BRAIDOTTI CHAIRS THE WOMEN'S PROGRAMME IN THE HUMANITIES AT THE UNIVERSITY OF UTRECHT AND IS IN CHARGE OF THE EUROPEAN EVALUATION OF WOMEN'S STUDIES FOR THE EUROPEAN COMMISSION'S SOCRATES PROGRAM. HER BOOKS INCLUDE PATTERNS OF DISSONANCE (1991), AS WELL AS WOMEN, THE ENVIRONMENT AND SUSTAINABLE DEVELOPMENT (1994), AND NOMADIC SUBJECTS (1994).

Released from the fantasy of being the center, a European space that would be capable of self-reflexivity might develop a sense of accountability for imperialism, colonialism, and fascism. This in turn could put the making of multicultural spaces, where the relationship of "sameness" to "difference" would be renegotiated, at the center of the reframing of Europe. This would allow for the strategic relocation of cultures in an antiracist, situated European mode.

The risk, of course, is that this progressive aspect would be drowned in more reactionary trends at work within the European Union, leading instead to the recreation of a Fortress Europe that would be as problematic for those it locks in as for those it locks out. The two options make European identity one of today's most contested areas of political and social philosophy. (The reactive tendency toward a sovereign sense of the Union is also known as the Fortress Europe syndrome, which has been extensively criticized by feminists and antiracists such as Helma Lutz, Nira Yuval-Davis, Avtar Brah, Floya Anthias, and Philomena Essed.[5])

"European identity" today is a contested zone where entitlement and access, exclusion and participation are crucial. "Europe" today means – also, but not only – a site of possible political resistance against the nationalism, xenophobia, and racism that accompany European unification.[6]

Is the reframing of Europe (yet again) a utopian project? It is, if by utopian we mean the impulse to create ethical and political solutions that may engender hope and empower change. As such, the reframing is not only useful but necessary.

THE POWERS OF REPETITION

If the point of repetition is to engender difference, it follows that conceptual creativity is accomplished always and already by doing it *again*. Repetition is not to be understood in any recognizable Hegelian dialectical mode but rather in a stubbornly nomadic mode of sequential retakes. Foucault argues that we are historically condemned to our historicity, which in his frame of reference means that postmodernity is condemned to critical theory, in the absence of a new conceptual or fundamental breakthrough. We are condemned to the patient task of revising and revisiting the archives of philosophical discourse, without the comfort of a primary philosophy.

Deleuze is definitely more optimistic. He believes that conceptual creativity can be engendered by releasing the nomadic potential of a philosophy that would invest in intensity and becoming, rather than in rationality and Being.

The concept of repetition is crucial to both Foucault and Deleuze, but it functions in very different ways in their respective philosophies. What they share is the conviction that subjectivity needs to be reconceptualized according to different degrees, colors, intensities, and speeds of repetition, without the comforting option of dialectical release.

Social theorists like Appadurai have suggested that at this end of the millennium the spent dialectics of sameness and difference have regrouped in a joint hijacking of the twin Enlightenment ideals of the triumphantly universal and the resiliently particular.[7] This calls for conceptual and political responses that move beyond the falsely universal, even monological discourse of classical binarism. New balances among dynamic forces are needed. New frames of becoming must engender positive differences through carefully framed repetitions. It is our task as critical thinkers to divide the diagrams that are adequate to the subjects we have already become or will have been.

Bernard Tschumi

Through a Broken Lens

Program/Project/Future are the three themes requested of my discussion panel. I will make three brief points to match the three themes, in a slightly reshuffled order. Their common denominator is a questioning of the primacy of vision – by extension, the apparent primacy of form, old or new – underlying these proceedings. It is entirely coincidental that my reading glasses broke yesterday on Friday the 13th – a minor event.

PROGRAM

The Deleuzian, even Bergsonian undertones of several interventions both at this conference and in a recent body of theoretical discourse in architecture are worth addressing briefly. Continuities, organic forms, and movement images are all interesting notions to map against the category of program that, for the sake of today's discussion, I will define as "the repetition of activities located in spaces and intersected by movement." If program-spaces belong to a single homogeneous and predictable space, the movement within them is generally heterogeneous and often unpredictable, as Gilles Deleuze notes in his introduction to *Cinema 1* (1986). This distinction between the homogeneous and the heterogeneous leads to a distinction between

"organic" architecture and "dialectical" architecture, once important in certain educational circles and no doubt a formative concept when I was an architecture student. One was not necessarily better than the other; they were simply alternative attitudes that also implied different processes in the making. No value judgment was intended: the example for the organic was Frank Lloyd Wright, the American, and for the dialectical, Le Corbusier, the European. The organic was about continuity, a so-called organic spatial continuum; the dialectical was about opposition. For example, the dialectical opposed the generic regularity and repetition of structure, say, a column grid, to the specificity of a ramp or a circular staircase. It opposed the homogeneity of structure to the heterogeneity of movement.

While such a "dialectic" was inherently formal at that time, its implications for today lie elsewhere. It now suggests that two systems – a static spatial structure and a dynamic movement vectorization (ramps, stairs, catwalks, etc.) – can intersect and make an event out of their planned or chance encounter. What is significant here is that the two systems are irreducible and mutually exclusive – once the movement of

bodies enters the equation, no organic synthesis between them can be reached. Let me expand the programmatic issue by using two other examples of mutually exclusive forms. The first is from my own work in the 1970s, which used movement and spatial notations mapped against a film sequence in which the film sequence acts as the program. Only when combined with space and movement notations – the dynamization of space and the spatialization of time – does architecture occur. Architecture is seen as inherently heterogeneous, as the place of crossovers between other disciplines and other media. Any autonomy of disciplines is abolished if architecture is defined as a crossover between, say, space constraints and film, or space constraints and philosophy or art, and so on.

A second example of dialectic raises a further question about which terms are opposed. *La dialectique peut-elle casser des briques? (Can Dialectics Break Bricks?)*, a 1968 film by Guy Debord, recycled a pornographic film as the image track and a Mao Zedong political speech for the sound track. Nothing organic here, but it is no regular dialectic either: the dialectic presupposes an opposition of comparable terms. If you take a film sequence, a philosophical statement, a computer program, or a sun diagram as analogous to an architectural program, there are no comparable terms. They are not logically related, namely, they cannot be opposed in a one-to-one relation, nor can they be constructed as a cause-and-effect relationship. There cannot be linearity.

This again suggests Benedict Spinoza's impossible paradox: "The concept of dog does not bark." The architectural implications are: architecture does not need to be

ceases to be comfortable to look at; it is no longer "what it looks like" that counts.

THE FUTURE

What good are space and time analogies when technologies are changing so radically? Deleuze expands on the reading of the cinema by Bergson, who had indicated that cinema is the art of producing movement through image stills. Confronted with evolving time, our knowledge of the universe proceeds in the same manner.[1] For Bergson, movement was inside the

space and the movement of bodies in space (our subjective experience) and the construction of technology (our technological tools: camera, projector, computer). The first example is a film by Bernardo Bertolucci, *The Conformist*. The second is a Nintendo 64 video game, Super Mario 64, but could include computer animation in general.

The Conformist mode of construction applies to classic as well as to avant-garde cinema. It uses devices — frames, sequences, montage, camera movements — all

The Conformist,
Bernardo Bertolucci, dir.

defined as object or as space but as the meeting between, say, event and space, two terms that are irreducible to one another — a dialectical and heterogeneous opposition that can never reach a synthesis because one term always acts as an irritant to the other, *ce qui n'est pas récupérable* (that which cannot be absorbed). For example, form can always be absorbed when considered culturally, aesthetically, and hence must always be challenged. When confronted with an unabsorbable element, such as the dynamics of moving bodies, in the equation of form, architecture

machine, either in the 24 frames per second of the movie camera/projector or in its equivalent, in our machine of knowledge that controls how we apprehend reality — an abstraction.

Deleuze expands upon this by saying, "In short, cinema does not give us a still image to which movement is added, it immediately gives us a movement-image. It does give us a section, but a section which is mobile, not an immobile section + abstract movement."[2] This film metaphor is what I intend to question — not only in philosophy but in architecture. I will consider two issues:

well documented since film directors David Griffith and Sergei Eisenstein. In a famous sequence, the actor walks through monumental interior spaces of a rationalist neoclassical palazzo. Spaces are shown mostly as static: the hero enters the film frame on the left, exits on the right. It is the body that is in motion.

In Super Mario 64, the body of the hero remains fixed at the center of the screen. The illusion of movement is given by the fast-moving or receding perspectival plane surrounding the still figure. The hero's constantly flapping

1 Gilles Deleuze, *Cinema 1: The Movement-Image*, trans. Hugh Tomlinson and Barbara Habberjam (Minneapolis: University of Minnesota Press, 1986), 2.

2 Ibid.

little feet do not alter the stillness and centrality of the body. More importantly, "space" is created through the juxtaposition of infinitely thin surfaces or textures. For example, if you quickly flick the controller to the edges of this virtual space, the dark emptiness that lies behind these immaterial textures is revealed.

In *The Conformist* and in Super Mario 64 the place of the body in relation to the materialization of space has deep architectural implications. While architectural theory

sion of still sections (24 frames per second), the computer screen and the spaces that it depicts work on variable times. Different parts of the pixelated screen change at different rates; compression devices allow part of the image to remain still while others vary at enormous speeds, limited only by the calculating power of the machine. Interactive devices make such discrepancies even more striking, as the rather primitive perceptual capability of the human user limits interaction to, say,

replaced by differentiated time or heterotopic vision. Once again, it's not only what it looks like that counts anymore.

THE PROJECT

The project that I want to present addresses some of these issues. This large student center for Columbia University in New York is set in a loaded historical context in which the neoclassical architecture of McKim, Mead & White is considered sacred. The project is also in the middle of a highly designed campus, planned

Super Mario 64.

(as well as the philosophers quoted earlier) still discusses the body-in-space as depicted in classic film, a major change may be in the making. This lies in part in the technology of image-making, which completely alters the Bergsonian/Deleuzian frame of reference. The Deleuzian "movement-image," used as part of a larger argument on time, duration, memory differentiation, élan vital, and so on, inevitably comes under question at a time when the very technology used to illustrate the concept is becoming obsolete. In contradistinction to cinema's regulated succes-

30 images per second while other parts or layers change at a rate which far exceeds that perceivable by the human eye. Sampling is, of course, the name of the game here: not a simple succession of still images, as in film, but the variable speed of regeneration of the image. The very technology of film, through the relentless and predictable repetition of ever slightly changing film frames, lends itself to coding and ruling. While Deleuze explores this predictability, today homogeneous time, homogeneous vision, and homogeneous image are under question,

through an ideal diagram, framed by a series of buildings flanking the avenues. The original (and mostly unbuilt) plan shows double rows of volumes proceeding from a pattern of solid-void-solid. We decided to implement that part of the original plan, for we were not particularly interested in what the solids would look like.

On the contrary, the project's main focus lay in revealing a series of potentialities stemming from a combination of the volumetric McKim logic with a change in ground level between Broadway and the campus. (The campus is a half-story higher than the street around it.) This change in levels is the interstitial movement inherent in the logic of the McKim system. It provided us with the opportunity to generate a new and staggered relation between the intended volumetric components of the plan.

The staggering of the McKim solids coincides in our project with the "void" auditorium requested by the program and the "void" for a place of exchange where the various programmatic aspects would meet. We call this place

is different from the one at Le Fresnoy National Studio for Contemporary Arts, where we designed the conditions for creating a nonprogrammatic space by taking a large roof and superimposing it over a landscape of existing roofs [see ANY 21 (1997): 32–35]. At Columbia, the in-between is not residual but manufactured and activated by the movement of bodies in space. In other words, the surrounding programmatic density activates the main space of the project. The in-between here is not a formal device but a

neous dialectic, a technology of differentiated time and vision, and a revealing of potentialities through programmatic dialectics (rather than Corbusier-like formal dialectics) are not unlike the intact lens and the broken lens: together they shift perception away from the logic of homogeneous vision.

I do not think it is very important to discuss "what buildings look like." It is what they do that is important. Architecture is about identifying and then actualizing potentialities. Architecture

Bernard Tschumi Architects/Gruzen Samton, Associated Architects, Lerner Student Center, Columbia University, New York, New York (scheduled completion 1999).

Left to right: Exterior view of Lerner Center at night; View through glass curtain wall toward center of campus; Perspective view of interior central space.

the Hub. One enters the Hub and either goes down to the bookstore, the auditorium, or a nightclub or up to a cinema, game room, dining halls, or meeting rooms via ramps along which 6,000 student mailboxes are located. Other facilities include student clubs, a black-box theater, a radio station, and so on.

We were interested in locating these various activities in such a way that the space of circulation, of movement, of motion would become charged and would generate a new intensity that would be not formal but programmatic. The in-between of this project

strategic and programmatic one. The in-between results from a spatial structure of a normative context combined with a dynamic movement vectorization. It suggests an inherently heterotopic spatialization of time.

CONCLUSION

Architectural history, even the most immediate and contemporary, still seems to strive for formal coherence and visual continuity. New theories of organic form seem to reinforce such genealogical lineages. The three points I tried to introduce here – a new heteroge-

is never static; it is always dynamic. Architecture is about the meeting of mutually exclusive terms: concept and experience, virtual and real, envelope and body.

That meeting takes place in an in-between, an interstitial space – but that space is not *poché*, not geometric, not merely physical. I have no name for it yet. Maybe it is close to what Liz Grosz described as an impure, soiled, and paradoxical state, an "interval that is neither space nor time."[3] It is an impossible but carefully designed dialectical relation between diagram and program.

3 Elizabeth Grosz, "The Future of Space: Toward an Architecture of Invention," presentation at Anyhow conference (Rotterdam, June 1997); see essay page 242.

BERNARD TSCHUMI IS AN ARCHITECT AND DEAN OF COLUMBIA UNIVERSITY'S GRADUATE SCHOOL OF ARCHITECTURE, PLANNING, AND PRESERVATION. HE HAS DESIGNED SEVERAL AWARD-WINNING PROJECTS INCLUDING THE PARC DE LA VILLETTE IN PARIS, AND IS THE AUTHOR OF MANHATTAN TRANSCRIPTS AND ARCHITECTURE AND DISJUNCTION. HIS LE FRESNOY NATIONAL STUDIO FOR CONTEMPORARY ARTS IN TOURCOING, FRANCE OPENED IN 1997.

Elizabeth Grosz

THINKING

What can philosophy bring to architectural discourse and its practice (the practices of design, cost analysis, siting, building)? And what can architecture bring to philosophical discourse and its practices (reasoning, arguing, formulating problematics, framing questions)? What are some pertinent points of overlap or mutual investment that may implicate each in the other in mutually productive ways? Perhaps more pertinently, what are the blindspots within the self-understanding of each? And how can each be used by the other, not just to affirm itself and receive external approval but also to question and thus to expand itself, to become otherwise, without assuming any privilege or primacy of the one over the other and without assuming that the relation between them must be one of direct utility or translation? One very small strand draws these two disciplines together, an idea of newness or virtuality, latency or becoming, which may be highlighted and productively developed within both disciplines through the help, the overlap, and the difference that each offers the other. This idea of the virtual, a concept prevalent if undeveloped in philosophy since at least the time of Plato, introduces a series of questions to both architecture and philosophy (with different effects) that may force them to change quite fundamental assumptions they make about space, time, movement, futurity, and becoming.

Architecture has tended to conceive of itself as an art, a science, or a mechanics for the manipulation of space, indeed probably the largest, most systematic and most powerful mode for spatial organization and modification. Space itself, the very stuff of architectural reflection and production, requires and entails a mode of time, timeliness, or duration. Indeed, space must always involve at least two times, or perhaps two kinds of time: the time of the emergence of space as such, a time before time and space, a temporalization/spatialization that precedes and renders the organization or emergence of space as such and time as such and thus emerges before any scientific understanding of a space-time continuum.[1] This is the space-time of difference, of *différance* (Jacques Derrida discusses *différance* as precisely the temporization of space and the spatialization of time), or differentiation (in Deleuzian terms, differing from itself), which is a precondition of and prior to the space and time of life, of understanding, of science.

Derrida, for example, claims that the insertion of an interval that refuses self-identity and self-presence to any thing, any existent constitutes *différance*. This interval, neither clearly space nor time but a kind of leakage between the two, the passage of the one into the other, propels any being beyond itself, in space and in time. Neither space nor time can exist as such "before" this interval, which expands being into a world in order that it paradoxically be both itself and other to itself:

An interval must separate the present from what it is not in order for the present to be

[1] Such a continuum – the space-time of contemporary science – always derives from a more primordial understanding of time and space: this was Henri Bergson's critique of Albert Einstein. It is not clear to me, however, that access to this more primordial space and time is provided, as Bergson suggested, by experience.

itself but this interval that constitutes it as present must, by the same token, divide the present in and of itself, thereby also dividing, along with the present, everything that is thought on the basis of the present, that is, in our metaphysical language, every being, and singularly substance or the subject. In constituting itself, in dividing itself dynamically, this interval is what might be called *spacing*, the becoming-space of time or the becoming-time of space (*temporization*). And it is this constitution of the present, as an "originary" and irreducibly nonsimple . . . synthesis of marks, or traces of retentions and protentions . . . that I propose to call archi-writing, archi-trace, or *différance*. Which (is) (simultaneously) spacing (and) temporization.[2]

The time and space of architecture, and for that matter, of philosophy, can rarely afford to consider this primordial differential, the movement, the shimmering of the differing of a time and space not yet configured, enumerated, mastered, or occupied. This time before time, the time of the interval, the time of nontime, enables space to emerge as such and is that to which space is ineluctably driven, the "fate" of space.

There is a second kind of time, the time of history, of historicity, the time of reflection, the time of knowledge — a time to which we are accustomed in the history of architecture and of philosophy in the very idea of history, of orderly progression, of the segmentation or continuity of time and space. Architecture has tended to face time and temporality through the questions posed by history and through its

response to the ravages of that history, its orientation toward monumentality. Architecture has thought time, with notable exceptions, through history rather than through duration, as that to be preserved, as that which somehow or provisionally overcomes time by transcending or freezing it.

I am more interested here in the relevance of this earlier sense of time, which I will represent through the concept of the virtual and virtuality, a concept that requires not only a time *before* time but also a time *after* time, a time bound up not only with the past and with history and historicity but also, perhaps primarily, with futurity, thus providing a mode of resistance to the privilege of the present and the stranglehold that the present and its correlatives, identity and intention, maintain on space and matter. The times before and after time are the loci of emergence, of unfolding, of eruption, the spaces-times of the new, the unthought, the virtuality of a past that has not exhausted itself in activity and a future that cannot be exhausted or anticipated by the present. This past, which layers and resonates the present, refuses to allow the present the stability of the given or the inevitable. It is the past that enables duration as a mode of continuity as well as heterogeneity. Both Derrida and Deleuze, in very different ways, indicate this central role of difference as a vector in the modalization of space.

In articulating a notion of virtuality linked to futurity, to becoming and to differentiation,

2 Jacques Derrida, "Différance," *Margins of Philosophy*, trans. Alan Bass (Chicago: University of Chicago Press, 1982), 13.

I want to explicate what I understand as a particularly underrepresented philosophical mode, which it may share with architecture, what might be called a "logic of invention" as opposed to an Aristotelian logic of identity, reflection, reason, self-containment. A logic of invention has yet to be invented: only such a logic can mediate between the reflective categories of philosophical thought and the pragmatic requirements of any empirical project, here the architectural project. It is a linkage that invents new philosophies and new architectures. Instead of the self-containment of the syllogism (in which conclusions are logically entailed in validly constituted premises), a logic of invention is necessarily expansive, ramifying and expedient, producing not premises so much as techniques, not conclusions so much as solutions, not arguments so much as effects. Such a logic can never be regulative (distinguishing valid from invalid arguments) but is always descriptive (do this, then this, then this).

Philosophy, according to Deleuze, is both a mode of solving problems and a mode of thinking or theorizing multiplicities. Architecture too is bound up with problem solving and with multiplicities, though the multiplicities with which it deals are not simply conceptual or simply material. Philosophy is not, for Deleuze, a mode of mastering the real, framing its rules, understanding its principles; rather, it is what deals with the coagulation, the alignments between the actual and the virtual, the ways in which the actual feeds off and grows in distinction from the virtual and, conversely, the ways in which the virtual continually enriches and diminishes the actual by forcing it to diverge from itself, to always tend toward and to be absorbed by virtuality. Architecture, like philosophy (and for that matter, biology and physics), is perpetually verging on, irresistibly drawn to, its own virtualities, to the ever-increasing loops of uncertainty and immanence that its own practices engage and produce. The future of each discipline requires that each open itself up to a reconsideration of the virtual and the promise it holds for newness, otherness, divergence from what currently prevails.

What does the notion of the virtual mean? Here I only have the time (or is it the space!)

to deal with one conception in any detail, Deleuze's reading of Bergson, and Bergson's understanding of the virtual and the return of the virtual image to the actual. Deleuze claims that Bergson is one of the great thinkers of becoming, of duration, multiplicity, and virtuality. Bergson developed this notion of duration in opposition to his understanding of space and spatiality. This understanding of duration and the unhinging of temporality that it performs are of at least indirect relevance to the arts or sciences of space, which may, through a logic of invention, derail and transform space and spatiality in analogous ways.

Space is understood, according to Deleuze (who followed Bergson at least up to a point on this) as a multiplicity that brings together the key characteristics of externality, simultaneity, contiguity or juxtaposition, differences of degree, and quantitative differentiations. Space is discontinuous, infinitely divisible, static, and always actual. Space in short is the milieu of things, matter, identities, substances, entities that are real, comparable, and calculable. It is the natural home of science, of the actual, where there are differentiations of degree but not in kind:

"Space, by definition, is outside us . . . space appears to us to subsist even when we leave it undivided, we know that it can wait and that a new effort of our imagination may decompose it when we choose. As, moreover, it never ceases to be space, it always implies juxtaposition, and, consequently, possible division. Abstract space is, indeed, at bottom, nothing but the mental diagram of infinite divisibility."[3]

Duration, by contrast, is a multiplicity of succession, heterogeneity, differences in kind, and qualitative differentiations. It is continuous and virtual. It is divisible, of course, but it is transformed through the act of division – indeed much of Bergson's work explores the implications of dividing time, among the more serious of which is the freezing of all motion into discrete momentary units. Duration is perfectly capable of subsisting without division, which is always imposed on it from the outside. Duration is not, through its continuity, homogeneous, smooth, or linear; rather, it is a mode of "hesitation," bifurcation, unfolding, or emergence.

3 Henri Bergson, Matter and Memory, trans. N. M. Paul and W. S. Palmer (New York: Zone Books, 1988), 206.

If space and time are represented as discrete phenomena, as separate, indeed opposed, in their various qualities and attributes, then not only are these primordial processes of temporization that induce space ignored, but the primitive processes of spatialization through which the notion of duration and temporality exists also fail to emerge. Bergson himself acknowledged this, though only rarely, when he qualified and refined his understanding of space. It is not that space in itself must be or can only be the space of quantification; rather, it is a certain mode of doing science, particularly science under the determinist, predictive Laplacian model, that effects the mathematization and ordering of space and makes this seem to be the very nature of space itself. In a certain sense Bergson acknowledged the becoming one of the other, the relation of direct inversion between them, when he conceptualized space as the contraction of time, and time as the expansion or dilation of space.

Space is mired in misconceptions and assumptions, habits and unreflective gestures that convert and transform it. Architecture, the art or science of spatial manipulation, must be as implicated in this as any other discipline or practice. According to Bergson, a certain habit of thought inverts the relations between space and objects, space and extension, to make it seem as if space precedes objects, when in fact space itself is produced *through* matter, extension, and movement:

> Concrete extensity, that is to say, the diversity of sensible qualities, is not within space; rather it is space that we thrust into extensity. Space is not a ground on which real motion is posited; rather it is real motion that deposits space beneath itself. But our imagination, which is preoccupied above all by the convenience of expression and the exigencies of material life, prefers to invert the natural order of the terms. . . .Therefore, it comes to see movement as only a variation of distance, space being thus supposed to precede motion. Then, in a space which is homogeneous and infinitely divisible, we draw, in imagination, a trajectory and fix positions: afterwards, applying the movement to the trajectory, we see it divisible like the line we have drawn, and equally denuded of quality.[4]

Space in itself, space outside these ruses of the imagination, is not static, fixed, infinitely expandable, infinitely divisible, concrete, extended, continuous, and homogenous, though perhaps we must think it in these terms in order to continue our everyday lives (and the architect is perhaps more invested in this understanding of space than anyone else). Space, like time, is emergence and eruption, oriented not to the ordered, the controlled, the static but to the event, to movement or action. If we "shut up motion in space," as Bergson suggested, then we shut space up in quantification, without ever being able to think space in terms of quality, of difference and discontinuity. We do not think of spaces but can at best allow ourselves to utter "places" in a gesture to localization. Space seems to resist this kind of pluralization: it asserts itself as continuous, singular, and infinite. Space presents itself as ready-made, as given in its constancy, fixed in its form: it is then a mode of the capture of both space and time when time is understood as the fourth dimension of space common in post-Einsteinian ontology.

It is relevant that Bergson called for a space, spaces, sensitive to the motion and actions that unfold in them. Rather than seeing motion in its scientific terms as distance or space over time, Bergson indicated, though did not develop, a different understanding, where space emerges through specific motions and specific spaces, where motion unfolds and actualizes space.

> Space, in effect, is matter or extension, but the "schema" of matter, that is, the representation of the limit where the movement of expansion would come to an end as the external envelope of all possible extensions. In this sense, it is not matter, it is not extensity, that is in space, but the very opposite. And if we think that matter has a thousand ways of becoming expanded or extended, we must also say that there are all kinds of distinct extensities, all related, but still qualified, and which will finish by intermingling only in our own schema of space.[5]

This kind of space could no longer be considered static, infinitely extended, smooth, regular, amenable to gridding, to coordinates, to geometric division, the kind of space one can leave behind and return to intact, independent of

4 Ibid., 217.

5 Gilles Deleuze, *Bergsonism*, trans. Hugh Tomlinson and Barbara Habberjam, (New York: Zone Books, 1988), 87.

what has occurred there. In opening up space to time, space becomes amenable to transformation and refiguring; it becomes particular, individualized. It is not clear that we need to return, as Bergson suggested, to the space of immediate, lived experience. For one thing, our lived experience at the end of the millennium involves spaces that were quite literally unimaginable in Bergson's time and moreover, the immediacy of experience is itself not unmediated by the social modes of inhabitation of space. For another, it is not clear that immediate experience is any more the point of proliferation of virtualities and intensities than, say, the most intensely artificial and manufactured movements and spaces.

In a rare moment, Bergson contemplated the possibility of thinking space otherwise, understanding it in terms other than as the binary opposite of duration. Space too could be conceived, instead of being the pure medium of actuality, as the field for the play of virtualities:

> In regard to concrete extension, continuous, diversified and at the same time organized, we do not see why it should be bound up with the amorphous and inert space which subtends it – a space which we divide indefinitely, out of which we carve figures arbitrarily, and in which movement itself . . . can only appear as a multiplicity of instantaneous positions, since nothing there can ensure the coherence of past with present. It might, then, be possible, in a certain measure, to transcend space without stepping out from extensity; and here we should really have a return to the immediate, since we do indeed perceive extensity, whereas space is merely conceived – being a kind of mental diagram.[6]

Bergson suggested that we can reinvent, or rather, return to a conception of space that does not so much underlie or subtend matter, functioning as the indifferent coordinates of the placement of matter, as function as an effect of matter and movement. It is not an existing, God-given space, the Cartesian space of numerical division, but an unfolding space, defined, as time is, by the arc of movement and thus a space open to becoming, by which I mean, becoming other than itself, other than what it has been:

> [I]f we try to get back to the bottom of this common hypothesis [shared by philosophical realism and idealism] . . . we find that it consists in attributing to homogeneous space a disinterested office: space is supposed either merely to uphold material reality or to have the function, still purely speculative, of furnishing sensations with means of coordinating themselves. So the obscurity of realism, like that of idealism, comes from the fact that, in both of them, our conscious perception and the conditions of our conscious perception are assumed to point to pure knowledge, not to action. But now suppose that this homogeneous space is not logically anterior, but posterior to material things and to the pure knowledge which we can have of them; suppose that extensity is prior to space; suppose that homogeneous space concerns our action and only our action, being like an infinitely fine network which we stretch beneath material continuity in order to render ourselves masters of it, to decompose it according to the plan of our activities and our needs. Then, not only has our hypothesis the advantage of bringing us into harmony with science, which shows us each thing exercising an influence on all the others and, consequently, occupying, in a certain sense, the whole of the extended. . . .[7]

The same attributions of becoming that Bergson accorded to duration can now be seen to accompany spatiality: just as the whole of the past contracts, in various degrees, in each moment of the present, that is, just as the present is laden with virtualities that extend it beyond itself – the ballast of the virtual past being enough to propel an unpredicted future out of an uncontained and endlessly ramifying present – so too the whole of space, spatiality, contracts into the specificity of location, and the occupation of any space contains the virtual whole of spatiality, which is to say, the infinite possibilities of my action on and being acted on by matter in space and time. To remember any moment is to throw oneself into the past, to seek events where they took place – in time, in the past; to experience any other space is to throw oneself into spatiality, to become spatialized with all of space. To remember (to place

6 Bergson, *Matter and Memory*, 187.

7 Ibid., 231.

8 Ibid., 68.

9 Ibid.

10 See figure 5, Bergson,
Matter and Memory, 162.

Figure 1

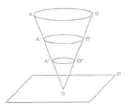

The cone SAB represents the
totality of memory, in its
different degrees of contraction. The base AB is situated
in the past and is unable to
link with the present, while
the point S indicates my
continuing present. The
plane P is my actual present
representation of the universe. S is the locus of the
sensori-motor functions.
The segments AB, A'B', A"B",
are repetitions of memory
more or less compressed.
The more expansive and
detailed, the less accessible
is memory to present action.

oneself in the past), to relocate (to cast oneself elsewhere), is to occupy the whole of time and the whole of space, even admitting that dura-tion and location are always specific, always defined by movement and action. It is to refuse to conceptualize space as a medium, as a con-tainer, a passive receptacle whose form is given by its content, and instead to see it as a moment of becoming, of opening up and proliferation, a passage from one space to another, a space of change, which changes with time.

Instead of a return to the prescientific immediacy that Bergson suggested as a remedy for the containment that science places on space, I would suggest a different approach to the reenervation of space through duration, the restoration of becoming to both space and time. If time is neither linear and successive nor cycli-cal and recurrent but indeterminate, unfolding, serial, multiplying, complex, heterogeneous, then space too must be reconfigured not as neutral, nor as singular and homogeneous but as opening up to other spaces, not regulating processes and events so much as accompanying them. We do not, as Bergson claimed, need to *experience* or live such a space (or time): this does not seem possible or necessary. We need more adequately intellectual, but above all pragmatic models by which to understand and actively seek the maximal paths of proliferation for vir-tual time becoming virtual space. These models are not simply modes of self-complacency that enable us to live our lives as before, now with a justification and a rationale; rather, these models may help us to understand, see, think, build differently, according to other logics of invention and experimentation.

PERCEIVING

If we want to understand how the virtual may enrich conceptions of space and thus of the architectural project, it may be necessary to make a brief detour through the role that the virtual plays in duration and especially in inserting the past into the present as its state of virtuality. This may in turn provide some of the key concepts or terms by which to think spatiality in terms of virtuality.

Bergson wants to define perception and memory, our modes of access to the present

and the past, in operational or pragmatic terms: the present is that which acts, while the past can be understood as that which no longer acts or whose actions are at best virtual.[8] Perception must be linked to nascent or dawning action, action-in-potential. Perception is actual insofar as it is active and thus relates primarily to an impending future. By contrast, instead of memory being regarded as a faded perception, a perception that has receded into the past, as is commonplace, it must be regarded as ideational, inactive, virtual. "The past is only idea, the present is ideo-motor."[9] A present per-ception and a past recollection are not simply different in degree (one a faded, diminished version of the other) but different in kind. Perception is that which propels us toward the real, toward space, objects, matter, the future, while memory is that which impels us toward consciousness, the past, and duration.[10] If perception impels us toward action and thus toward objects, then, to that extent, objects reflect my body's possible actions upon them.

The present is that which acts and lives, that which functions to anticipate an immedi-ate future in action. The present is a form of impending action. The past is that which no longer acts, although in a sense it lives a shad-owy and fleeting existence. It still is. It is real. The past remains accessible in the form of rec-ollections, either as motor mechanisms in the form of habit-memory, or, more correctly, in the form of image-memories. These memories are the condition of perception in the same way that the past, for Bergson, is a condition of the present. Where the past in itself is pow-erless, if it can link up to a present perception, it has a chance to be mobilized in the course of another perception's impulse to action. In this sense, the present is not purely in itself, self-contained; it straddles both past and present, requiring the past as its precondition, oriented as it is toward the immediate future. Our perception is a measure of our virtual action upon things. The present, as that which is oriented toward both percep-tion and action, is the threshold of their interaction and thus the site of duration. The present consists in the consciousness I have of my body. Memory, the past, has no special link with or proximity to my body. Most significant for the purposes of this argument is that as the present functions in the domain of the actual, the past functions as virtual.

The past cannot be identified with the memory images which serve to represent or make it actual for or useful to us; rather, it is the seed which can actualize itself in a memory. Memory is the present's mode of access to the past. The past is preserved in time, while the memory image, one of the past's images or elements, can be selected according to present interests. Just as perception leads me toward objects where they are, outside of myself and in space, and just as I perceive affection (which Deleuze would refer to as intensity) where it arises, in my body,[11] so too I recall or remember only by placing myself in the realm of the past where memory subsides or subsists. Memory, the past, is thus, paradoxically, not in us just as perception is not in us. Perception takes place outside ourselves, to where objects are (in space); memory takes us to where the past is (in duration). In Deleuze's reading, Bergson goes so far as to say that the only subjectivity or life is time and that life participates in this subjectivity to the extent that it is submerged in duration.[12]

Bergson seems to problematize a whole series of assumptions regarding our conceptions of the present and the past. We tend to believe that when the present is somehow exhausted or depleted of its current force it somehow slips into the past where it is stored in the form of memories. It is then replaced by another present. Against this presumption, Bergson suggests that a new present could never replace the old one if the latter did not pass while it is still present. In place of the more usual claim of the succession of the past by the present, this leads to his postulate of the *simultaneity* of past and present. The past is contemporaneous with the present it has been. They exist, they "occur" at the same time. The past could never exist if it did not coexist with the present of which it is the past:

> The past and the present do not denote two successive moments, but two elements which coexist: One is the present, which does not cease to pass, and the other is the past, which does not cease to be but through which all presents pass. . . . The past does not follow the present, but on the contrary, is presupposed by it as the pure condition without which it would not pass. In other words, each present goes back to itself as past.[13]

Bergson argues that the past would be altogether inaccessible to us if we can gain access to it only through the present and its passing. The only access we have to the past is through a leap into virtuality, through a move into the past itself, through seeing that the past is outside us and that we are in it rather than it in us. The past exists, but it is in a state of latency or virtuality. We must place ourselves in it if we are to have recollections, memory images. This we do in two movements or phases. First, we place ourselves into the past in general (which can only occur through a certain detachment from the immediacy of the present) and then we place ourselves in a particular region of the past. Bergson conceives of the past in terms of a series of planes or segments, each one representing the whole of the past in a more or less contracted form. We move from one set of memories to another through a leap into a virtual time. We must jump into the milieu of the past in general in order to access any particular memories. The present can be understood as an infinitely contracted moment of the past, the point where the past intersects most directly with the body. It is for this reason that the present is able to pass.

Each segment has its own features although each contains within itself the whole of the past. Memories drawn from various strata may be clustered around idiosyncratic points, "shining points of memory," as Bergson describes them, which are multiplied to the extent that memory is dilated.[14] Depending on the recollection we are seeking, we must jump in at a particular segment; in order to move on to another we must make another leap: "We have to jump into a chosen region, even if we have to return to the present in order to make another jump, if the recollection sought for gives no response and does not realize itself in a recollection-image."[15] For Deleuze, this provides a model for Bergson's understanding of our relations to other sys-

11 Bergson, *Matter and Memory*, 57.

12 This is already an indication of the strangely postmodernist, indeed, surprisingly posthuman character of Bergson's writings, even those characterized as the most committed to humanism. Indeed, this seems to attract Deleuze's bastardized, anal reading of Bergson: Bergson's own wayward, quiet peculiarity and complexity relative to the simplified characterizations generally used now to discount his work: Bergson is not one of those philosophers who ascribes a properly human wisdom and equilibrium to philosophy. To open us up to the inhuman and the superhuman (*durations* which are inferior or superior to our own), to go beyond the human condition: This is the meaning of philosophy, in so far as our condition condemns us to live among badly analyzed composites, and to be badly analyzed composites ourselves. (Deleuze, *Bergsonism*, 28.)

13 Deleuze, *Bergsonism*, 59.

14 Bergson, *Matter and Memory*, 171.

15 Deleuze, *Bergsonism*, 99.

16 Deleuze argues that "this time-image extends naturally into a language-image, and a thought-image. What the past is to time, sense is to language and idea to thought. Sense as past of language is the form of its pre-existence, that which we place ourselves in at once in order to understand images of sentences, to distinguish the images of words and even phonemes that we hear. It is therefore organized in coexisting circles, sheets or regions, between which we choose according to actual auditory signs which are grasped in a confused way. Similarly, we place ourselves initially in the idea; we jump into one of its circles in order to form images which correspond to the actual quest." (Deleuze, *Bergsonism*, 99–100.)

17 *Bergsonism*, 61–62.

tems of images as well (and hence Bergson's suitability to Deleuze's analysis of cinema).

It is only through a similar structure that we can detach ourselves from the present to understand linguistic utterances or make conceptual linkages. The structure of the time-image also contains that of the language-image and the thought-image. It is only by throwing ourselves into language as a whole, into the domain of sense in general, that we can understand any utterance, and it is only by leaping into a realm of ideas that we can understand problems.[16] In all three cases, this leap involves landing in different concentrations of the past, language or thought, which nonetheless contain the whole within them to different degrees.

Along with the simultaneity or coexistence of each moment of the present with the entirety of the past there are other implications in Bergson's paradoxical account. Each moment carries a virtual past with it: each present must, as it were, pass through the whole of the past. This is what is meant by the past in general. The past does not come after the present has ceased to be nor does the present become or somehow move into the past. Rather, it is the past which is the condition of the present; it is only through a preexistence that the present can come to be. Bergson does not want to deny that succession takes place – of course, one present (and past) replaces another; but such real or actual succession can only take place because of a virtual coexistence of the past and the present, the virtual coexistence of all of the past at each moment of the present – and at each level or segment of the past. This means that there must be a relation of repetition between each segment whereby each segment or degree of contraction or dilation is a virtual repetition of the others, not identical, certainly, but a version. The degrees of contraction or dilation which differentiate segments constitute modes of repetition in difference.

In Deleuze's reading, Bergson systematically developed a series of paradoxes regarding the past and present that run counter to a more common, everyday understanding:

(1) we place ourselves at once, in a leap, in the ontological element of the past (paradox of the leap); (2) there is a difference in kind between the present and the past (paradox of Being); (3) the past does not follow the present that it has been, but coexists with it (paradox of coexistence); (4) what coexists with each present is the whole of the past, integrally, on various levels of contraction and relaxation (*détente*) (paradox of psychic repetition). These Bergsonian paradoxes, which are only paradoxical if duration is represented on the model of space, are all, Deleuze claimed, a critique of more ordinary theories of memory, whose propositions state that:

(1) we can reconstitute the past with the present; (2) we pass gradually from the one to the other; (3) that they are distinguished by a before and an after; and (4) that the work of the mind is carried out by the addition of elements (rather than by changes of level, genuine jumps, the reworking of systems).[17]

It seems clear that a series of analogous unhingings of the self-containment and fixity of spatiality can also be developed, though Bergson himself refrained from doing so. Duration contains as part of its conceptual content the ideas of (1) unevenness, heterogeneity, states of contraction and expansion, such that time exists in a state of detailed elaboration, or in a state of compressed schematism; (2) difference, specificity, and multiplicity: each movement has its own duration, each event its own unfolding. These durations, though, are never simply isolated or self-contained but always both intersect with other durations (the duration of my actions may interact with the durations of the objects and materials with which I work) and participate in a kind of mega-duration, a world duration which renders them in a web or weave of comparable and interlocked durations and becomings; (3) simultaneity, the coexistence of the past in the present, the anticipation of the present as the actualization of the past (in other words, the coexistence of two kinds of time, one frozen and virtual, the other dynamic and actual). These two kinds of duration are irreducible in their difference: the past is contemporaneous with the present it has been; and (4) succession, the complication of the past, present, and future. Each is necessarily involved in the function of the others, not by way of determinism (which in fact annuls the existence of the future and enables the effectivity of the past only) but through the divergence of the present from the past, and the future from the present, the interlocking of the past and the future (both virtual, both productive without emerging as such through the present) without the mediation of the present.

The question now remains: Do these rather strange and paradoxical formulations regarding duration have any spatial counterparts? Can the ways in which we conceive, indeed live, space be subjected to a similar unhinging, a similar destabilization of presence and habitual self-evidence? To return to my earlier question: What would virtual space be like? What does such a conception entail? How can it be thought? (My questions.) How can it be built, lived, practiced? (Your question.)

I spoke earlier about the need for a logic of invention. Instead of requiring logical certainty, the guarantee of universal validity, the capacity to provide rules of procedure independent of the particularities of space and time, such a logic would instead require ingenuity, experimentation, novelty, specification, and particularity as its key ingredients. It would not seek to be certain but rather to incite, to induce, to proliferate. Rather than direct itself to questions of consistency, coherence, and regularity, such a logic would focus on an intuition of uniqueness, the facing of each situation according to its specific exigencies, the openness to failure as much as to innovation. I am not proposing that we replace Aristotelian logic with such a logic of invention; only that we acknowledge that each may work and be relevant in its particular spheres. Such a "logic of invention" has always governed architecture. The question is: What are the best terms by which to articulate this logic? How, in other words, to extract its *own* theory from its architectural practices rather than simply import or impose a theoretical frame from the outside? This is to inquire about architecture's own (theoretical) latencies, its virtualities.

I can offer only a more general understanding of virtuality and what it implies for rethinking or perhaps reinventing space. I have two thoughts: one regarding the rethinking of space in terms of becoming and duration; the other

regarding what the virtual can offer to architectural theory and practice.

To look, then, at some possibilities for the reconceptualization of space in terms of its openness to its own processes of differentiation and divergence. It seems possible that many – or at least some – of the qualities that Bergson attributed to duration may also be relevant to a considered spatiality, especially given that the time-space of primordial experience links space, before mathematization, to the movement of duration. It may be that many of the attributes particular to duration have some spatial equivalent. For example, if duration exists in states of contraction and expansion, in degrees of uneven intensity, either elaborated in increasing detail or functioning simply as "shining points" of intensity, then perhaps space too need not be construed as even, homogeneous, continuous, infinitely the same. Perhaps space also has loci of intensity, of compression or elasticity, perhaps it need no longer be considered a medium. Perhaps it can be considered lumpy, intensified, localized, or regionalized. I am not talking here simply of locale or landscape but also of the fundamental or ontological space that underlies a specific region. Nor am I simply confirming the insights of an Einsteinian space-time, in which there is still a relation of smooth, mathematical alignments between the expansion of time and the contraction of space. The very configurations of space itself may be heterogeneous, just as the movements or configurations of duration vary. Perhaps, in other words, there is a *materiality* to space itself, rather than materiality residing with only its contents.

This implies that space itself, if it is heterogeneous, is multiple, differential, specific. There are specific locations, places, regions that have their own modes of extensity: like intensity, the extensive always radiates from a point, given spatially as "here," the spatial present. The spatial present defines its own region but this regionality both intersects with the regionality of other heres and, like world duration, links to a larger space, a world space or even a universal space, which in no way qualifies or marginalizes the concrete differences between different spaces. Cosmological spaces are not the master or overarching space within

18 Ibid., 97.

19 Ibid.

20 Constantin Boundas
states this well: "Virtualities
generate disjunctions as they
begin to actualize the tendencies which were contained in
the original unity and com-
possibility. Differenciation
does not happen between
one actual term and another
actual term in a homoge-
neously unilinear series, but
rather between a virtual term
and the heterogeneous terms
which actualize it along the
lines of flight of several ramified series." Constantin V.
Boundas, "Bergson-Deleuze:
An Ontology of the Virtual,"
in Deleuze: A Critical Reader, ed.
Paul Patton (Oxford: Blackwell, 1997), 81–106.

ELIZABETH GROSZ IS
PROFESSOR OF CRITICAL
THEORY AND PHILOSOPHY
AT MONASH UNIVERSITY IN
AUSTRALIA. SHE IS THE
AUTHOR MOST RECENTLY
OF SPACE, TIME AND PER-
VERSION: THE POLITICS OF
BODIES. A SHORTER VERSION
OF THIS ESSAY FIRST
APPEARED IN ANY 19/20,
THE VIRTUAL HOUSE, 1997.

which places, regions are located in a mode of neutralization; cosmological space could itself be regarded as patchwork and uneven.

If two types of time coexist, one virtual (the past) and the other actual (the present) and their coexistence is necessary for the functioning of either, then perhaps there is a spatial correlate for this unhinging of temporal continuity through Bergson's paradoxical idea of the temporal simultaneity of present and past. Obviously spatial relations happily admit relations of simultaneity: space is that which enables simultaneous or coextensive relations. Perhaps it would be more intriguing to consider spatiality in terms of the coexistence of multiple relations of *succession*, space as a layering of spaces within themselves, spaces enfolded in others, spaces that can function as the virtualities of the present, the "here." Here a notion of virtual space will be of crucial relevance. If past, present, and future are always entwined with each other and make each other possible only through their divergences and bifurcations, then perhaps there is a way to consider spatiality in terms of relations of nearness and fairness, relations of proximity and entwinement, the interimplications of the very near and the very far, rather than of numerals or geometry.

This returns us once again to the vexing question of the virtual and its particular spatial resonances. One cannot of course directly specify what a virtual is, for insofar as it is, insofar as it exists, it exists as actual. In the process of actualization, the virtual annuls itself as much in order to reemerge as an actual that thereby produces its own virtualities. At best one can specify what it may produce, what effects or differences it may generate. We need to remind ourselves for a moment how Deleuze distinguished between the virtual and the possible. He claimed that the possible is the correlate or counterpart of the real. There are two distinctive connections between the possible and the real: the real both resembles the possible and is a limitation of the possible. The possible, or at least one of them, is a preformed real: the real is simply the coming into material form of this nonmaterial possible. The real is a mode of conformity with the possible, its plan or blueprint. Or equally, the possible is simply the retrospec-

tively conceived past of the real. By contrast, the virtual is counterposed with the actual rather than the real (indeed the virtual has a reality without any actuality). The actual in no way resembles the virtual nor does it limit or select from the virtual. It is linked to the virtual through "difference or divergence and . . . creation"[18]:

It is difference that is primary in the process of actualization – the difference between the virtual from which we begin and the actuals at which we arrive, and also the difference between the complementary lines according to which actualization takes place. In short, the characteristic of virtuality is to exist in such a way that it is actualized by being differentiated and is forced to differentiate itself.[19]

This means that the virtual *requires* the actual to diverge, to differentiate itself, to proceed by way of division and disruption, forging modes of actualization that will transform this virtual into others unforeseen by or uncontained within it. In other words, virtuality functions evolutionarily: it functions through the production of the novelties that remain unforeseen by, yet somehow generated through the virtual materials ("genes" or seeds). The virtual is the realm of productivity, of functioning otherwise than its plan or blueprint, functioning in excess of design and intention. This is the spark of the new that the virtual has over the possible: it is the capacity for generating innovation through an unpredicted leap that the virtual brings to the actual, the capacity of the actual to be more than itself, to become other than the way it has always functioned. It is differentiation, which, while propelled by a tendency or virtuality, can only actualize itself through its encounters with matter, with things, with movements and processes, and thus with obstacles, through which it produces itself as always other than its virtuality, always new, singular, and unique.[20]

How then can space function in ways other than the ways in which it has always functioned? What are the possibilities of inhabiting otherwise? Of being extended otherwise? Of living relations of nearness and farness differently? Architects are no doubt more able to reflect on and produce with these questions than I am.

Discussion 5

Alejandro Zaera-Polo John, you seemed to start by saying that we live in an incredibly complex world where it's very difficult to diagram things. As a result you propose a practice of what you call indetermination, but I don't see the relationship between living in a complex environment and using indetermination as a tool to operate within that environment. Also, if I understand you correctly, you explain the diagram as a tool that introduces complexity in the process of production. I would like further explanation about the diagram as something that produces indetermination. The diagram produces determination and leaves certain things open; it doesn't produce absolute determination, but it is definitely a tool of determination, even, for example, in the case of Foucault's panopticon prison diagram that you presented. It identifies something; it's not a tool that releases noise, it's a piece of a system that actually makes a statement without words. That's the potential of the diagram and that's also why everyone is so interested in it.

John Rajchman I don't think Foucault's panopticon diagram was a way of determining something but of seeing how things are already determined. That's what makes it a "tool" of a rather different kind, I would say a diagnostic tool. I don't think Foucault was even saying that things are in fact determined along those lines — that everybody is in fact disciplined. Rather, he was trying to pick out an anonymous strategy that industrial societies devised to deal with their accumulating populations, a strategy that was no longer working so well. While concerned with techniques of spatial and temporal distribution, his was a diagram mostly in words, the point of which was not to make a statement but to open up a problem. That is how indetermination comes in — a kind of indetermination that is not to be confused with the problem of indeterminacy of observation of physics. In short, Foucault's diagram was not a tool of determination but rather a way of seeing a problem that arises when a previous kind of determination no longer works. Deleuze's idea was then to associate this kind of historical indetermination with powers or virtualities of another kind, requiring different kinds of action that, while pragmatic, would not be instrumental.

Complexity, on the other hand, is not a feature of environments but rather of the powers or potentials in them that diagrams can be used to bring out – something more like a pattern of dissonance than noise. That is what connects the idea of diagram to Henri Bergson, who was a great philosopher of vital indetermination – an indetermination that distinguished his vitalism from organicism and linked him to William James, to pragmatism. In particular we then see why diagrams are needed for other geometries or sorts of forces that are shown through them. But, Alejandro, if it is true that with the word **diagram** you are instead looking for some wordless tools to determine things in situations you otherwise find too complex, then that's a bit disappointing.

Chris Dercon Rosi, at the beginning of your presentation you said that diagrams of the present are in trouble. Could you elaborate on that?

Rosi Braidotti When I said that they are in trouble, I meant that as a gesture of diagnosis of the historicity of the present, diagrams have undergone a number of in-depth critiques, one of which is that an effective diagram is a cartography of the present that can only take place if the subject drawing the map is him- or herself inscribed in the cartographic gestures. It becomes a form of embeddedness of the subject, or a form of self-reflexivity, or a form of the deconstruction of the historicity of the disciplines within which a particular map is being drawn. It is a translation of it. Consequently, working with some insight from families of epistemology, if this diagram of the present has embedded in it a subject position, that position is necessarily partial, is necessarily blind. There is a blind spot in this dream of symmetry. The classical example of this is the critique that Donna Haraway has made of Foucault's representation of science – his completely out-of-date notion of biology, physics, and mathematics. In his diagrams of biopower, Foucault depicts a situation that no longer exists. He depicts a situation – as Haraway puts it – showing biopower at the moment of its implosion, when that sequence changes into the informatics of domination. The resulting diagram is the best we can get but it is always already out-of-date. Connected to that is the inscription of the subject, the idea of partiality, and the idea of politics of location. I would like to understand more of the difficulties of putting together the programmatic with the diagrammatic because my lack of knowledge of architecture leaves me fascinated but a bit aporetic.

Bernard Tschumi The link with Foucault is very troubling because it was also made by an architect called Aldo Rossi, who used the diagram as a way to justify a definition of the constant, of certain kinds of spaces: the archetype of the prison, the archetype of the hospital. The notion of the diagram seems to work only if you take into consideration that society today is no longer the society that Foucault described. Foucault's was a society of fixed institutions, which is no longer the case. The question is, to what extent can the nature of fixity be challenged by architecture, itself perceived by culture or by society as something fixed? It challenges the fixity of spaces through a paradoxical use of those spaces.

Dercon Liz, do you think that architecture has the weapons to challenge that problem of fixity?

Elizabeth Grosz I don't know if it has self-contained weapons, but when external techniques are imported – external tools, philosophical tools, intellectual tools – they often misfire, partly because the tools weren't designed for those particular practices. I find the incredible attraction that theory holds disturbing — I have it, too, but I'm allowed to have it insofar as my practice is the production of theory. I'm not a new empiricist but I support a certain empiricism that says that there are practical issues at hand. I have all sorts of tools and theory is one of them, but it's not the most important. It isn't the most important one in architectural practice either, but it's necessary. Science is just as necessary; anthropology is just as necessary; political economy is just as necessary. It's a useful device, but nothing more.

Dercon Joost, you seemed to favor an architecture that is outside of discourse.

Joost Meuwissen We are always in a situation where rhetoric already exists, so why would I add my own to it? I like to speak with the existing rhetoric. We use diagrams, but how do we formulate the diagram in a theoretical way? Deleuze comes up with an interesting interpretation of Foucault's notion of the diagram when he refers to Francis Bacon, who called his own paintings "diagrams." The diagram can be used in a highly modernist way as a direct translator toward a reductive aspect of the reading of the diagram, or you can use it in a more generative way, in a more unfolded way, so that the diagram becomes a possible virtual transformation of normalization. In Bernard Tschumi's work, the computer game is transformed toward organization but referred to the plain organization, which means that you transform the diagram in an almost modernist organizational way; it's not proliferated toward a way of conceptualizing the diagram three-dimensionally. Let's say the diagram is actually transformed in a rethinking of organizational spatial effect. In other words, you refer to the diagram almost linguistically instead of instrumentally. That is the difficulty I see in the way you use a diagram.

Sanford Kwinter The diagram, as I always understood it, was not a spatial thing at all. It was really a germ of directed development. Deleuze makes the point that the great innovation of Foucault's concept of diagram was to have successfully formed a bridge or a link between the discursive and nondiscursive domains. What was effectuated was a bridging of two previously irreducible domains. I would like to ask anyone on the panel if the architect's embrace of the diagram is not in fact a device to effectuate just that sort of cosmopolitanization or hybridization or extension of architectural practice to adjacent domains that for a long time have been marooned as islands without bridges or links.

Rajchman In attempting to bring Foucault into this discussion I wanted to expand on the types of exchange that Sanford thinks are interesting. I agree that there should be interferences and exchanges with other disciplines in which philosophy wouldn't be an overarching theory but would be a participant. What's interesting about Foucault in part, and Deleuze's interpretation of Foucault, is that he introduces the diagram in a political context or a context of power. The diagram of discipline, he says, is a diagram of a strategy of power. When one listens to architects describe how they use diagrams in their work, this dimension is not strongly represented. I liked Liz's suggestion that this time of the diagrammatic belongs to the political as such, time invention and time is as if, what you would call the same time. I want to ask Bernard whether these more political senses of diagram have any role in his work.

Tschumi Sanford's distinction between the discursive and the nondiscursive is absolutely crucial because architects have a tendency to take certain things literally. The word **diagram**, whether it's a three-dimensional diagram, a motion diagram, or a diagram that hints at multiple geometries, is interesting only at the moment it is challenged by the nondiscursive, by what cannot be mapped. If it can be mapped, it is always within the realm of architectural certainty and within the total coherence of architectural history for the past 500 years. The moment that diagrams start to enter the real, the diagram is challenged. So, to what extent do you consider the diagram as a literal possibility of architecture, as a way of forming the envelope? Or is it already implicitly containing its own contradiction? Instead of designing the diagram for the condition, diagram the conditions that you want to encourage.

Charles Jencks I want to be really reactionary and quote a person who's been called the "so-called Aldo Rossi," as Bernard called him a minute ago. Rossi used to talk about the representational nature of architecture. Architecture used to represent a public language. In the 1960s, however, Aldo van Eyck talked about the in-between of so-called Bernard Tschumi. In other words, "in-between" has been a poiesis of architecture for about 40 years, as well as in other discourses. In literature, Leslie Fiedler spoke about jumping between this and that, and everybody used to talk about the in-between. But Bernard, you said, "I don't want to hybridize; I want to dialecticize." You said it's trivial to combine things, to build bridges in the way that Fiedler and van Eyck spoke about. You also said, "It's not important what it looks like, but what it's going to do." I hadn't seen your scheme for the Columbia student center before today, but it looks on the outside like something McKim, Mead & White would do. You say it doesn't matter what it looks like, but the minute you say that it becomes a question of consciousness. Who is reading it, and how do they read it?

Tschumi It's not about reading.

Jencks Who's giving the text? Who's understanding how we get into their consciousness? Who's perceiving it and in which of the six senses?

Tschumi It's not about reading, and it's not about perception. I'm very glad you raised the question. Here we have an influential member of the architectural body of consciousness putting all of the emphasis on the form of the envelope and its meaning and what it represents. Representation is by now irrelevant. We are talking so much about those virtual images and those media images because they are interchangeable. It doesn't matter if you use a McKim, Mead & White facade, a modernist facade, or one of your postmodernist facades. The reason to bring the diagrammatic and the programmatic together is not about reading, it's about living and experiencing. It is about another perception of space and not about the reading of the institution through its elevations.

Jencks Then it's no longer public.

Tschumi I don't think that publicness deals necessarily with the image of facades.

Rem Koolhaas The point is clearly not the facade. I have been highly involved with that part of New York and I have always found it to be a very depressing part. If I analyze why it is depressing, there are a number of reasons: first, in a city that depends on heterogeneity it is disconcerting to see such a stretch under a single architectural control; second, there is the equally disconcerting element of horizontality when your nervous system is used to verticality; and third, there is also the unfortunate character of the color scheme that McKim, Mead & White imposed on the facades. Broadway is particularly depressing, somber, and pompous — an American kind of pretension. The facade may not be the point, but your contribution can never be neutral or indifferent or unimportant to that piece of New York.

Tschumi The building has two wings linked by a social space between them. That social space is the locus of the activities of the building. Under no circumstance was it interesting to put the emphasis on the McKim envelope. In other words it was found as a readymade. The discussion you are suggesting by questioning McKim, Mead & White and horizontality is not the issue of the project.

Koolhaas You have to question.

Tschumi You choose your question. This is irrelevant. It's a readymade; it's a found object. It could have been there before, except that it's not going to look exactly like that. If you want to put the emphasis on the locus of activity, on movement, you don't work in this particular case. There are no fixed strategies; each problem is viewed individually. It is very conscious. We decided to negate the facade part of the problem and only focus on the place of exchange, on the hub, on the social space. In other words, I was not naive; I knew that people would get upset about seeing something contemporary. We can eradicate the notion that the facade is part of the symbolism of the building. It is not. It's not where the action takes place.

Braidotti I am interested in the question of whether the hybridization of cosmopolitanism is a way of relandscaping what Arjun Appadurai calls the "ethnoscapes of postmodernity." In order to answer this very complicated question one has to be inside a diagram, to be situated somewhere. If I situate myself seriously as somebody who lives in Europe right now, I would say that there is an enormous contested zone. What kinds of figurations of the ethnoscapes do we go for? Cosmopolitanism is a very classical one and also very complicated. Nomadism isn't much better. There is a long list of figurations of these new situated forms of subjectivity, from the pilgrim to the homeless to the alien immigrants to the cross-border prostitute to the new au pair girls to the mail-order brides. These are not just metaphors but real interstitial social places where new types of subjectivity and, I dare say, European citizenship are at work that need to be framed and consequently represented adequately. There is a real clash of adequate figurations for these types of social subjectivities that fall in between the established category. Martha Nussbaum went for cosmopolitanism when she said, "As a woman I have no country; as a woman my country is the whole world." People are pitching the figurations of their situated conditions one against the other. To compare those figurations we are comparing diagrams. You can only do it from a situated, localized perspective.

Dercon What's your reaction to Rem's work on China or to the configurations and comments from the European-American architects who want to be key players in these sorts of adventures?

Braidotti The positioning and place of enunciation from which the statement was made are very different from the position I've chosen. The description of the all-encompassing city, whether it is the periphery of Paris or a city in China, shows some of the conditions of postmodernity. This has nothing to do with postmodernism, but with the condition of postmodernity, which is this paradox of globalization and fragmentation, the simultaneity of very contradictory effects whereby there are pockets of the so-called third world that are completely analogous to the first world and vice versa, where you can talk about the differences **within** geopolitical blocks and not the differences **between** them anymore. I recognize a portion of Rem's diagrams, but he's looking at it from a very different location, and consequently our maps are different. I would call social theory in the 21st century a comparison of our respective cartographies. You could say that I'm looking at this from the angle of discipline, from the angle of geopolitics. The comparison of maps would make interesting philosophical discussions. Rather than actually looking at the answers right away, we need to look at the ways in which we frame the questions.

Saskia Sassen What Rosi just said is extremely important. One of the ways in which I think about this new figuration is the formation of new geographies of centrality that cut across the old north-south divide and install themselves in various places, be they geographically confined centers or more complex digitalized forms of centrality. One of the questions I have vis-à-vis Rem's China project is whether Shenzhen is or is not part of this new cross-border geography of centrality. Similarly, there are new geographies of marginality that also cut across the old north-south divide. The **banlieue** of Paris are part of that new geography of marginality, as are the favelas in São Paulo. A whole series of new questions leads back to the question of the relocation of borders and edges. The politics of this are enormously important because they're in the making; they're somewhere in the future. Many of the components of this new politics are invisible, though they are happening. There are micropolitics all over the place. Rosi's presentation raised a whole set of issues that don't fit comfortably in the discussion here. The most direct connection to the discussion of architecture and especially the discussion about Shenzhen is, how does this part of China fit in the geography of centrality that connects it to European centers and to other Asian centers?

Ignasi de Solà-Morales The discussion of diagrams is not about the need to consider the problems in China or to compare China with the suburbs of Paris. If we mix everything, we will never solve any problems. The discussion was a little confusing, ranging from the idea of diagram in Foucault and Deleuze to the use of the diagram in these different presentations. In the tradition of internal tools of architecture, diagrams are instruments related to function. The diagram in Foucault could be translated as a very precise concept having to do with the spatial synthesis between construction, organization, and place. At what point do Foucault's diagrammatic ideas of prisons and stadiums have to do with a preestablished system of control as a complete ideological approach without any space for producing invention in the project?

Grosz There can't be a space, project, or program that doesn't leave room for indeterminacy. There can't be such a thing because to be a thing is to be open to what befalls you. You can't produce a thing, an entity, or an object that doesn't leave space for indeterminacy. This is what it is for a thing to live in time. You can't create an object with a guarantee that it remains the same. This is one of the challenges facing postmodern architecture. There has been a historical understanding of the staticness of building, yet historically this has been proven false and will continue at ever-increasing rates to be false. One of the most interesting questions that could be extracted from this event is how to design a building open to an inherent indeterminacy, to an inherent incapacity to have a function before the event, before the building, given that the function will inevitably transform itself, will change over time.

Greg Lynn I remember the very first Any conference in Los Angeles as having metadiscourses and hierarchical subdiscourses going on. Architecture cast itself in the first inning as trying to attack philosophy, or being a launch pad into philosophy from which we could throw questions to philosophy. The papers given on this panel by John, Rosi, and Liz were very similar to mine, but I felt a strange uneasiness because I'm not in close contact with any of you – I've never even met Rosi. How is it that we all came with a similar paper about motion, time, and space without a shared base? This kind of meta-status for philosophy, where a philosopher would establish the program for architecture, doesn't really exist anymore. There may be some kind of a space race, and philosophy becomes a place where you get a language to describe things, but if I gave a paper in mathematical terms or geometric terms, it would be pops and whistles. The term **diagram**, however, is more accessible. It offers more of a common ground between philosophy and architecture.

Braidotti One of the most cheerful things I heard in my happy days at the Sorbonne, when philosophy was dead and agonizing, was that the essence of the philosophical debate would be happening outside the hallowed walls of the discipline, and that is exactly what is taking place here. It's not where you expect philosophies actually to take shape. One of the greatest things I take away from this panel is the extent to which a lot of those philosophical concepts are taking place in nonarchitectural spaces, which again proves that philosophy is continuing outside its domain and is doing very well, especially when there are fewer rather than more philosophers involved in the activity of creative thinking than even the discipline itself would allow.

Grosz What's significant here is that the same kinds of openness, the same kinds of transformation are occurring not only in a range of the natural sciences but also in a range of the arts at the moment. The most interesting philosophy right now is going on in biology but biologists don't know it. What seems to differentiate architects is that architects are interested in how philosophers think and biologists absolutely aren't. This is an exciting milieu to work in because architects – the architects here at any rate – are more interested in philosophy than the philosophers I work with.